Wow! This book does not hold back on issues not normally talked about! I am quite sure that we would encourage our single members to read such a book. I think it would also give non-single people an insight into the struggles of single people and help us to be more understanding. (**Gary Colvin,** *Head of HR, Mission Aviation Fellowship*)

While this book will be of particular benefit for singles in mission and those sending them out, it will also be helpful for single people in general. (**Rev. Uel Marrs,** *Secretary of Board of Mission Overseas, of the Presbyterian Church In Ireland*)

Singleness is a real and difficult issue for many people in cross-cultural mission, yet I have not found a helpful book on the subject until now. So I am delighted that Debbie Hawker and Tim Herbert have put together this book. It fills a massive gap and we will certainly use it as a resource for training, preparing and supporting our mission workers. (**Philip Bingham,** *Mission Personnel Manager, Church Mission Society*)

This will fill a gap in a much neglected area in missions... The topics addressed in this book are very relevant and I believe it will contribute a lot to a better understanding of the needs of single missionaries and how to care for them more effectively. (**Marina Prins,** *Director, Member Care Southern Africa*)

There is a lack of books on this topic written by experienced singles living in cross-cultural contexts from all continents. The joys and deep satisfaction, the abyss of pain, the threats and the journey of resilience and victory, and more... described in this new book is what singles who are called to serve Christ cross-culturally will not find in a pastoral book written by one author, from one country, who might have theoretical knowledge but has not lived it worldwide for any length of time, and cannot write from both the female and male perspective. (**Hanni Boeker,** *WEC International, Indonesia*)

Your book will be a valuable and required resource for all of our present/veteran long-term cross-cultural workers and especially for our new candidates as they prepare to go. Of course this book will also be a great addition to our membercare workers both in the home office and field settings. (**John Kennedy**, *Associate Executive Director, Interserve USA*)

All Nations Christian College trains and equips men and women for effective participation in God's mission in his multi-cultural world. We seek to equip the whole person and are always on the look out for appropriate, contemporary resources. The new book edited by Hawker and Herbert will be a valuable addition. There is a real gap in this area. As a multi-cultural community of learners the diversity of cultural perspectives will be important. (**Ruth Wall**, *Programme Leader, All Nations Christian College*)

There are few materials available that recognise the needs of this cohort and aim to inform the single mission personnel themselves as well as those in a position to offer support and encouragement. This resource should be useful to all those involved in the care and welfare of single mission workers. (**Storm and Richard Hann**, *Managers, Penhurst Retreat Centre*)

I'm particularly glad for the multicultural approach and the willingness to address issues of single sexuality directly. (**Elizabeth Pennock**, *Member Development Consultant, Pioneers USA*)

The book would be a great resource for carers and workers alike. (**Kerrie McGibbon**, *Counsellor, Salvation Army*)

I wish that such a resource had been available for me when I went to the field single. I didn't thrive as a single, quite the opposite, got into strife and nearly ended up in being sent home. (**Anonymous**, *Australia*)

Single Mission:

Thriving as a single Christian in cross-cultural ministry

Edited by Dr Debbie Hawker and Rev. Tim Herbert

Copyright © Debbie Hawker and Tim Herbert 2013

All rights reserved. No part of this publication may be reproduced or transmitted in any form or by any means, electronic or mechanical, including photocopying, recording, or any information storage and retrieval system, without permission in writing from the authors.

ISBN 978-0-9892440-3-9

All Scripture quotations, unless otherwise indicated, are taken from the *Holy Bible New International Version* ©1984. London: Hodder & Stoughton.

References cited as MSG are taken from Peterson, E.G. (2004). *The Message*. Colorado: NavPress.

To order this book, visit www.condeopress.com

Cover © Maddy Sargent, www.maddysargent.com

Condeo Press

Acknowledgements and dedication

Over thirty people have written material for this book, and we thank each of them for doing so, including those we are unable to name for security reasons. We are sincerely grateful to Maddy Sargent (www.maddysargent.com) for designing the cover at no cost, to David Hawker for editorial assistance, and to Dr Brent Lindquist for help with publication.

This book is dedicated to single people all over the world who are serving God, and especially to Heather and Kat.

Contents

Preface   1

Part 1: Single mission workers from different cultures

Voices from Western Europe
- 1. Lessons learned in ninety years (Dr Marjory Foyle)   7
- 2. My single mission: Loving and serving God (Rev. Tim Herbert)   13

Voices from South America
- 3. Longing for protection, like a newborn bird (Verônica Farias)   18
- 4. The pain of saying goodbye (Telma Santos)   22
- 5. An Argentinian working with the Japanese in London (Anny Rosciani-Woodhams)   24
- 6. A single mission worker in turbulent times (Antonia van der Meer)   32

Voices from Asia
- 7. Why aren't you married? Asian single men in missions (Philip Chang)   35
- 8. Where is my helper? A Chinese woman in Central Asia (Little Dove)   47
- 9. Community in Cambodia (Chami Nagai)   52
- 10. Being shot in Nepal and India (Debbie)   55

Voices from Africa (see chapter 33 for another voice from Africa)
- 11. A Zambian mission worker's single journey (Annie)   57
- 12. From Namibia to the ends of the earth (Martha)   66
- 13. Singled out in Cameroon (Marius)   71

Voice from the Middle East
- 14. A single woman in the Middle East (Melinda)   72

Voice from Eastern Europe
- 15. Single parent – is mission impossible? Fostering children (Paula)   76

Voices from North America
- 16. The joy of children and friendship (Eunice Hill)   84
- 17. Returning 'home' to care for parents (Deb Rupe)   93

Voice from Australasia
- 18. Papua New Guinea back to Australia : Returning 'home' (Joy Atkinson)   98

Part 2: Sexuality
- 19. Scantily clad temptation in Burundi (Simon Guillebaud)   105
- 20. Single in South-East Asia (Dr Glenn Miles and Dr Debbie Hawker)   107
- 21. Why cross-cultural mission is high-risk for sexual challenges (Dr Roni Pruitt)   110
- 22. Sexual desire (Dr Roni Pruitt and Dr Debbie Hawker)   113
- 23. Masturbation (Dr Debbie Hawker)   122

24. Pornography (John Steley)		127
25. Same-sex attraction, homosexuality and bisexuality (Dr Debbie Hawker)		132
26. Sacred sexuality: A positive view of single sexuality (Dr Roni Pruitt)		140

Part 3: The journey from singleness to marriage (and, for some, back to singleness)

27. Waiting, dating, or stating that you are called to be single (Dr Debbie Hawker and Rev. Tim Herbert)	149
28. Love on-line (Jo Swinney and Dr Debbie Hawker)	154
29. Against all odds: How one woman found love over the internet (Lizzie)	160
30. Dating during cross-cultural ministry (Dr Roni Pruitt and Janet Fraser-Smith)	166
31. Journeying on (Dr Debbie Hawker)	173
32. Open doors: Can God use a married woman? Can God use a widow? (Dr Lois Dodds)	184
33. Singleness and widowhood: Married for two weeks (Catherine Bezold)	193
34. Single for the second time, after separation or divorce (Dr Debbie Hawker)	207

Part 4: What we know about single people in ministry

35. Cold comfort: What not to say to single mission workers (Alison Clarke)	215
36. Isn't it better if single people stay home? (Dr Jessie Ritchey and Dr Debbie Hawker)	227
37. Understanding and enhancing the resilience of single mission personnel (Dr Nancy Crawford and Dr Karen Carr)	233
38. Singularly significant: The value of single people in ministry (Dr Debbie Hawker)	242
39. Issues to consider prior to starting cross-cultural ministry (or changing team) (Dr Debbie Hawker)	246
40. Conclusion: Responding to the challenges and reaping the benefits of being a single mission worker (Drs Debbie and David Hawker)	250

Appendices

1. Topics to discuss if you are considering a cross-cultural marriage (Janet Fraser-Smith)	277
2. Useful resources (Dr Debbie Hawker)	286
3. 40 ideas for coping with loneliness and sad times (Dr Debbie Hawker)	289
4. Abuse (Dr Debbie Hawker)	291

Footnotes   292

Preface

"Marriage isn't for everyone. Some, from birth seemingly, never give marriage a thought. Others never get asked – or accepted. And some decide not to get married for kingdom reasons." (Matthew 19:12, MSG)

Tens of thousands of single people are serving short-term or long-term as Christian mission workers outside their home country. It has been estimated that about 60 per cent of Western mission personnel in the past 200 years have been single women.[1]

Some people enjoy their single lifestyle, or don't think much about it. Some feel they have been called to singleness, and they don't consider marriage; they might even make a vow of celibacy. For others, singleness is a 'cross to carry' or a 'thorn in the flesh', with a constant hope of marriage one day, and a feeling that until that day comes, something important is missing. Some feel they have never been loved or chosen. Others have had opportunities to marry, but not with a person they felt was right for them. Some have experienced the pain of broken relationships. Some are separated, divorced or widowed.

Evangelical Christians who are single, unlike their secular friends, are expected to refrain from sexual activity and pornography. Evangelical teaching encourages Christian single people to be celibate.[2] This makes them unusual in today's society. They may feel that being a Christian reduces the potential partners available to them as they would only marry someone who shares their faith. Among Christians, there are many more single women than single men, so many single Christian women are unable to find a suitable marriage partner within the Church.

Marriage prospects reduce further for single people committed to ministry outside their home country, as there may be fewer potential partners they can relate to who are willing to share their lifestyle. This is especially true for women, as among mission personnel, single women outnumber single men by about ten to one.[3] Mission workers may have less time or opportunity to meet people of the opposite sex than they would in their home country. Single mission personnel can face particular challenges, related to the culture they are in and being far from home, family and friends.

Some Christians, ignoring the advice of many a pastor, date someone in the hope of converting them to Christianity, so that they can marry them. This is known as 'missionary dating', but is not the sort of missionary activity which this book is about!

Some people assume that there must be something wrong with single people or else they would be married. This book challenges that assumption. Jesus was a single man, and Paul wrote that it is good to be single (1 Corinthians 7:7-8). This book contains testimonies from normal people who are single and thriving in ministry. We give God the glory for what he has done in their lives, around the world. We pray that these inspiring stories will encourage you in your own faith and ministry. Singleness is not a disease or a problem. Single people can be fruitful and happy, and there are advantages of singleness.

People will read this book for different reasons. You might read it because you find it challenging to be a single person in ministry. If so, we want you to know that you are not alone. Many people experience similar difficulties. We hope you will be encouraged and that these pages will help you find ways to thrive, and not merely to survive.

You may have chosen this book in order to improve your understanding of what it is like to be a single person serving far from home. You may be supporting or working alongside people in this position. We hope this will help you care for and pray for them effectively. Deep friendships and support mean a lot to single people.

You might have picked up *Single Mission* because you are interested in cross-cultural mission. We trust that these stories will inspire you. Perhaps you are preparing for ministry yourself. We hope you will appreciate the insights from different cultures.

In a book of this size it is impossible to include authors from every nation, but we have tried to reflect some of the diversity of the topic. We apologise to those from countries not represented here.

The chapters have been written by more than 30 people from many different cultures, backgrounds and ages. Most of the authors are women to reflect the proportion of single women on the mission field, but some men are included. There are more authors from some continents than from others, and some chapters are longer than others, but we regard each individual and every culture as equally important. The mission personnel who have contributed chapters include Bible translators, health workers, preachers, teachers, (friendship) evangelists, administrators, church planters, counsellors, 'tent-makers', and those in leadership serving with different mission agencies and churches. The editors have both served as single mission workers in a number of countries.

In this book, you can discover the challenges and joys of being single in different cultures. You can read about friendships, involvement with children, and returning home. We include a section on dating and marriage, for those who are considering that option. We refer to those who are single for a second time. We also discuss sex, masturbation, pornography and same-sex attraction.

We are very grateful to everyone who has shared their comments and experiences with us, and helped in the writing of this book. Some authors have chosen not to give their full name or location, and some details have been disguised in order to protect people working in insecure locations.

Our prayer is that this book will help encourage, equip and support many in ministry, so that they can be even more effective in the important work done in bringing hope to people around the world.

We would love to hear your feedback about this book, to assist us in our ministry and in any future editions. You are welcome to contact us with any comments, through the website www.resilientexpat.co.uk.

Part 1: Single mission workers from different cultures

VOICES FROM WESTERN EUROPE

Chapter 1 - Lessons learned in ninety years

Dr Marjory Foyle initially worked in India and Nepal as a missionary doctor. Then she began an itinerant ministry, travelling the world advising mission personnel about mental health. Her book Honourably Wounded: Stress among Christian workers[4] *helped mission organisations take seriously the needs of their workers. Marjory is now in her 90s, and still travels the world speaking at conferences. In this chapter, she relates lessons she has learned about singleness, and describes how a single person can remain happy and fulfilled even in old age.*

Having attended many weddings as a child, I learned a lot about the joys of the wedding day and looked forward to standing at the altar with a lovely man someday. There were, however, some problems to be overcome. Marriage was assumed to be a valuable commodity, but I could see that some marriages were not happy. My childhood had been difficult in some areas, although we were well cared for. I grew up thinking that getting married was fine, but afterwards it would probably deteriorate.

My other problem was that I knew few boys. When I was growing up in the 1920s, children were taught nothing about sex. My brother was six years older than I was, and was away at boarding school most of the time. Anyway, in those days it would have been a total 'no no' to ask a brother about how babies were made. When I studied biology in school I began to understand it all and to look at males with a new eye. I went on to become a doctor. I got to know some men, and found out they were really nice people. Only one man was interested in my becoming his wife, which I refused because I was intending to go to India as a medical mission worker, and so I have always been single.

I obtained a Diploma in Obstetrics, having learned a lot about babies and where they come from. I have also learned lessons about singleness.

Lesson 1: Single mission workers may be misunderstood by nationals
Single mission workers overseas, especially women, are often misunderstood by nationals. Marriage is very important in most

countries, and local people have strict expectations about how marriages are made and maintained.

My own experience may serve as an example of the difficulties single mission workers may encounter. I worked in India and Nepal as a doctor for many years, and in both countries people could not understand why I was single. The women used to say, "Why did your parents not make a marriage arrangement for you?" I tried to explain that we did not have the dowry and cultural marriage systems that they had in their country, and that most marriages in England were based on love, with the couple themselves deciding to marry, often with no involvement from the parents. Such a situation was almost unheard of in the places where I worked. I heard later that the women had talked together about me, and had arrived at the conclusion that I had been married to the head doctor (an American) who had cast me off because I had no children, and that he had then taken another wife! They believed that the reason I worked so hard was that I was trying to make restitution for my sin of being childless. We were all very amused by this. Mercifully, they accepted me with gratitude as "their doctor".

We let the Nepali hospital staff explain that I was *not* a cast-off wife, nor had I committed any serious sin because of which no-one would marry me. The staff explained to the local women that things worked differently in my country, and hence it was all right for me to work with a married man. Things eased up as time went by and more single men and women arrived to work with us.

When I had to leave Nepal to cover a hospital in India, the local women went to the hospital and asked "Where is that doctor who speaks like a baby? She really understands us." I had a stammer so they thought I spoke like a baby, but at least they felt I understood them. It was at this point that I think they realised that I was not a cast-off wife!

Lesson 2: Single mission workers need to behave very carefully
Because we can be misunderstood, we need to behave very carefully. For example, in the situation I have just described, I was careful to avoid visiting the house where the American doctor and his family lived unless there was a staff party. I never invited my male colleague to my home if the nurse I shared it with was not there. Instead we would sit on the balcony outside where everyone could see us as we discussed our business. In another hospital I worked in, I never interviewed a male without keeping the door open. Then everyone could see we were just

talking. This helped to avoid suspicions of sexual misconduct. Married people need to be careful as well, but singles are treated with even more scrutiny and suspicion in cultures where there is no understanding of an adult who is not sexually active.

Lesson 3: Seek to understand and to be understood
It helps if we can explain to local people the customs of our own countries (including regarding singleness and marriage). We should also make an effort to understand the culture we are serving in. We should invite nationals to visit us, and accept invitations to their homes. Wonderful friendships can develop, and these reduce the likelihood of misunderstandings.

Lesson 4: We need privacy
Although hospitality is important, we also need some private space in our living area. Mission personnel work hard, and we need opportunities for solitude, where we can be alone with God, as well as enjoying wider relationships.

Lesson 5: Ways to handle sexuality
How can single mission workers deal with sexual frustration? Jesus was single all of his earthly life. He understands us well. He has been there, done that and 'got the t-shirt'.

The biggest thing I learned was to take my singleness to God, and give it back to him. Taking things to God included the normal sexual urges of a normal woman – me! I asked God to help me when I saw a really marvellous man who had no interest in me at all. I took up the traditional ways of handling singleness such as taking exercise to reduce the urges. Best of all, I learned to take my singleness from God's hand. (See chapter 22 for more on this topic).

Lesson 6: Ask God what he wants you to do, and do it
Whether married or single, we should ask God what he wants us to do, and do that. He may lead us in unexpected ways. I have found great fulfilment in following his leading. When I reached 60 years of age I decided to retire from hospital service. Then God revealed to me what he wanted me to do next. By a strong mental conviction, I understood that he wanted me to start travelling to any area of the world where I was invited, in order to investigate the selection, training and care of cross-

cultural workers. I felt I needed confirmation that this was what God wanted me to do, so I asked him to send me a sign. Within a week I received an invitation to go and speak at a conference in Bangladesh, and also to meet with people needing to discuss problems. I accepted this at once, realising this was exactly what God had put into my mind to do. From there things opened up and I was invited to many parts of the world to visit and discuss the welfare of mission personnel. Since then member care,[5] the care of mission workers, has developed into an important ministry.

Lesson 7: There are benefits of singleness
God would have made other arrangements for me if he wanted me to be married. Hence he had a purpose in my remaining single. I realised that when I turned down the request to marry a man I had known for some time. Refusing a marriage proposal, if that is what God wants, can lead to later developments in your life that would have been impossible if you had married.

Being unmarried meant that I have been free to travel round the world, accepting invitations to speak. I am not a threat to anyone. I am just an old lady who can befriend people. These days the ministry I can offer is to talk to people who look sad or lost on the London underground train network. I can smile at men without it being misinterpreted, because I'm an old lady.

As I move towards the end of the day, I know that God has walked with me the whole way. It has not always been easy, but now, aged 92, I believe that singleness enabled me to do many things I would not have been able to do if I was a married woman.

Lesson 8: Appreciate what God has given us
I thank God I accepted what he has planned for me to do on earth. I am amazed how much he has helped and rewarded me for times when singleness became a bit lonely.

God brings great happiness into our lives, through many different channels. Thanks to a wonderful family and many friends I have been loved and cared for. I am able to work freely for God as long as he gives me health and strength. I have learned to thank God for all the good things he gives us.

Lesson 9: Live life to the full
It is good to celebrate life. I travel a lot. When I do, I enjoy treating myself to a free squirt of the expensive perfume available at the airport, followed by a tasty treat. I carry a travel kettle and teabags with me, so I can enjoy a nice cup of tea wherever I land.

As I have got older, I started to get grumpy about the things I can no longer do. I grumbled at God that I had not been able to do athletics, or to run the London marathon. I felt that God challenged me to stop complaining and instead be grateful for the things I *can* do. Ageing is a normal process which God created. I can't run a marathon, but I can walk it, so now I do that every year. At the age of 90 I had to choose between speaking at a conference in Thailand or taking part in the London marathon. What a great choice to have at my age. I chose the marathon. Complaining about getting old wastes our later life, and so I have stopped complaining, and instead live life to the full.

As well as walking, I also enjoy bird-watching, taking holidays in Scotland and going on cruises. On one cruise I befriended the hard-pressed musicians who played each day to an uncaring crowd. I listened and thanked them. One piece of music made me realise that I'm in love - with God and with life. It inspired me to write the following poem:

The Musician

All of a sudden the music began, and I lost the world.
I felt I could dance, pirouette, arabesque,
And even do points.
I saw myself whirling, stooping,
Rising again to the music,
Graceful, and free.
Then the music stopped – over, finito, right back to the world.

"What's it called" I asked?
Gazing at me with cows' eyes, and using a smoochy voice,
"Woman in LUURV", he said, heavy with emphasis.
And I laughed and blushed, and went off like a young girl.

Was I really in love? Surely not. Not at my age.
But then I saw – I am always in love,
I am in love with life,

In love with God,
In love with the people he leads me to.

And the day will come when I shall dance –
Pirouette, arabesque, swooping, gliding,
Whirling and praising and loving with total freedom,
And even do points.

Chapter 2 - My single mission: Loving and serving God

Rev. Tim Herbert, who is from England, served for five years as an administrator in Mozambique, Zimbabwe and Zambia. He now supports mission workers by visiting them as well as running a practical and pastoral support service. He reminds us to focus on God, not on marital status.

I never intended to be lifelong single. It just happened. And now I've been doing it for 30 (adult) years, it is starting to feel good. I wonder if I would have felt the same about being married for 30 years.

When I was younger, I always assumed that I'd get married. That's just what everyone did, so I thought I would as well. I don't think I ever particularly wanted to, any more than I wanted to stay single. It was an unconsidered assumption about the way things were. As I got into my thirties, I began to wonder if it would actually happen, and in my forties I began to doubt it would happen. The question people asked me started to change from "How come you're not married?" to "Have you ever been married?" I've now got to the point of assuming it's not going to happen, but not yet to the point of hoping it won't! I guess that means I'm comfortable with the way things are, and who I am.

I like being single. I like being able to get up in the morning and choose what I want to do. I like being able to do stuff on a whim without having to schedule it in with someone else. I'm glad I don't have to do things I don't enjoy or be with people I don't really like, just because my wife does. Some people call that selfish. Is enjoying yourself selfish? Should I get married just to prove I'm not? Is it more selfish than getting married because you want to have a life partner? The very accusation of being selfish implies that marriage is sacrificial. That doesn't make it sound that attractive an option to me!

We all know that being single has its downsides. One of them is being alone, which of course is not the same as feeling lonely. My parents are both dead, and Christmas Day is usually pretty hard for me. So is Valentine's Day. But two hard days in a whole year, well that's probably better than most married people manage.

I grew up largely alone, though not lonely. My father died when I was a child and I didn't get on very well with my Mum. I have a younger sister who has Down's Syndrome, and after I started going to school we seldom played together as the gap between us socially and physically widened. We lived in a large house on the outskirts of town in an area mostly populated by retired people, so I had few school-friends around. The result was that I learned to occupy myself. Reading, making models, walking in the nearby woods, playing with trains and keeping pets were some of the activities that I developed. I learned at an early age to occupy myself and to be successfully alone.

I've never been too concerned about being on my own. I'm comfortable going on holiday alone and going to the cinema alone. I have long walks in the country by myself. I decided long ago that I wasn't going to waste my life not doing things because I didn't have anyone to do them with. When people ask, for example "Isn't it hard going skiing alone?" my response is, "it's not as bad as not going skiing at all". It seldom bothers me that I don't have somebody to share the experience with. If something is so good I can't keep it to myself, I tell God. He usually enjoys it too.

What makes being single hard for me is not that I'm on my own. It's got more to do with other people's expectations. I don't fit into their idea of society and they have to find a reason for it. Married people can be particularly insensitive towards single people, as if somehow their experience of marriage has completely wiped their brains of any memory of their own singleness. Some say crass things like asking when I'm going to 'settle down'. Some ask if I'm gay. Church leaders say, "we want young families" without realising that they're implicitly saying "we don't want old singles". And I get angry just thinking about the patronising comment, "I'm sure God's got somebody special for you"!

A patient and gentle education process is needed to help people realise the impact of what they're saying. We shouldn't be like the woman who got her revenge on all the old ladies at weddings who said "It'll be you next" by saying the same thing to them at funerals! Instead, we should respond with love, reminding people that we need to be inclusive. We might ask if they can imagine what it feels like to have something like that said to you. I recently reminded a friend who was due to present a sermon on marriage that there would be single, widowed and divorced people in his audience whose hurt needed to be addressed, or at the very least, not aggravated.

Being single has sometimes been hard because I have felt like I've been rejected. It hurts to think that nobody wants me. I guess we can all feel like this from time to time. We wonder what is wrong with us and why nobody finds us attractive, whether it's our appearance or our character. Expressions like 'left on the shelf' reinforce this feeling, by suggesting that all the best partners have already been taken, leaving only the substandard ones. On reflection, for me it isn't true. I'm sure I could have got married, if I'd really wanted to, if I'd made an effort to smarten myself up, or gone on the internet to meet somebody. So I'm not exactly rejected. I'm as much responsible for my singleness as I am a victim of it.

To feel that we need the reciprocal love of just one special person is to denigrate the love of many friends. Over the years my friends have been very good about incorporating me into their lives. They've invited me to spend Christmas with them, to be a godfather to their children, and to be a regular presence at their family table. Some people have given me keys to their house, and I am free to come and go as if it was my own home. This is an amazing affirmation for a single person - to feel that we belong somewhere, to someone. *Belonging* is important. It helps you to feel that you're not a leftover, a mistake, an outcast. It reminds you that people value you, that you are part of not merely a community but a family.

Ultimately, these issues about whether somebody loves us, whether we belong to a family and whether we can manage being alone, all boil down to what is for me one central issue: what is our identity in Christ? It is at this point that we run the risk of platitudes, but actually, if in Christ we are pleasing to God, why are we so fixated on that one flawed, fallible human being to somehow make us happy? Surely we should be focussing instead on how to find our complete fulfilment in Christ.

The Bible often talks about us being servants of God, or slaves, or bondservants. However you translate it, the biblical imagery is not of an employee who lives his own life and is rewarded for his service. It's more like slavery. The slave has no right to his own opinion, choices, or relationships. The slave's obligation is to live to serve his master. If this is genuinely true of us, uppermost in our thoughts every day of our lives should be serving God, not our own enjoyment, fulfilment, recreation or procreation.

When my last serious relationship ended, along with the inevitable pain I also had a feeling of relief. I'd got my life back! On further reflection, I realised that one has to pour a lot of time, money and emotional energy into maintaining a successful relationship. It occurred to me that I'd rather put those resources into serving the Lord.

How does this all pan out on the mission field, with its special challenges for single people? I spent five years working as an administrator in southern Africa. I didn't find it any harder being single on the mission field than at home. Admittedly, I was always fortunate enough to live in pretty tight communities so it's not like I was the only European for miles around. Yet such intense communities have their own challenges, and in those contexts, you have to make friendships work. As a result I still have good relationships with people I might not have connected with if I'd had more choice. I was happy going on holiday by myself, to visit friends or just relax on my own. Evenings alone were no problem – I always had a good supply of books and DVDs. I never felt lonely or left out; in fact most of the communities I was part of went out of their way to incorporate people like me, and often had a significant number of singles in them. I always had the great fortune of being welcomed for a meal on Christmas Day by the same Danish family, which worked well for all of us. They had their intimate family time on 24th December, and saw Christmas Day as a time to catch up with family and close friends, which was ideal for me.

One challenge I faced as a single mission worker was the temptation to overwork. Because there was nobody waiting at home for me, I often stayed late at work after others had left. At first, I thought this was a brilliant privilege which gave me extra flexibility and productivity. However, as I began to suffer with stress, I realised the benefits of having a reason to go home. So I took up gardening, which meant I had to go home to water the plants every evening before it got too dark – usually around 7.00 pm. I called this 'family time' – just me and my roses!

Although being married in the culture I was working in did technically improve one's status, this wasn't really a problem for me, since being a white mission worker trumps marriage. People may have wondered what the problem was, but nobody mentioned it to me. Only on one occasion did the issue come up: an African matron said to me in frustration: "Ah, what do you know? You have no wife. You are just a boy!"

I found that relationships with other mission workers could become challenging. Feelings of unrequited love (both for me and by me) complicated life, as well as doubts about whether somebody might have those feelings, or what might happen if she did. While these confusions are part of everyone's life and relationships, they become much more significant in a small, tightly-knit community operating as an island of mission in a surrounding sea of local beliefs. Just socialising with someone could become problematic. Before I learned the rule that you always have to have a chaperone even if you are sitting reading a book on the opposite side of the room from somebody you don't even like, I upset everyone in our mission by going for a walk in the bush with a young lady who had only been there a couple of weeks longer than me. There was nothing in it but companionship, but everyone there believes there is only one reason why two people of the opposite sex will go off into the bush together, so they were scandalised. In their outrage, nobody was concerned that they had not explained this rule to either of us.

When I started working on this book, I was asked if I am single by choice. I said "no", equating that idea with the sort of vow of celibacy that would be expected of a monk or a Roman Catholic priest. I've certainly never felt called to go that far. Yet in some ways, it is a choice for me to be single. I have had opportunities to pursue relationships that might have culminated in marriage, but I didn't take them up. I've not taken active steps to get out there and meet a partner. Now my priorities are such that I am far more concerned about serving God faithfully than I am about getting married. I see marriage as a tangential issue not a core one: if I can serve God better by being married, then fine, but if not, then I'd rather be single.

VOICES FROM SOUTH AMERICA

Chapter 3 - Longing for protection, like a newborn bird

Verônica Farias *from Brazil has been a single mission worker for the last 20 years. She has observed that Brazilian single female mission personnel often report a longing for protection.*

I was about to start my devotional by the beach in South Asia one morning when I glanced at something small moving near my feet on the sand. It was a newborn bird, still not able to see. I thought how fragile that baby bird was without its mother and away from its nest. The bird's suffering was obvious to me. He was lost, alone and lacking any protection or provision. The ants were already attacking him, and because he was so immature he could not feed himself. Death was imminent for such a small, helpless creature. I left my Bible study, took the bird on the palm of my hand and started a desperate search for a nest in the nearby trees.

As I contemplated that little bird, a thought came to mind. I have worked as a member care provider for the last seven years, helping many Brazilian mission workers to take care of their emotional health. Each is unique, but single women often express the need for protection.[6] Like the bird, they feel unprotected. This seems to be regardless of personality, pre-field preparation, age or success in ministry. Single men, on the other hand, rarely mention protection. They are more likely to speak about loneliness.

Pondering on the bird, I thought about the verse which says, "Like a bird that strays from its nest is a man who strays from his home." (Proverbs 27:8) The word which struck me that day is "home". In the Bible this term can be connected to family or home country. "Nest" brings to mind the image of a bird protecting its young, making them warm and nourished. Mission personnel leave their place of protection and fly off to areas where they are vulnerable to illness, accidents, attack, conflict, persecution, harassment, loneliness or stress. Where is their protection?

I cannot speak for other cultures on this matter, and I must be careful not to generalize the behaviour and mindset of all Brazilian women, since we have a very diverse culture throughout Brazil. But I have observed a pattern among Brazilian single women. During pre-field preparation, they are usually very independent and excited. They want to leave Brazil quickly and head to the mission field. After all, they have worked hard towards that goal. In our discussions, I intentionally highlight their dreams and expectations about marriage and having a family. Most of the responses I hear are spiritual. Many women say that they are content with their single status.

When these women return to Brazil for home assignment after a few years, many begin to complain about being single. They now see it as a burden and a source of distress. I sense disappointment in their hearts and a weariness caused by the pressures which the mission field imposes on single women. Brazilians are relational people and are used to living with their family. I often hear how hard it was to live alone, while they watched families with children growing and running around them. Some women have feelings of regret or bitterness in their hearts. Sometimes I notice a subtle resentment against God behind their words.

I hear the tick of the woman's biological clock. As each year passes, fertility slips away. In general, the closer a single woman gets to her forties the more she worries about her loneliness and empty nest. It is a natural process. Even married women may feel the anxiety of the approaching years when having children is no longer an option. This is true both for women who have not had children yet but would like to, and for mothers who would like to have more children. When women are younger they go overseas without a sense of urgency in this area, yet later some find this very difficult to deal with. Some women feel that they can not continue in mission without a husband. If not properly understood, they or others may perceive this as weakness, failure or turning back.

Like a newborn bird away from its nest, female mission workers desire protection. Instead of this they receive criticism from many sources. Many host cultures do not understand why a woman would be unmarried, and bombard them with unpleasant questions and judgments. Well-intentioned people from the home country, including counsellors, may also make insensitive comments such as: "You need to fix yourself up, take care of the way you look, and make yourself more attractive so that you can marry", "You can't be praying or believing enough in the power of God, or else you would get a husband", "You are too independent, and no one will come near you if you don't show that you have needs", or "You have neglected this part of your life for years doing your ministry, now you are just reaping the consequences".[7]

The Bible is our main source of knowledge in all areas of life. We can also learn from psychology. Every man and woman needs to belong to someone and some place. In the case of cross-cultural workers, this security is constantly challenged due to the kind of life they are forced to live, moving many times. It is not a normal life but by the grace of God, they overcome the obstacles and live well.

Mission families are able to encourage each other along the journey. I notice that families tend to become more united and cooperative when they are living abroad than when they are living in their home country. This is probably because they know that they must depend on one another to survive when they are on their own with no relatives or home comforts around. They know that even when they relocate they will stick together as a family. They belong to each other. Here we find the best picture of home: wherever we go, we remain together as a family, and we are at 'home'. Being a family provides a kind of emotional roof, creating home wherever we move and this helps a lot.

Single cross-cultural workers do not have any family with them to create this sense of home, belonging and stability. They have left their parents, but not to join a spouse. They have no nest. They need to learn how to survive emotionally on their own. Even when they have team-mates around, it is not the same as living with family. Team-mates come and go, as they leave on home assignment or move on to new locations.

Single mission personnel have been uprooted from their homeland. Living abroad among foreigners and multicultural teams, and deprived of their warm Brazilian culture (which is full of hugs and open doors), they can become overwhelmed. Who will listen to their deepest desires, frustrations and needs?

If a single woman feels isolated, we should not deny her feelings, but should allow her to express them honestly. In supporting such a woman, we can help her to consider her options, respecting her as an individual. How can she enhance her ability to respond to loneliness? (See chapter 40 for some suggestions). Instead of feeling ashamed, a failure and incompetent because she is single, she should hear the words, "Well done, good and faithful servant" (Matthew 25:21).

In conclusion, it is not wrong for a bird to fly from the nest. It is necessary. But the bird needs protection, and to find a new nest. Missionaries also need protection and a sense of home. Some feel unable to express this need as they are afraid they will be misunderstood. They don't want people to respond by limiting them, or telling them to go back to their family, or to get married. They want to accept challenges and to use their gifts where God has called them.

Marriage can bring protection, but it is not the only form of protection. Mission workers can continue to serve as singles. What they want is for people to understand their feelings, and to pray for them and sometimes to offer practical help, such as accompanying them at night. They need families, friends and supporters to provide care and a sense of belonging, and a safe place to rest – a 'protective nest'.

The following tips may help singles along the way:

1. Try not to be sensitive to public opinion, as people can be wrong. Instead, seek God's opinion.
2. Have a healthy perspective on life, giving balance to personal and ministry areas and enjoying each part of life with creativity and self-care.
3. Find a mentor who is able to listen without judgment to whatever you need to say from the depth of your soul. This can bring relief like a stream in the desert.
4. Consider that everything in your life is under the sovereign control of God and his endless love. Live the life that God gave you with integrity and wholeness, considering suffering as a natural part of it.
5. Remember that Jesus understands how you feel. He was single, childless and had no home. He said, "Birds of the air have nests, but the Son of Man has nowhere to lay his head" (Matthew 8:20).
6. Remember that you belong to God. Trust him to give you a sense of belonging and to be your protector.

We may suffer in this life, but when we take an eternal perspective we know that God "protects the way of his faithful ones" (Proverbs 2:8). He will bring us to nest in our eternal home.

By the way, I did find a nest for the baby bird. And Jesus said, "Don't be afraid; you are worth more than many sparrows" (Matthew 10: 31).

Chapter 4 - The pain of saying goodbye

***Telma Santos** is a Latino single woman. She has served in Peru, the Philippines, Bangladesh and India. She is involved with church-planting. She points out that saying goodbye to close friends can leave a sense of grief, particularly for single people (for whom friends replace family), and for Latinos (who are famously relational).*

I have been in mission work for 24 years. Every day I learn something from God. To depend on him is crucial for my work. I depend on God for words when I talk to someone about him, hoping that God will open their heart to him. I also depend on God to help me in my personal life, as I often face loneliness.

During these years I have been in many different living situations. I have lived with other single people, with a couple, with a local family, and nowadays I live on my own. I have always been careful with relationships when my housemates included men, whether married or unmarried, making sure I behaved appropriately.

As Latinos we function better when we are part of a team and each member has an important role. We are very relational, caring and emotional. Not every culture is like this. When you work in a multi-cultural team the differences between the cultures can be challenging. We naturally have difficulties at times, but we try to overcome them with mutual respect, being flexible and putting Christ above all else.

If single people have a good team environment, are responsible and love the people, then they can play an effective role in mission. They often stay long-term because they don't have family responsibilities such as children's education which might lead them to return home.

When you work together as a team you become very close. Single people can become especially close to team members, as these are the main people we relate to each day because we do not have a partner and children. Because Latinos are very relational, it can be hard when friends leave (or when we ourselves need to leave). People are always coming and going in mission, whether for home assignments or relocating. I find it particularly hard when children leave, because I love children. When I lived with one family I often helped with the children, playing with them or looking after them. When they left it was very hard for me. The book *Praying our goodbyes*[8] offers some help in dealing with this sort of loss.

Although goodbyes are painful, I am happy. I want to continue to serve God until he says, "Okay Telma, your work here is done, come to me."

Chapter 5 - An Argentinian ministering to Japanese people in England

***Anny Rosciani-Woodhams** describes how she coped as an Argentinian ministering in England. She struggled with English culture where people seemed busy and private, and it was hard to make deep friendship. The keys to Anny's well-being and effectiveness included making sufficient time to spend with God and to develop friendships, and spending time with children. With these priorities in place, Anny not only had a fruitful ministry, but also overcame personal difficulties including coping with cancer while she was far from her family.*

"God said, 'It is not good for the man to be alone; I'll make him a helper, a companion'" (Genesis 2:18, MSG). This is one of my favourite verses of Scripture. God hasn't made us in isolation. He made us inter-relational people. As a Latin American, I highly value community.

I grew up in a very inclusive family. When I was young, at my parents' front door was a picture of a house and the words "Bienvenidos, nuestra casa es su casa" (Welcome, our home is your home). Even today my Mum never closes the front door, and everyone is still welcomed.

My family consisted of my parents, my two sisters, my brother, my grandparents, my aunt and her husband and their four children who all lived with us. Everyone was welcome at the Rosciani family home, and the doors were never closed. Our friends and neighbours were our extended family. We shared the ups and downs of life with them.

We were brought up as Catholics. I had my first communion when I was eight and was confirmed at the age of twelve. I experienced God as strict and distant. I liked Jesus though, because he suited my socialist views. Sex was unthinkable as it was considered 'a ticket to hell'. The fear of condemnation put us off from sexual temptation for a while.

In the 1970s in Argentina, the Bible was forbidden by the Militia who were in power. One of my sisters met with a group of college friends to secretly study the Bible. Soon after that she became a Christian. I was amazed to see the changes in her. Before, she had been the grumpy one in our family, and suddenly she became a jolly person. She became more confident too. I decided to find out what it was all about. I was a popular and rebellious teenager, but I felt extremely lonely and hungry for truth and meaning.

One day I stole the Bible from my sister and opened it randomly and put my finger in the Gospel of John. The words in chapter 14 verse 6 pierced my heart, "I am the way and the truth and the life". From that day on, something changed in me. I became aware of God's presence. I felt in love with Jesus, and God became a real person to me. I developed a passion for Jesus and for prayer, and my life began to change for good.

Before my conversion I was going out with a nice guy who later 'dumped' me because he felt I had become too religious. It was hard for me as the relationship was going well and could have ended in marriage.

A few years later I met a Christian mission worker. I wondered if he was 'the one'. I was shocked when he suddenly left Argentina with a married lady who left her husband for him. I was confused and angry; I didn't expect to be hurt by a Christian man. It took a lot of prayer and forgiveness to overcome that experience. I was helped by the love and testimony of a group of male Christian friends. I was very blessed to have a group of Christian friends to spend time with. It was impossible to feel lonely or left out.

In my culture, women were generally viewed like objects. 'Mothers or lovers', that was the view of a 'macho' orientated society. By the age of 23 you were expected to be married or at least to have a child and be a single mother. If that didn't happen you were considered weird or a lesbian. I dreamed of becoming a wife and a mother, as any woman in her twenties did. I developed a special love for children. Somehow they liked my company. I became an adoptive aunt for many of my friends' children. I worked for several years with children with special needs. I enjoy the laughter and the affection shown by these little ones.

By the age of 30 becoming a biological mother was becoming a real concern for me. As the possibility became less and less likely, I offered my longings to God and prayed for grace to cope with the desire. I grieved for a few months. One day a lady from my church approached me out of the blue and timidly shared with me that God had spoken to her about my desire to be a mother. I took her words seriously as only God knew about that desire. The word I received was that I would become 'a mother of many'. The promise from God was that I would bring spiritual children into God's Kingdom. I received those words with a mixture of feelings, as they seemed to indicate that I would not have natural children. God sustained me when my longings for a child were intense, and he gave me the passion and conviction to bring many people to his feet.

Sometimes I felt the pressure of the expectations from my culture and family was too much to handle. When I felt like giving up, I reminded myself of my identity in Christ. My identity is not defined by my status (single or married) but by what God has said and done for me.

Once I had a picture of two mirrors. One represented the world and the other represented God. I had a choice, to find myself in the reflection of the world or to see myself in God's eyes. I discovered by looking at 'God's mirror' that I am not a product of society; I am God's masterpiece, an ongoing work of the Holy Spirit. I am God's beloved daughter. Even today in my fifties I still remind myself that I am who God says I am. Single or married, I know that I am loved and valued. Over the years, I came to understand that when the Bible said in Genesis that God didn't mean for a man to be alone, he wasn't talking about marriage. He was talking about the need of human beings to be in relationship. I learnt that loneliness has nothing to do with being single but is about being disconnected from others, and that is a choice!

In my late twenties I felt a strong call to become a mission worker among Japanese people. I was very single-minded. Internally I longed for a companion, but I wouldn't put my life on hold until Prince Charming came to me. Life has to be lived to the full. So I spent all my energy in serving the Lord among students and developing a prayer ministry. I was busy until I was ready to go to England to a Bible College.

In July 1993 I arrived at Heathrow airport in London, full of excitement. I was ready to serve God and be surprised by him. My passport was stamped with the word 'alien', anticipating the feelings and the experiences I was about to have in years to come.

After six months of a 'honeymoon' period in England, I began to feel deflated. I had had enough of the rain, the cold, and grey days. Winter seemed eternal, and when the sun finally came out it felt like it was just painted in the sky! People I met seemed to only talk about the weather, and not to be interested in cultivating friendships. I felt like a palm tree planted at the North Pole.

I had left the warmth of relationships, hugs and family far behind. I felt lonely and depressed. In England I was no-one, just an alien with big aspirations for God. I felt for the first time very single, very female and very vulnerable. Despite all the anguish the culture shock provoked, I knew deep in my heart that I was not alone. God was closer than ever, he was 'walking the walk' with me.

During my first week at language school I had a chest infection. My English was very poor, but I managed to see a lady doctor. She prescribed me the contraceptive pill without even looking at me or asking me what was wrong. After explaining many times that I didn't need the Pill because I never had sex, she turned to me for the first time and asked me what was wrong with me. At that moment I felt my Latin blood rising up quickly. I managed to get off the hook by telling her that I was a nun and that sex was not allowed in the convent! The trick worked. I left the clinic with antibiotics, but emotionally wounded. I felt so unfashionable. I was in my thirties, I was single and I felt suitable for the Guinness World Record for celibacy.

After a few months of English language school I realised that six months was not enough to acquire the language skill I needed to get to Bible college, so I had to defer college for a year. There I was, without enough English or the money to survive another month. God encouraged me with Psalm 68:6, "God sets the lonely in families". God came to my rescue, and this verse became my experience. A friend of a friend was willing to receive me in her home in the south of England. I was warmly welcomed and soon after my arrival I felt part of their family. I had left my nephews and niece in Argentina, but God provided three lovely boys in England whom I played football with on Sundays, and a loving family who made me feel nourished.

The year passed quickly and I was excited to start my life in a multicultural community. At All Nations Christian College I met amazing people. I was enriched by the whole experience. God gave me a great opportunity to learn and be polished there. Even though the majority of students were single, there were times when being an unmarried person in a Bible college was a great challenge. Some of these challenges were due to cultural differences and people's expectations. Later I understood that this was the setting where God wanted to shape my character.

I made three very meaningful relationships with prayer partners that still continue today. The downside of my time at college was my difficulty to relate to male students. Being seen with them brought suspicion. I missed my male friends back in Argentina. I was just looking for a male friend, not a potential husband, but the fear of being misinterpreted put me off even trying. I look back to that aspect of my life at college with sadness, because I could have enriched my life even more during those two years if we had had the freedom to enjoy mixed friendships – I think it is easier nowadays than it was then.

In my first year at college my best friend, whom I had lived and worked with in Buenos Aires, came to England to get married. Our friendship was a covenant friendship, like David and Jonathan, unbreakable. I was happy about her news, but I also felt anxious. I wondered if I was about to lose my friend, my sister and soul mate. Still, I rejoiced with her at the wedding, and I was privileged to be her bridesmaid. Far from losing the friendship I gained a family. A year later, I became the godmother of her son and I was honorary 'Aunty Anny' to both of her children. I was there when her children walked their first steps. This helped greatly when I felt sad that I didn't have children of my own. Her family became mine. When I missed being hugged and touched (as people are very tactile in Argentina and not in England), I was able to get hugs from her children.

God has also blessed me with many other children, just as he promised. Some of these I brought to birth spiritually, and others I adopted in my heart and prayers. I am a mother of many, and I trust God that more will be born out of my ministry, my prayer and my love.

It was important for me to know what the things that enliven me were. Spending time with friends, my godchildren, and most of all spending time in prayer and worship were the necessary ingredients for me to function well in life. So I made sure that I spent plenty of time enjoying these.

Soon after Bible college I started my ministry among Japanese women in Oxford. I was blessed by living in a house for students from all over the world. We met regularly for prayer and parties. It was great to be able to share my life with others. I had flexible time but also I was very busy working.

One of the frustrating experiences of being single was that I could not choose when to take my holidays, as those who had children were given priority in our team when choosing holidays. I sometimes felt discriminated against and taken for granted. I had to learn to be humble and forgive. Money was an issue too, as I was supported by my home church in South America and they had little money. In order to afford my rent I agreed to help with the washing up at the communal breakfast. If I wanted to spend time with the Lord before the hectic day I had to get up very early. These times of prayer enabled me to be more aware of God's presence and become more dependent on him.

One day when I felt very tired and lonely, I prayed that God would provide someone to go on holiday with, and the time, the money and the opportunity to do it. I felt stuck and exhausted. I was surprised when my friend's father-in-law and his wife invited me to join a group of people from their church on a trip to Israel. Everything was paid for, and all I needed to do was to pack and go! God was so amazingly generous. I spent two refreshing weeks in the Holy Land and I didn't pay a penny.

After a few years in Oxford I sensed that God wanted me to move to London to start a Japanese group there. I joined a church and started my ministry among Japanese people in the north of London. Living in London was great, but also challenging. People seemed busier and more reserved and private than I had ever experienced. It was easier to socialise with the Japanese people than with the British, although it was difficult with those who had young children. But I didn't want to just have friends who I was ministering to. I wanted reciprocal friendships, with other Christians, separate from my work. I was happy with my own company but I realised that I was becoming like a hermit. After long hours of work I just wanted a ready meal or a pizza in front of the TV, watching *Eastenders*. I knew that if I wanted to make friends I would have to leave my comfort zone.

I understood by reading the Bible that isolation wasn't God's purpose for human beings, and I was a human being. So I began to take the initiative and stay longer after services at church, instead of rushing home to avoid people. Sometimes I invited people from church to my home. I discovered a gift that was hidden: I liked providing hospitality. I learned to cook and enjoyed it. I was having a great time with friends and a successful ministry when suddenly I faced the dark night of my soul.

In July 2003 I was diagnosed with breast cancer. For a few weeks I felt shocked, confused and terrified. I didn't know what the future would look like. I was far from my family, but throughout this time God's presence was tangible. I knew he was with me; I was never alone. I was overwhelmed by a sense of deep peace. I was comforted by the Holy Spirit and by friends who faithfully remained with me at such a difficult time, even though I wasn't very good company.

Despite the uncertainty with my health, while I waited to get a bed in hospital I went to a Christian festival called New Wine. In the midst of thousands of people worshiping God I experienced the presence of the Lord lifting me up and carrying me. I even had the strength to sing from my heart "You give and take away, blessed be your name". Whatever the future held, I knew that the Lord would meet me there. I went forward for prayer, and a well-known pastor in his 80s prayed for me. He said without knowing anything about me, "Sister the Lord is going to turn your life upside down, from now on your life is going to change forever". That was a very true statement, as in the next year my life turned upside down.

A few weeks later I was in hospital waiting for a mastectomy. In the hospital I heard about a lady vicar, mother of two children, who was dying. I poured out my anger and confusion in my prayer journal. I wrote, "Lord, why? Why has this happened to your children?" Then I tried to bargain with God. I had lived a fulfilled life, and those children needed their mum. I found myself praying that God would take my life instead of hers, so that those children could still have a mother. The woman died, leaving behind her grieving husband and two children. So, I wrote again, "Father, remember this family and look after them".

I left hospital after having my mastectomy. One part of my body was lost, but I gain a much deeper sense of the purpose of life. My experience of mortality put me in touch with the reality of eternity, and God become even more real. I developed a sense of urgency to live with purpose and a passion. Nearly a year after my time in hospital I was completely restored. I felt strong and ready for the next challenge. I decided to go back to my country and set up a drop-in centre for women who suffered from domestic violence. I prayed that God would bless my decision and vision.

As I was carefully planning my future, my best friend rang me one day to introduce me to a man who wanted to socialise. Peter was a widower who would like someone to go to the theatre with. I had a plan for my future so I was not interested in getting involved with anyone who could stop me going back to Argentina. She reassured me that Peter's motives were just to socialise. I accepted the invitation to meet him at her house. My two godchildren didn't leave me alone, as if they guessed that I needed to be shielded from any possible trouble! A few weeks later we met again, and soon after that I gave in. We started to date.

It was very stressful at times as Peter's daughter was hostile towards me. This was understandable as she was still grieving for her mother, and didn't want her father to remarry. I decided to take a break and went to Argentina for a couple of months, to pray and ask God what direction to take. I loved Peter and wanted God's approval. My only reservation was the hostility of his daughter.

I was going through an old journal when I was amazed to read a prayer that I had made in the hospital the year before, which I had forgotten. I had asked God to look after the family of the lady vicar who died. I felt that I had become the answer to my own prayer. Peter was her widower! It seemed that God was placing me in that family to love them and care for them! Instead of moving back to live in Argentina, I married Peter. Our wedding was a testimony that God had brought good out of something bad. God had freed Peter's first wife from pain and given her eternal life with him, and God was caring for her family. The wedding invitation read "Those who sow in tears will reap with songs of joy" (Psalm 126: 5). My best friend preached at the wedding, her husband married us and her children carried our rings. I had never lost her friendship as I had feared years before. My stepson was my husband's best man and my stepdaughter, despite the pain she was feeling, was there sharing her Dad's happiness. I respect her for that.

I was 43, and in a blink of an eye God turned my life upside down as he said he would. I suddenly became a wife in a cross-cultural marriage, a stepmother to two teenagers, and I gained permanent residence in England. These had not been on my agenda. God's ways are different from mine, and his plan works even better.

Life was not easy during the first three years of our marriage, and we cried many prayers for our blended family. God restored each one of us and taught us to respect and love each other. We became a loving family, with my stepchildren accepting me. My husband has enriched my life and I love him dearly. I love his children as if they were born from me. I choose to embrace them as God's gift.

I have learnt that God's main purpose for me is to make me more like him and I know that he is committed to doing this. God walked with me for 43 years as a single woman, and he is still walking with me as a married one. Singleness and marriage are tools God can use to make us the people he planned for us to be.

Chapter 6 – A single mission worker in turbulent times

Antonia van der Meer, *from Brazil, was a single mission worker for ten years in Angola and Mozambique. This was during a time of war and Marxist governments (1984 – 1995). She served with the International Fellowship of Evangelical Students (IFES), working in theological training, visiting victims of the war in the hospitals, and serving as a Personal Assistant to the General Secretary of the Evangelical Alliance of Angola. She is now serving at the Evangelical Missions Center in Brazil.*

What was it like to be a single mission worker in Angola during the 1980s and 1990s? Most Brazilian mission personnel serving during those years were single. We were used to kissing or embracing friends at home. We had to adjust to a culture where there are many restrictions on touch. Some of my friends related to men in a way which was too liberal for Angola, and people started to consider them 'easy women', not really serious and pure.

The Angolan people lacked basic supplies, and long-term military service was enforced. Because of this, many young Angolan men wanted to find a way to leave their country. Marrying a foreigner seemed like a good option. They liked the Brazilian single women, who were happy, friendly in relationships, and usually adapted well to the culture. As a result single mission workers kept receiving proposals from men. Some mission workers married nationals. Some marriages were happy, while others brought much suffering.

One friend, a medical doctor, married an Angolan doctor. The country became divided into parts dominated by the government, and those run by UNITA (who fought the government). Her husband stayed in the UNITA part and became a leader. My friend was left at home with her children in the capital. People caused her much distress as they knew who her husband was. For years she lived on her own, not receiving much news from her husband, though he sent her letters and money. Much later she moved back to Brazil for the education of their children. Finally her husband was allowed to rejoin his family.

Some of us resisted all these interesting men, and remained single. That was not easy. Sometimes we would feel lonely, especially when our friends were out of town. We did not have cars and we were not free to move around much, especially in the evenings. When I had to go out in the evenings, I would walk over a mile from my home to the meetings. I prayed for special protection. There was no public illumination on the streets and to take a torch would attract too much attention, so it was best to walk in the dark.

One 27-year-old woman was kidnapped in her own car. By God's grace the car stopped functioning at a busy roundabout, and after threatening her, the kidnappers decided to flee. She breathed deeply, prayed, and then the car drove without any problem. Her agency thought single workers should live alone, but she was too afraid to face that again. She invited a young single Mozambican who was pregnant and had problems at home to stay with her. That was a blessing for both women and for the baby.

In Angola and Mozambique, remaining single is considered very unusual. Even many Christian families would prefer their daughter to become a man's second wife, or to have a baby outside marriage, rather than to remain single and childless. Childlessness is considered the worse destiny for a woman. In Mozambique, single cross-cultural workers suffered from people trying to arrange marriages for them.

People in South America could not generally afford to visit those of us who were ministering in Africa, so it was very rare for us to receive a visitor from home. Some singles did finally receive a visit from a leader of their church or mission, but this was not always helpful. In some cases the leader made fun of her singleness, and had no time to listen and pray with her. Some leaders seemed to come for a sightseeing tour, asking a church member to show interesting places where they could buy handicrafts. The local 'tourist guide' who was very poor was shocked that pastors had money for souvenirs but not to help them.

I moved back to Brazil after ten years because my regional IFES leaders considered that I had prepared those who could lead the work onwards. My new work in Brazil focused on preparing Brazilian mission workers for their ministry, and providing care for them. I interviewed mission personnel for my doctoral dissertation, and found that the lack of member care was a strong unmet need among those who were single. Another felt need of the single mission workers was the lack of opportunities to relax. Sadness and depression were more common among singles than among those who were married.

In Latin America, single people often continue to live at home with their parents. They experience warm relationships with family and friends and in their churches. They have people to share with, to talk to, and to have fun with. There is freedom to embrace and to kiss, with due respect. Moving to places with many restrictions, very little freedom and few close relationships is hard for Latinos. A friend went to a country for which she had been praying for years. She adapted well to the local people, learned the language and made friends. But she had no Christian fellowship. The only other person from her agency was from a very different culture, and they could not relate. After suffering from extreme loneliness my friend returned home and needed a time of restoration.

Is it right to send these single Latin American women to serve in other countries? Yes, they love the Lord and the people, and they desire to adapt and integrate well, and to serve with creativity and mercy. But they need good pre-field preparation. This should include cultural training (to equip them for possibly living alone, coping with loneliness, and living in a culture where there may be little touch). There should also be security training (see resources below) to reduce the risk of being kidnapped, attacked or injured, and to help them cope if they encounter any traumatic events. Spiritual preparation is also vital, to help people be effective, depending on God and remaining aware of his presence.

In addition to pre-field preparation, mission personnel should receive on-going training and care, so that they will be able to face challenges. This might include appropriate visits (avoiding the problems mentioned above), or communication by phone or internet.

God still sends the weak, foolish and lowly, and he enables them and cares for them (1 Corinthians 1: 26-29). From this perspective I am not ashamed to be a foolish and weak person. In Angola, male mission workers were often perceived as a threat to local leaders and so there were some tensions. But how could a single, childless woman be a threat to anybody? I had greater freedom to serve because of my singleness. I thank the Lord for his wisdom.

For information about security, see
- Global Connections (2006) *Crisis Management and Prevention Guidelines* (www.globalconnections.co.uk/ codesandstandards)
- Roberts, D.L. (1999) *Staying Alive: Safety and security guidelines for humanitarian volunteers in conflict areas*. Geneva: ICRC (www.icrc.org/eng/resources/documents/ publication/p0717.htm)
- Spencer, T. (2013). *Personal Security: A Guide for International Travelers*. Boca Raton, FL: CRC Press

VOICES FROM ASIA

Chapter 7 - Why aren't you married? Asian single men in missions share their insights

Philip Chang, who is from Malaysia, is a single man who has been mobilizing and caring for Asian mission personnel for many years. In this chapter he shares insights derived from interviews and conversations with Asian single men in missions as well as those who used to be single but met their 'match' in the mission field. He interviewed 11 Asian male missionaries from six different organisations, and three male mission executives. These men come from various parts of Asia, and the majority are serving or previously served within the Asian continent. He also interviewed two female mission executives about their observations regarding single Asian men. To protect privacy, pseudonyms have been used.

Questions, questions, and more questions
"Why aren't you married? When will you invite me to your wedding? Do you want us to introduce a nice girl to you? Why are you so fussy? We have so many godly sisters in our church who are still single – shall we arrange a meal together with one of our lovely lady friends? Are you being too choosy?"

These are typical examples of the questions that an Asian single male mission worker will regularly encounter. In most parts of Asia, it is common for a man of marriageable age to experience pressure from his family and community to settle down and start having children. Parents make remarks such as:

> Oh, how we wonder if we'll ever live to drink tea served by a daughter-in-law. When can we expect to see any grandchildren? When are you going to produce offspring to carry on our family name? Look at our friends - they already have grandchildren. How we long to embrace our very own grandchildren and play with them. We are not getting any younger, and neither are you!

A son might hear such comments repeatedly like a record being played over and over again. Some mothers have the knack of making such laments, usually with a deep sigh, in the presence of visitors. The son is trapped because, like all good Asian sons, he has to keep quiet in order not to show disrespect to his parents in front of the visitors.

The pressure doesn't only come from parents. As soon as an eligible Asian man turns up at a family wedding celebration, one can be sure that within minutes he will be asked many times (especially by aunts), "When is your turn?" The Cantonese people have an expression "Aunty number three and Grand-Aunty number six" to describe someone who is a busybody. The best way to respond is probably to put on a big smile and reply "Soon, hopefully", and immediately change the subject of the conversation.

Well-meaning church friends or mission colleagues may also embarrass the single man with their comments, whether due to curiosity or genuine caring concern. Sometimes personnel in mission societies are concerned when applications are received from single men to serve in mission. They might ask each other "Why is he single? Does he intend to remain celibate or not? What happens if he falls in love and marries a local believer in the mission field? What does our policy say?"

Single Asian male mission workers: A small but growing number
"Single male missionaries are a rare breed," says John, a single man from Malaysia who has been working in the mission field for almost thirty years. While Asian mission statistics are not easily available because of the lack of detailed research from many countries, single Asian women mission workers far outnumber their male counterparts. According to a friend who leads a mission organization with well over a thousand long-term mission personnel, the ratio of single women to single men in his organization is greater than ten to one.

However, while there are far fewer single Asian men serving in mission than their female counterparts, they are no longer as rare as they were. We can think of at least four reasons why.

1. Increasing numbers of Asian mission personnel
The number of Asians in global mission has grown significantly in the past few decades. Countries like South Korea, India, and the Philippines are significant senders of cross-cultural workers. In addition, Chinese Christians from all over Asia are emerging as a major mission workforce.

Steve Moon, CEO of the Korea Research Institute for Mission, has studied the explosive growth of Korean mission personnel. He reports that from 1988 to 2013, the total number of mission workers from South Korea grew from 1,178 to 19,798, a phenomenal 1680% growth in 25 years. Between 2000 and 2012, the proportion of Korean mission workers who were single increased slightly from 12.7% to 13.8%.[9]

India is another major sender of mission workers, ranking among the top ten sending nations in the world. A recent report by the Center for the Study of Global Christianity indicates that in 2010 India sent out approximately 10,000 mission workers.[10]

Concerning the Philippines, Pastor Nono Badoy, Executive Director of the Philippines Missions Mobilization Movement, explains, "More than 5,000 Filipinos are leaving the country each day for overseas employment, and the total number of overseas Filipino workers (in secular jobs) is estimated to be more than ten million. Among them are more than one million evangelicals, many of whom are tentmakers." [11]

As the overall number of Asian mission workers has risen, so has the number of single men among them.

2. Increasing number of young Asians in short-term mission

There is an increasing number of young Asian men (as well as women) entering the mission field for short-term mission service, perhaps for a year or two, before returning home to further their studies or careers. Some use this period as a practical training stint before returning to full-time ministry in their home church or home country. Others simply wish to gain some experience living and working overseas before returning to settle down and start a family. Some mission agencies focus on recruiting students and young people to join in their short-term missions and discipleship training programmes. Most young men are still single when they joined these agencies.

These young men might marry later, but are able to serve as single men first. Chen from Hong Kong says, "When I first entered mission at the age of 25, I was still considered young and there was no pressure from my parents to settle down yet." Likewise Joseph, who is now serving in Taiwan, relates "I went into missions when I was quite young, and later returned home to enter Bible school. After graduation, I worked a few years before getting married, and went back to the field together with my wife."

3. Changing worldviews and traditions
Traditionally, men in Asia were expected to 'bring the bread home' and look after the needs of the extended family. In most Asian societies, the eldest son felt obliged to care for his elderly parents, get married, and produce offspring to carry on the family name and customs. These traditional obligations used to deter many Asian men from mission.

These age-old traditions are eroding in a rapidly modernizing world and a changing socio-economic climate. The younger generation of Asian men and women are increasingly making important decisions and actions based on their personal choices and preferences, rather than meeting the expectations of their family or community. They may feel free to move to another culture, away from their family, as this is becoming more common.

4. Rising costs of getting married
Getting married today can be very costly, as couples are expected to throw a big wedding feast and move into a new home with increased financial commitments. Wedding banquets in some Asian societies can be a lavish and costly affair, with guest numbers running into hundreds or even over a thousand. In some communities, the local customs require the bridegroom to pay a huge dowry to the bride's family and to have prepared all the necessary amenities like a new home prior to getting married. All of this contributes to a huge financial commitment that may take years to save up for.

In some affluent Asian societies, there is a common jest that a good male suitor ought to possess at least six Cs: cash, career, car, credit card, condo[12], and club membership. Some single men opt to focus on their career first and save up some money, leaving marriage to a later stage. Such changing social norms may have also influenced some who are considering a career in mission, as it is becoming less unusual to delay marriage until later.

Some snags of singleness
Some of the challenges which are most commonly encountered by single Asian men in mission involve not being trusted or respected, loneliness, sexual temptation, and pressure to get married.

1. Not being trusted
Single male mission personnel are sometimes viewed with suspicion. People wonder why they are single, when most adults are married. Is it because there is something wrong with them? Are they paedophiles, more interested in having sex with children than with adults? Are they likely to go off with someone else's wife?

Sadly, in recent years, there have been some reports of affairs and abuse by Christian workers around the world. Some of these men were involved in ministries with women and children, in churches and non-governmental organizations.

We have no evidence that single people are any more likely to abuse children or to have affairs than married people. Perpetrators of sexual offences are usually (although not always) male. They can be either married or single. In one study of around 10,000 child sex offenders, only 37% of child molesters and 27% of other child sex offenders were single. The majority were married or previously married.[13]

There is no reason why single mission workers should be trusted any less than married ones. Very few mission workers abuse children, and those who do are as likely to be married as to be single. It is good practice to get a police report or a reference for everyone involved with ministry with children or vulnerable adults – whether they are single or married, male or female.

Most people in missions are trustworthy, but it is not possible to prove innocence. Consequently some people treat single men with unwarranted suspicion. One pastor from West Asia who served in Thailand for several years stated, "People do not trust you so much when you are single. Sometimes people are suspicious of your intentions, especially if they have daughters. Somehow they do not treat you like a fully qualified pastor even if you are one."

Another full-time minister from West Asia who is serving in South Korea remarked, "When I was still single, I did not feel welcome or comfortable visiting families... After my marriage, however, the men did not mind me visiting their homes and their families even if they (the men) were not at home."

Each of the male mission workers interviewed who had since got married confirmed that the trust factor improved significantly after they married. "People respected me much more when they knew I was a married man", says one mission worker from an ethnic Chinese background.

A Filipino mission worker relates that when he started in mission, his team mates lacked faith in him because he was single, and did not encourage or support him. "When I initially entered the mission field, I was shocked to discover that my married team mates did not expect me to last long there simply because I was a single guy... They anticipated that I would succumb easily to the pressures and temptations faced by a single man, and they waited to observe how long it would take for me to drop out". He managed to prove his critics wrong, and stayed a long time.

2. Lack of respect
In some Asian societies, marriage is a sign of maturity and adulthood. A single man, even if he has grey hair or no hair, is seen as not having reached maturity. Even his sending church and mission colleagues may lack confidence in a single male mission worker. Mark, who initially served eight months in Central Asia as a single man, said, "Seeking full support from my home church was a major challenge. They did not really understand how a single male mission worker can contribute in the field". After he married and returned to serve with his wife, he was treated with more respect. He offers a word of advice to churches: "You should treat a single male the same as you would treat a family in terms of offering member care, financial support, and prayer."

In some countries and communities, local people are very curious about single men. Some communities consider marriage and having children as a sign of being prosperous and blessed by God, and important in order to enlarge the community of faith. Alan, who served in Central Asia for several years, states, "In a Muslim culture, they may think that you are a strange person if you are not married". Wang, a mission worker from China, says, "The local people cannot accept for a man to be single. They think he is a sinful person for disobeying the teachings of their holy book and prophet. According to their beliefs, every man should marry and reproduce to enlarge their community". The community has a different attitude towards a single woman. "They think she has a pure heart and chooses to remain a spinster to serve the community, so it is acceptable for a woman to remain single." Men, on the other hand, are expected to marry and have children (preferably lots of them), in order to be accepted into the community.

3. Loneliness

Many single Asian male mission workers find loneliness a huge challenge. This is especially difficult if you are from a large close-knit family and always used to having people around. "Probably the biggest challenge I can think of is that of getting sick and miserable and not having someone around to cheer you up and lend a helping hand during such moments," says John. "Also, there are times when you come home frustrated and discouraged due to ministry problems, and you don't have your own family to share your frustrations and feelings with. You only have the regular planned sharing time with mission colleagues and friends."

To overcome his loneliness, Lee (who worked in South Asia) says, "I shared a house with other single guys... I had to learn how to relate to people from other cultures." This helped a great deal in Lee's ministry because he found it easy to form friendships with the young local men on the street where he lived. He adds, "I am thankful for the support of fellow workers as we labour together. There were a number of single guys with whom I was able to have fellowship."

Some single workers even die alone. Steve Moon, who has interviewed many Korean mission workers in the course of his research, reports that "It is usually very sad at the funeral of single male mission workers in Korea. There are hardly any family members there. Usually only a few mission workers and former mission colleagues turn up at their funerals to pay their last respects."

4. Sexual temptation

"Missionaries are men too, not super-spiritual or neutered beings who only think holy thoughts all day long," says Paul, an athletic man who used to be active in sports before entering the mission field. Mission workers, like any other human beings, are not perfect, and are subject to all forms of temptation. This can come at any time and in the most unexpected places. Peter, who was single when he pastored a church in Thailand, explains candidly, "Sometimes the young girls will approach you for prayer or ministry. All kinds of thoughts can go through your mind." He adds, "Attraction to females can simply be due to loneliness rather than sexual. On several occasions I was tempted to find a girlfriend or wife who is not a Christian, simply for the sake of companionship."

Alan describes his personal experience in Central Asia. "There is some temptation from local girls, because most of them are willing to marry a foreigner due to their bad situations or poor economic conditions."

It is wise to avoid compromising situations like being alone with a girl during ministry. However, there are times when the work requires travel alone. In some countries, as soon as a man checks-in to a hotel and walks into his bedroom, the phone will ring and a voice on the other end will ask, "Sir, do you want any massage? Do you want any special services?" If your response is negative, then the voice may persist and ask, "If you do not want a lady, would you prefer a boy instead?"

Peter raised the taboo topic of masturbation, saying, "Whether or not masturbation is a sin, you should not make it such a habit that your mind is affected and you become controlled by it".

Single men are not alone in facing sexual temptation. Single women and married people also face sexual temptation. The single men I interviewed had successful strategies to overcome temptation. Joseph managed to avoid getting into unwanted relationships despite being surrounded by older women colleagues who showered him with unwanted attention. "I kept my focus on my ministry, set boundaries with the opposite sex, and kept strictly to the agency's rules which did not permit anyone to start a relationship with any team mate for at least one year."

Peter, who was based in the city where he was surrounded by plenty of nightlife, relates how he kept himself from moral failure. "Being afraid of being seen in compromising situations or locations kept me from going to such places," he says. "Being seen there might be a stumbling block to others." Strong self-discipline is a great deterrent from falling into sin.

Whatever measures one may take, it is natural for men to have sexual urges that need to be cooled down. "I have to do lots of sports and take cold showers to overcome my sexual urges," admits Darius, a 30-year old from West Asia who is tent-making in South East Asia. "I try really hard to control myself and sometimes resort to fasting and praying".

A good practice in Asia is to avoid local 'heaty' foods or aphrodisiacs that can act like sexual stimulants.[14] Abstinence and learning to control sexual desires are essential. All the single Asian men interviewed agreed that ultimately, the key to overcoming loneliness and sexual temptations is maintaining a strong spiritual life and to have good accountability to protect you from falling into sin.

See chapter 22 for more on the topic of temptation, and chapter 23 for more about masturbation.

5. Pressure to get married

"To be or not to be (married)?" That is the question. As described at the start of this chapter, a single Asian man will inevitably attract a lot of questions and face unwanted pressure to be married, even if he wants to remain single. Steve Moon reports, "In Korean society, there is tremendous pressure from parents for a son to be married... Also, when the single Korean mission worker gets together with his peers, he may feel out of place, and feel pressure to be married like the others in order to fit in with them."

For some, the pressure comes from mission colleagues. As there are many more single women than single men in missions (and in the Church generally), a single man can be put under pressure to marry one of the many women who are looking for a husband. Joseph was quite young when he first entered mission, and he experienced unwanted attention. "I felt a lot of pressure from the ladies in the team who were still single, especially those over 30 years old". Friendship with local or expatriate women may be misunderstood, and be perceived as your intention to marry them, so great care must be taken. Sometimes the pressure comes from within, from a strong desire to marry. Paul acknowledged, "When I was single, it was customary to check out single sisters, and they were checking me out. I was always wondering which one the Lord had in mind for me. It was both exciting and frustrating!"

Some mission teams have strict policies regarding relationships between a single man and a single woman in the team. While a relationship may be permitted in some circumstances, it is not easy for a single Asian man to develop relationships in a multi-cultural team. Chen explains, "Coming from a more conservative Chinese background, I found it more difficult than others, especially the Westerners who interact more easily with girls on the team."

Matchmakers – a blessing or a curse?

Although matchmaking is no longer a profession in most Asian societies these days, it is still a popular pastime for many Asians. You can be sure that many Asian friends or colleagues will jump at any opportunity to introduce potential suitors to a single male mission worker.

While such introductions may be appreciated, it would be better if well-meaning friends could avoid creating awkward situations for the mission worker. Some try to pair up two persons who are not really suited for one another or not interested in being married. One retired mission worker who has remained single explains, "Some kind people think that it would be good for you to be married, so they try to matchmake you with someone they think would be ideal for you. This makes the relationship with that person rather awkward at times."

In some instances, friends can become too enthusiastic about matchmaking two interested persons so that it completely backfires, instead of allowing the relationship between them to develop naturally at its own pace. While both parties may be willing to enter into friendship that might lead to serious courtship, too much interference or pressure can spoil things between them.

Advantages of being single
Male mission workers find that being single has a number of positive factors. John, who is serving in Latin America, emphasizes one advantage of living alone: "One significant aspect is being able to have the space and time to reflect, contemplate and relate with God without any distractions when I am home and alone."

Paul, a Malaysian who went to the mission field as a bachelor and later married a fellow mission worker, observes two significant advantages of being single: lighter burden and lower budget. Marriage has inevitably made a huge difference in terms of his freedom of movement and lifestyle. "I could travel more and accept invitations to speak in many places when I was a single. I didn't need a big place to live either, and I could move at my own speed."

Lee, a Malaysian who has retired from mission, highlights the convenience of being single. "One is able and available to go at any time to any place without having to consult or consider the needs of other family members." Similarly, Cheong, another Malaysian, adds, "I could come back home at odd hours without disturbing or waking up anybody, and accept invitations to eat anywhere at any time without prior consideration from a family."

Life becomes very different after getting married and having children, as Bambang from Indonesia discovered. He explains, "Before marriage, I had the freedom to do what I liked. There were no worries about safety or security. Now, after marriage, I always worry about my family. I miss home whenever I travel, and have to think about managing finances more carefully."

Flexibility in terms of time management, mobility, and decision-making in ministry are some of the compelling reasons for male mission workers to remain single while serving in mission.

Words of wisdom from experienced men (and women too)
Pramila, a single mission executive, offers this practical advice for mission teams from a woman's perspective: "If the team leader is a single male, it can be awkward if the team has many single ladies. Just make sure there is another woman leader in the team to supervise the single ladies."

Being certain about one's calling to ministry while having a good sense of humour will be very helpful, especially when confronted by the usual questions. "From time to time people ask me about my family (meaning my wife and children). When I mentioned that I am not married, they are amazed and some of them offer to help me find a wife" says John. "I find those times amusing rather than awkward. Once I had somebody telling me that I am not complete until I am married, and I responded that I am very much complete as I find my life and purpose in Christ!"

"Preconceptions regarding singleness are predominant not only in Asia but also in other countries that emphasize family units and values", says Cheong. "Effectiveness and fruitfulness in any ministry is about God's calling and finding our purpose in him and then surrendering our will to do his will. Single male mission workers need lots of encouragement and moral support."

Peter recalls the time when he was forced to be in a situation where he had to minister alone for a long period without any team members. "Looking back, it would have been helpful if I had had a more mature person around as my mentor, someone who could provide guidance and encouragement especially to deal with the challenges of being single amidst all the temptations around me," he says. Having a mentor, good friends or a support group helps.

John adds, "For those single male missionaries who are about to throw in the towel due to the factors mentioned above, I want to encourage you to keep your eyes upon Jesus and remain focused on him".

To single men who wish to get married, we say do not give up hope. Those who have found a wife while in ministry offer some practical advice. "Get educated about ladies and relationships. Learn how to date and court a girl." Some even suggest taking a sabbatical to study at a seminary for a year or two. Many of these mission workers met their wives at Bible school. A good number also met their wives while serving in the mission field.

Asian mission workers are increasing in number and here to stay. They bring their wisdom, virtues, and values to the mission field. Whether single or married, there is plenty that they can contribute. If they are single, they have many unique advantages that can be helpful in their ministries and they can be a great blessing in the mission field.

Chapter 8 - Where is my helper? A Chinese woman in Central Asia

Little Dove *is a single mission worker from Hong Kong. She has been in Central Asia for 17 years.*

There have been many changes in Hong Kong in the past 15 years. The average age for a woman to marry has increased from around 25 to 30. More women in Hong Kong are single now, whether they are Christian or not. This is because more women are achieving highly academically and seeking their own career. Significant work pressure and long working hours leave employed people with little time to develop their personal interests and social life. Many women find it difficult to find a dating partner with a compatible level of knowledge and career status. For Christian ladies it is even more difficult to find a man with the same level of faith. Some women from Hong Kong solve the problem by going to Mainland China to work and search for a husband. This option is not right for everyone though.

When I was growing up there were fewer single people. People in my parents' generation are not used to considering singleness as an option. Most parents in Hong Kong who are over the age of sixty are not Christians. If their daughter does not have a boyfriend the parents ask why. Some try to arrange an appointment for their daughter to meet a son of their friends, whether or not their daughter wants to meet him. After several years of struggling like this, parents (especially mothers) became tired of their unmarried daughter continuing to pursue only her faith, and not seeking a husband. My mother told her friends that I was out of my mind, or was not a lovable person in the eyes of men. Once or twice she made such complaints to people she did not know who were sharing the table when we were eating in a restaurant.

It is difficult for unmarried women to answer the question, "Why haven't you had a boyfriend?" The Chinese New Year festival can be especially difficult. Relatives come together, and married couples give red pockets (envelopes with money) to the children and also to single people. Then they usually ask the singles, "When will *you* give red pockets?" Another difficult time is Valentine's Day. Due to the promotion by the mass media and shops, there are pictures of sweet couples everywhere.

This can cause inner pressure for single people, especially those who hope to get married but don't have a partner.

Another difficult time is when good friends get married, leaving the remaining single friend feeling even more lonely.

Pressure to marry may come from relatives, peers or society, or there may be inner pressure. We have to deal with teasing words, loneliness, and the fear that nobody will take care of us when we become old. The Chinese have a proverb that says "Raising up children is a preparation for us in old age". Government and social facilities are very limited in caring for the elderly, especially those who are single and do not have many relatives nearby. The pension system for single mission workers provides little money compared to the average. Some single mission personnel fear how they will survive after retirement if they do not have their own property.

I received the call to become a mission worker on the third day of my Christian life, during my daily devotion when I was 16-years-old. In the very beginning of my Christian life, God showed me three verses:

> *Believe in the Lord Jesus, and you will be saved – you and your household. (Acts 16:31)*
> *Go into all the world and preach the good news to all creation. (Mark 16:15)*
> *The Lord God said, "It is not good for the man to be alone. I will make a helper suitable for him." (Genesis 2:18)*

From these verses, I understood that God will help my family to know him and accept him; what I need is to keep my eyes on him and try different ways to let them know that he is God. I would go out to the mission field where I could serve nations. And I did not need to worry about finding a life partner, because he promised to give me a helper. I realised that I would be a tentmaker, meaning that I should use my professional skills to serve God in an area where an evangelist would not be allowed to stay.

My youngest sister is 14 years younger than me, and became a Christian at the age of six. She saw how my parents scolded me and did not treat me with favour because I was a Christian. I did not want to leave her until she was in her final year at school. I asked God to give me ten years of preparation time, so that I could gain practical service experience in my church and get a recognised qualification to work overseas. I prayed that my family's perception of my faith would change. During the ten years I helped my sister as she grew up, and I provided my family with an apartment to live in, so that they would manage financially. I also acquired sufficient professional skills to be able to work as a professional abroad.

When I was 35, I went to work in Central Asia. I discovered that in my new country, when people meet new friends, the first questions are usually "What is your name?" "How old are you?" "Are you married?" "How many children do you have?" And for single women, "Do you want to marry a local guy?" Sometimes the men even ask, "Would you like to marry me?" A single Taiwanese woman who came here was angered by these questions, because she thought that the local people had invaded her personal private life too much.

I was fortunate because I look about ten years younger than I am. People asked these questions, and I had the confidence to reply politely that I am still single. I explained that by God's grace he can give me a suitable husband, and nationality is not important to me. What I want in a husband is a pure heart to serve God, and mutual understanding and love.

People in this part of Central Asia, whatever their ethnic group, tend to marry much earlier than those in Hong Kong. If ladies over 25 are still single, their relatives and peers put a lot of pressure on them to marry. Once I met a professional lady who was about 30-years-old. She told me that she had just got divorced, after being married for six months. She only got married to stop the constant pressure from her parents; she did not love her husband very much. She said she is now free to choose to live a single life, as a divorcee, because her family will no longer put pressure on her.

Being single and looking young helps me to develop close relationships with the university students (even though I am the same age as their mothers). When they hear my age, they ask me to tell them my secrets for looking so young. This creates an interesting starting point for me to share about the peace of God.

In the Muslim culture I live in, people believe that if someone is blessed by God, they will marry and have children. Therefore, local people think I don't have God's blessing, as I am single. If I try to counsel couples who have marital problems, the husband tells me to shut up, as I only know theory.

On several occasions local men who were divorced and alcoholic proposed to marry me, in order to solve my visa problems and their need of a wife. Some local sisters tried to arrange a date for me by inviting me to their homes for meals, without telling me that this was to introduce me to a man. Taxi drivers have also offered to date me and even to marry me, when I have needed to take a taxi home at night. Even though I told them that I am already 52-years-old, this still does not quench their sex drive.

I am a shy person, but when I came to the point of loving a man, I was bold in expressing my feelings. I have done this twice, and both times were unsuccessful. Once was to a Christian colleague in Hong Kong when I was around 25. He was unable to overcome his homesickness after a one-week trip to Macau, so he could never leave home to be with me.

The second time was when I was about 45. I fell in love with a local Christian where I was ministering. He was very gentle, sincere, and kind to me. He said that he wanted to be my helper. I wished I could hide my age, because it would be difficult for us to develop our relationship if everyone knew that I was 16 years older than him. But it was not possible to hide that.

We had several deep talks about our relationship. At first we were really close and seemed to develop the relationship, but there were too many obstacles. Besides age, there was a language problem – I couldn't speak his heart language fluently enough. In addition, people said unpleasant things about us. Finally he withdrew and married a lady of the same ethnic group. He had been my companion for a time and helped me overcome some difficulties in ministry, but now he has his own life companion, and I choose to bless him.

As a single female mission worker in a Muslim culture, without any team-mates for the past six years, it has not always been easy to remain full of joy and hope. My personal relationship with God is what has helped me most as I have dealt with loneliness, being abandoned, and being looked down upon. Last April during an eight-day personal retreat, God revealed himself to me as my friend, my Father and my lover. As I reflected on this, I suddenly thought about God's provision of a helper in a new way. I had previously thought God would give me a husband to be my helper. In an exegetical preaching, my former seminary teacher explained that 'helper' in Genesis 2:18 was a collective representation of all kinds of human relationships. What God did not want to see was a person living alone without any companionship. God has provided me with significant relationships with people. I have been living with some young single ladies. I have companions locally to have fun with and hang around with in the holidays. I have supporters who I see during home assignments. We need people to provide pastoral care and to keep track of our emotional health and our ministry performance. I am glad that my sister and some of my close female friends call me when they find out that I may be feeling low. They are soul friends. God has provided helpers for me, although not in the way I expected when I first read Genesis 2:18 as a new Christian.

My help comes from the Lord, the Maker of heaven and earth. (Psalm 121:2)

I will talk to the Father, and he'll provide you another Friend so that you will always have someone with you. (John 14:15, MSG)

Chapter 9 - Community in Cambodia

Chami Nagai *is a 27-year-old Japanese woman who has been serving in Cambodia for three years. She writes about community.*

I am part of a team serving with *Servants to Asian's Urban Poor*. This organisation has five core principles, one of which states:

> **Community** - As well as a commitment to the communities we move into, we have a passion to work together in supportive teams that model the love, care and community that Jesus spoke of. We work with people, not just for them[15].

This commitment to community, in a supportive team, has been helpful to me as a single person. My team members (who are all married) have generously included me in family life. They let me spend time with their children, and often invite me to join their family holidays. One family invites me to come to their house every Thursday, where I feel free to grab a drink from the fridge, take snacks from the cupboard, then help make food or relax while we spend the evening together.

There have been discussions on singleness within our organisation which have helped to cultivate a healthy perspective on singleness and sexuality. We have changed from talking about "issues that singles have", to "issues we all might have, related to our relationships and sexuality". When I share things, my team members avoid having an attitude of "you're single and we're married, so we can't relate to that". We look at the gifts that each of us can offer, as singles and married couples. As well as being generous with their time, team members have encouraged me to seek single friends for support.

Within *Servants*, we also value wholism. This means more than embracing both social action and care for the soul. It includes celebrating all aspects of what it means to be human, including our desire for intimacy and our sexuality. This approach has helped me feel free to share how I am feeling, including my loneliness or frustration at not having a spouse to share things with. We aim to accept each other as whole people, not just the spiritual part. We lift the whole of life to God, celebrating how we are indeed made in His image.

Sometimes conservative Christians speak as if sexuality is only about sexual intercourse, within the context of marriage. That view implies that single Christians cannot be sexual beings, suggesting that they need to be on the lookout for a partner if they want to become sexual. I have come to disagree with such a limited view on sexuality. One book which I have found helpful when it comes to discovering the gift of my sexuality as a woman, is *Being Sexual... and Celibate*.[16] The author explores sexuality in terms of intimacy, not just putting it into a romantic genital relationship. This has helped me look at different relationships which fulfil different needs I have, and enabled me to celebrate being a woman (see chapter 26).

In the past I had an approach to life that could be summed up as, "I am a strong, independent woman and don't need men". That is how I fended for myself while growing up and leaving home and living overseas for many years. But as I have encountered many moments of difficulty and weakness, I have been able to recognize that I cannot, and need not, always be self-sufficient and independent. Out of that realisation has come appreciation of the gifts that I have to offer.

Another of the core values for *Servants* is creativity. I had never thought of this word as being connected to how I see my sexuality, but the word 'generative,' which another single person shared with me, has become a framework for thinking about my femininity. I like to be creative, through words and music. I also enjoy cooking and decorating. I was able to link the gift of being a woman to being generative (generating beauty, music, etc). This is a broader way of looking at my femininity compared to seeing it as something that is only activated through marriage or child bearing.

One challenge I face is not having someone to share life with on a deep level. When a crisis arises, singles are more vulnerable. I have found that it is easy to get sucked into a 'go, go, go' mode and not take time to rest, since the flexibility singles have means that the rhythm of everyday life can be easily pushed aside. Families have the flow of breakfast then off to school, lunch, nap, afternoon activities, evening meal, bath, and downtime after the children are in bed, but I have sometimes found myself skipping meals or working straight through until night. It has to do with my own discipline, but since there is no immediate accountability (from a husband or children), it is easy to get away with an unhealthy lifestyle.

Many Cambodian people ask why I'm not married, since girls here tend to marry when they are 16 or 17 in the countryside, or in their early twenties in the city. I have not found it offensive when people have asked why I'm not married, because I know the culture. I tell them that in my home country (Japan) people get married later. There probably would not be a lot of understanding towards a Cambodian woman if she decided not to marry and have children. Because I am a foreigner, they just accept me as being different.

In Japan, the pressure to marry is not as strong as it is in Cambodia. The average age for marriage in Japan keeps rising and there are many more people these days who aren't married. My family has never put pressure on me. However, as I am now 27, my grandparents often ask when I will marry, or if I have met anyone yet. My grandparents' generation was probably more similar to how Cambodia is, with people getting married younger and with more arranged marriages.

As I have shared above, community has had a powerful effect on me. The hardest thing for me has been not having someone who speaks my own language where I live. Since our vision is to live in the community in an incarnational way, I have lived with a Cambodian family. This has been great, but there have been times when the cultural differences have made it hard to share with this lovely family. I have felt sad because other people have spouses to share with and I don't. When I was with *Servants* in Vancouver, we lived in a community house together, opening our home to our friends on the streets. I thrived in that kind of intense community living (as tiring as it can be). I miss living with people who speak my language, but this lifestyle also has many blessings, mainly in that I get to walk closely with my Cambodian family and neighbours.

For me, the gifts of being a single mission worker include close relationships, easier language acquisition (as there is more time, and no spouse to distract me from learning), productivity, flexibility, the ability to go deep into the culture, and being able to befriend many people. It has been a gift being a young Asian woman in Cambodia, as I am not seen as a benefactor (while Caucasian men may be seen as that), and I can befriend Cambodian families and singles quite easily.

Chapter 10 - Being shot in Nepal and India

Are you willing to be shot? If you travel in certain parts of the Indian subcontinent, you might be shot frequently, as **Debbie** *describes.*

"Do you mind if I shoot you?"

It was my last day in Nepal. A civil war was raging, and I had been invited to visit mission personnel around the country who were grappling with the question of whether they should stay or leave the country. Some families had had windows shattered by bombs. Curfews restricted movement. It was a dangerous place to be. I had updated my will before leaving home, and was prepared to die during the trip. But I didn't expect someone to ask permission before shooting me!

"Do you mind if I shoot you?" he repeated.

I was sitting at the hairdressers, looking forward to a cheap trim as prices are much lower in Nepal than at home. I couldn't see what was happening around me. I'm extremely short-sighted, and had taken my spectacles off for the haircut.

The speaker explained, "We're making a television programme on hair and beauty products. Do you mind if I shoot you?" I consented, and laughed throughout the filming as they asked me questions about beauty products. "I don't use any", I giggled, thinking they had definitely picked the wrong person. "What shampoo do you recommend?" they tried. "I go for the cheapest", I replied. Refusing to give up, they asked, "What does beauty mean to you?" "Um... I don't think outward appearance matters much. It's what's inside and how you act that makes you a beautiful person", I replied, vaguely remembering words in 1 Peter 3: 3-4.

I left Nepal the following day, which meant I never saw myself on the big screen. This episode left me wondering why people would film me. There were plenty of gorgeous Nepali women in the saloon, but the film crew picked the one white woman, although I obviously don't use beauty products! I suppose we take pictures of what is unusual in our environment.

On another occasion I was in India, sitting on my own outside the magnificent Red Fort. Scores of Indian tourists came to take a photo of me, some bringing their children to be in the picture with me.

One mission worker I know felt extremely distressed in India, because everywhere she went people took pictures of her on their mobile phones. She ended up refusing to leave her room, as she felt harassed by the phones which were repeatedly pushed in her face as people took her picture.

Personally, I don't like having my photo taken. But it's not a big deal. In the past I have travelled to many countries and photographed local people and their houses. People from resource rich countries have done this for decades. It is only in recent years that people throughout the world have gained the power that comes through owning a mobile phone with a camera. So why shouldn't they take our pictures too? It might help them feel more empowered, and brighten their day. Even if the guy taking the photo tells his friends that I'm his girlfriend, to boost his self-esteem, I'm not particularly bothered.

The one thing which I object to is if I think the photo will be used for dubious purposes. For example, some people deliberately try to take 'sexy' photos to put on 'creepshots' websites. If you are modestly dressed, they are not likely to be interested, so this is a good way to avoid this. People taking 'creepshots' try to do this without you noticing. If someone does not hide the fact that they are taking your photo, it is probably just because you are an object of interest, and not for any negative reason. You might like to engage them in conversation and ask what they want the photo for.

I have written this to warn you that you might be photographed more than you want to be if you travel outside your culture, to where you look different. Especially if you are a woman alone in parts of India. Be prepared for this to happen. It's a wonderful country, most of the people are lovely, and it's better to be shot by a camera than by a gun, isn't it?

VOICES FROM AFRICA

Chapter 11 - A Zambian mission worker's single journey

Annie *is a single mission worker from Zambia. She brings an African perspective to the experience of singleness in a culture where being single is considered abnormal, and travel without a protective male can be dangerous.*

I am a 45-year-old single African woman and I have been on the mission field for the past 19 years. When I started out in mission I never imagined for a moment that I would still be single at this age. In my culture marriage is considered normal and right, while singleness is thought of as abnormal and wrong. A single person is considered odd and is subjected to a lot of questions. These range from people wondering if you are single due to character or morality issues, to whether you have an alternative lifestyle. At one time I shared a house with another lady mission worker and one of our African colleagues asked if we were gay and were living as a couple. It was a challenge trying to explain things like choice and God's timing to a person who cannot comprehend how anyone can live as a single person without satisfying sexual desires.

Not only am I single but I'm also a woman in a male-dominated world. In terms of being worthy of respect, a single woman is only considered a little bit more important than a child. Being a single woman can be a hindrance to ministry. A single woman may be overlooked. I remember a time when I and two other mission workers, a lady and a man, went to a remote village to run a training program. I was the team leader but whenever we had meetings with the leaders in the community and churches, the men always referred all their questions to the man in our team.

In the Zambian culture, it is expected that the women in the family should serve the men (including spouse, father, brothers, uncles and cousins). If the woman is single, this is expected even more. I went to visit a cousin of mine in another town some time back. He had separated from his wife and was living with his two teenage sons. No sooner had I arrived at the house than I was told that I would be making supper for them all. I'm not the best of cooks and I don't like cooking. To make matters worse he got someone to buy a village chicken - that is the type you have to pluck yourself and whose meat is very tough. He asked me to cook the chicken as well as the staple mealie meal porridge. I had to boil the meat for ages to get it tender. I did my best but the meal was a disaster. My cousin was very gracious about it and made sure that for the next meal I could choose something easier to cook.

In my culture it is generally felt that a single person cannot speak into the life of married people or into the area of raising children. I cannot count the number of times I've been told, "Oh you don't understand, wait until you're married and have children of your own". I was particularly blessed some years ago by a couple who asked me to teach them how to raise their children. I was very humbled as this was so out of character in the culture but it was a great affirmation for me as a single person. This couple respect me a lot and I still speak into their lives today. Their daughter is now 15 years old and on a recent visit they asked me to counsel and pray with her.

A single woman may be viewed with suspicion, perceived as a threat and may not be welcomed by married women. In some situations men may even perceive her as being 'easy'. One has to be aware of the dangers that a single person in ministry may face. Being in leadership in a predominantly male world I find myself working closely alongside men most of the time. This can create a situation where I develop friendships with these married men whose wives are not in leadership. Friendship develops because we spend time together and have a lot in common in the leadership context. Without the fear of God I could easily find myself developing an inappropriate intimacy with a married man. I always have to be on guard and totally dependent on the Lord to enable me to be holy in thought and action.

All five of my siblings are married and have children and some even have grandchildren. One of the toughest things during the years has been going home to visit my family and church and repeatedly being asked if I was married or if there was someone in my life now. I grew to dread the question and always prayed that the next time I went home I would have the news that everybody was waiting for. I thank God that as I've grown older the questioning has diminished and now people say that I'm like a nun, one who has renounced marriage. As a single person I have also had to deal with matchmakers. People mean well and believe they are helping by trying to hook me up with guys they think would be perfect for me. So far none of these have caught my interest, hence I'm writing this as a single! There is a lot of pressure to get married, as if marriage was the end goal in life. I can think of many young ladies who were very active in church, but as soon as they got married they stopped doing any ministry as if to say, "I've attained my goal, I can rest now".

I love being single but one of my regrets is not having any children. When I was growing up I dreamed of having a daughter. In my culture having children is a big issue. It is generally believed that you must have children so that they can look after you physically and financially when you get old. Children are your inheritance.

Many young ladies and men will do anything to have a child, even if they are not married; hence our communities have many single parents. Many men have left their wives and married another because the wife was unable to bear children, and these men receive encouragement from their families to do so. A fellow Zambian mission worker in her late forties has recently started going through the menopause. One of the other ladies commented, "Oh how sad not to have experienced motherhood". She did not take into consideration that this lady has had many fruitful and satisfying years of ministry behind her.

A few years ago a gynaecologist told me that I needed to go out and have a child because time was running out. When I said to him, "But I'm not married", his response was "So?" Every time I go to a place to minister and the group is given an opportunity to ask questions, I know that among the questions there will be three that will always be asked without fail. These are, "How old are you?", "Are you married?", and "Do you have any children?" I have no biological children, but I have many spiritual children for which I am very grateful.

Loneliness is a big issue for singles in missions. I find myself surrounded most of the time by married couples, especially now as I'm involved in leadership. There are only a handful of single people involved in this area. When I attend a meeting or a conference I find that I may be the only single person. I remember being invited one time to dinner and as we left to go to the restaurant I realized that I was the only single person with four couples. I almost turned back but they all made me feel welcome and wanted.

Single people long for companionship and intimacy. There is a desire for someone who would be a permanent fixture in your life, someone who only death would separate you from. I've made many best friends over the years but friends get married and the relationship changes or they move away. Then I find myself alone and needing to make a new best friend again, which takes time.

Travelling alone in Africa as a single African woman puts you in a very vulnerable place. I especially feel the need for companionship when I have to travel long distances on my own. I would like a protector, and someone to process daily happenings with.

There have been times when I have found myself in real danger, such as the occasion when I went to the beach with my team mates on our day off. Not many people go there, and there is only one eating place, with the only restroom on the beach. I went off to use the restroom, which was some distance away, and then went back to the members of my team. Along came a worker from the eating place, who told me that the owner wanted to see me. I didn't suspect anything so I went with him. When I got there I was asked if I'd used the restroom and I said "yes". I didn't know that another lady had used it after me and had left it in a mess, and they thought it was me.

I tried to explain that I had left it clean, but there was no reasoning with the owner, who had been drinking and probably using drugs. He grabbed the front of my shirt and threatened to beat me up. I was very scared but then a supernatural courage came upon me and I pointed my finger in his face and told him that he would not beat me. Finally some people came and pulled him away and told me to forget the whole thing because the man was drunk. If I'd been married I would not have gone off to face those people on my own. I would have had a protector with me. Ultimately the Lord is my protector and he proved himself to be that on that day and every day.

Every trip I make I put my life completely in the hands of the Lord. I am a quiet, gentle, soft-spoken person but when I travel in Africa I almost become a different person because it is the only way to cope with the challenges that I face. I once travelled with a friend and she was shocked at the new me. When I travel I have to be almost aggressive and not show any fear. This usually works well, but not always.

I serve as a regional coordinator, and need to travel regularly between five countries: Angola, Malawi, Mozambique, Zambia and Zimbabwe. Public transport is getting better but when I first went into mission it was really difficult. At times I had to stand by the road-side for hours on end, waiting for transport. During the wait I would have to deal with advances from men. On the buses, if a man under the age of 60 sat next to me, whether he was married or single, I would be sure to be asked for my phone number or even asked outright for a relationship. African men can understand why a white woman would be travelling alone (as they assume she's a tourist), but it's hard for them to understand why an African woman would be travelling alone.

One time I was in a small town about 300kms from my home base. I was staying with friends. I bought a ticket to catch a small open pick-up truck home at four o'clock the next morning, but I overslept. I woke up at ten minutes to four and realised that I was late. I had been in Mozambique for ten years and in all that time I had never seen public transport leave on time. It just so happened that on this day the truck left on time! I got to the bus station at ten minutes past four and the truck was nowhere to be seen.

There was no other public transport leaving the area that day. I was upset as I had commitments back home that I needed to attend to. I prayed for a miracle and a short while later I saw a private truck going to the main road. There were two men in the truck and they offered me a ride. I had no choice but to get on. I put my life in the Lord's hands and trusted him to watch over me as I sat between these two strange men for the 300km trip through the middle of nowhere where there is no phone coverage or any means of communication with the outside world. Both men were Muslim and I was able to share the gospel with them. They were very interested, listened attentively and asked many questions. They made me feel safe throughout the trip and when I got to the place where I was going, they let me out. I thanked them and went on my merry way.

Many times I faced situations which were scary but which were in hindsight funny. One time I was travelling from Mozambique to Zambia to visit my family. I went via Zimbabwe and spent a night at my sister's house. The next morning I planned to take the bus to Lusaka, from the main bus station in Harare. This place had a reputation for having thugs and pick-pockets. A friend of my sister offered to escort me to the bus stop as he was familiar with the place and would protect me.

When we got to the bus station, my sister's friend was a few steps ahead of me carrying my backpack. Suddenly he was surrounded by about eight guys. This was a tactic to keep him away from me. One big guy grabbed me around the waist from behind and started to run with me. I had no idea what was going on but because of the stories I'd heard about the place I thought I was being kidnapped. I started screaming, kicking and trying to get away. A couple of minutes later he deposited me in one of the buses heading to Zambia. The whole episode was so that I would take that particular bus. Apparently the bus operators had a deal with these guys to make sure they helped load their bus and these guys would then get paid. I was scared out of my mind and shaking all over. Sitting on the bus, all I could do was thank God that I was safe. I felt very humiliated and angry that no one had come to my rescue. People just watched. After a while I started to see the funny side and now I can laugh about it.

In another incident I was travelling from Mozambique to Malawi. The route I had to use has a stretch of 250kms of dirt road with poor transport. I waited almost the whole day for a ride to the border town. Finally at around 4pm I got a ride in the back of a pick-up truck. I was the only female on the truck. I entrusted my life to the Lord as I knew that I would arrive at my destination very late and in that part of the country there is no way to book accommodation in advance. In the back of the truck there were two 100kg bags of dry fish. As we bumped along on the dirt road the bags began to move to the end of the truck where I was sitting, until they were up against me. I tried to push them away but they were too heavy. I would manage to push them a few centimetres and I would have a bit of space for a few minutes and then they would be against me again.

The six guys in the truck, including the owner of the bags, just looked at me and never lifted a finger to help. I travelled for seven hours like that. It was one of the most uncomfortable rides ever. We eventually got to our destination at 11pm. I looked around wondering where I would stay the night. A man came up to me and said he could show me to an inn. I had to trust God and go with the guy. He went ahead of me carrying my backpack and we walked through little dirt paths in the dark until we eventually got to the inn. As it is a small, undeveloped town the accommodation is very poor and basic. It was one of the worst places I've ever been in, with no door on the communal ablution block (just a curtain) and no running water. I paid and thanked the man and as soon as I was shown to my room I locked the door. As I went to close the curtain over the small window I saw a man peeping into my room. I asked him what he was doing and he walked away startled. It is not abnormal for a guy to pick up a girl like that. I had an uneventful night, woke up the next morning and continued my journey.

Over the past few years internet dating and other matchmaking services have taken off in Zambia. In desperation some ladies I know decided to try it out. I know of a few success stories but I also know of some disasters. A lady in her thirties connected with a man who said he was based in the USA. This lady was independent and owned her own house and vehicle. After some time they decided they would get married in the USA but before that the man came to Zambia for a visit. When he left he suggested that since they would be based in the USA it would be best for her to sell all her property and deposit the money in his account since it would be theirs. The lady sold everything, deposited the money in his account and got ready to go to the USA. From that moment on she could not get through to the guy by phone, email or any other way. She went to the American embassy for help but the man could not be located as he had used false identification. This lady lost everything, even her hope. She went into depression and died a few years ago. In my culture the pressure to marry is immense but one has to trust God for his time and for the right marriage partner. Even if he doesn't provide one, God is enough.

Living as a single person in a mission community has its challenges and its blessings. When it comes to housing, singles are usually the last to be considered. The best and biggest accommodation will be given to families and couples. Singles are usually squeezed into small spaces and can be moved around at short notice. Families are more stable. Singles can be in a mission community for many years but never get to the place where they feel they have a home. Singles also usually do more of the day-to-day work of running the place.

On the flip side though, a single in a mission community is assured of being part of a family with parents, brothers and sisters and children. Singles are invited for meals, get-togethers and all that goes along with family life. A single person can enjoy being lavished with love from the children and everyone else.

Singleness is a season in life. It may be a long season that one day comes to an end or it may be the only season in a life. Whatever the case we have to trust God who knows best and who allows these seasons. In the book of Esther chapter 5 we see Haman boasting to his wife and friends about all his achievements, wealth and favour with the king and queen. Haman had so much but we see him say later that all this for him was insignificant and worthless as long as Mordecai the Jew would not give him respect and bow before him. Haman forgets all the positive things and focuses on the negative. The one negative thing became his obsession to the point of planning and ordering the annihilation of an entire people group. My prayer is that I would not be like Haman and let the negatives of singleness become an obsession but would learn to be content with my lot.

Singleness has many advantages. Over the years it has opened doors for me to reach out, minister to and influence the lives of many young men and women. When I recall my ministry years in the north of Mozambique, one of my highlights was significant discipleship relationships with the local people. A few of these turned into deep friendships that continue even now that I'm in Zambia. Being single means the young people found me approachable. They felt free to share their needs, their struggles and their dreams with someone they felt they could identify with but who was at the same time more mature than them physically and spiritually.

One lady I ministered to was about 21-years-old. She came from a big family and like most such families they struggled financially. One of her older sisters had married a man who had a good job and so the family had some income. Her sister was barren and so her husband was allowed by the family to have a child by the younger sister, the girl I met. A few years later the older sister passed away and my friend was forced to become the 'wife' of the brother-in-law so that the family would not lose the financial support he provided. I met her at this stage where she was getting to know the Lord more and was aware that the situation she was in was not pleasing to the Lord. She was very unhappy and torn between wanting to do what was right before the Lord and also wanting to ensure that her family was not deprived of the income from her brother-in-law. It was a long process of discipleship and prayer support until she was finally free of this man and could stand up to her family in choosing what was right. I'm grateful to the Lord for this friendship and the fact that he allowed me to influence this life. When I was leaving to go back to Zambia, she said to me, "If you ever wonder why God sent you to Mozambique, know that he sent you here for me". Today my friend is happily married to a great man of God and both are mission workers in another part of the country.

Another highlight is a relationship I formed with a lady in her early twenties. She had lost her dad when she was young and was taken in by her aunt. They ran a little eating place to try and make ends meet. She helped out in the eating place when she was off school. When she was 14 she met a man there, and ended up living with him for six years. Her family approved of it because it meant they would not have to be responsible for her school fees or other expenses. I was privileged to be one of the people to speak into her life over the years and see her come to a place of firm decision for the Lord and for righteousness. Today she is married to a lovely man of God and both are serving the Lord in ministry.

There is a lot of freedom that comes with singleness. I'm free to set my own schedule with only myself to take into consideration. When I travel, all I need to do is pack my bag and go. I don't have to ask permission from anyone and I have no restrictions. When I come home I can throw food together and in a few minutes I have a meal. I don't have to think of cooking a meal for two or more, or plucking a chicken, as it's just me. I can have sleepovers and outings as often as I choose with my female friends. I have a lot of time on my hands in the mornings and evenings compared to a wife and mother. Yes, there's a lot of freedom to enjoy!

Chapter 12 - From Namibia to the ends of the earth: Patterns I have observed as a single woman

Martha from Namibia is 44 years old and has spent 20 years in cross-cultural mission. She worked initially in church planting in Siberia, and for the past 13 years she has been involved with intercession and leadership in Europe.

I have thought a lot about singleness. Many young women and men from a variety of nations have asked me about this topic, seeking God's purposes for themselves. I would like to mention a few patterns which people have discussed with me.

Socialising and conversation
In my experience, married couples (with or without children) often invite couples over for a fun evening, but rarely invite single people. Even if I am good friends with the hosts and the guests, somehow I find myself alone on Fridays while my married friends hang out together – going to restaurants, movies or playing games. The strange thing is that married women will invite me over when they need to talk, or for Saturday morning coffee or shopping, but when there is a fun evening out, singles are easily forgotten.

Single people get invited to baby-sit, or to house-sit while a family is away. This is often offered as if they do us a favour to ask us. If we accept, we are still on our own, without the adult company we ache for. Our real need is to be with people, not in an empty house, or one with just sleeping children.

Although I have no children, my social schedule works around children. I need to consider school pick-ups and bedtimes if I want to schedule a visit. It is a privilege to consider my friends and to make life easy for them, but can be less convenient for me.

Conversation can be very monotonous. Mothers are tempted to talk a lot about their children when you hang out with them and the buggies in the park, or if you try to have a conversation in the kitchen in the midst of dishes and *Teletubbies* (children's TV). As a result I sometimes prefer to hang out with the married men rather than with married women. It is not that I dislike children, or am jealous of people with children; it is simply not my world. I am happy to baby-sit, and I play with children a lot. I love spending money on the children of my friends and siblings. But I also need some stimulating conversation on a regular basis that is *not* about children. Without normal conversation on many topics and at different levels, loneliness can make us 'calcified' in our thinking. We get stuck in ruts, and become inflexible and even obsessive. We lose the confidence to try new things. I don't want to lose the art of conversation just because I don't have a partner or children.

This year, I was sad to realise that I regretted the pregnancy of a close friend of mine. I had prayed fervently for her to conceive, and I cried with joy when her pregnancy test was positive. But within three months of pregnancy many of our conversations had shifted to increased bra sizes, stretch marks, baby clothes and labour. I rejoice with her, but I feel I have lost a soul mate. I will now have to fit into her new life. I know I will be thoroughly blessed by her little one, and she will share her baby generously with me. I will be enriched. But as she steps out of her fast-thinking secular job, her world will inevitably become smaller. This relationship will demand commitment and honest conversation, as I deliberately embrace her new life and joy.

Gifts, and raising support
People are generous in different ways to single people and to families. Singles are often invited for Christmas meals, or Thanksgiving. Families don't want single friends to be alone on these major holidays. It is a fantastic blessing to be invited to join a family for these celebrations. But singles are not likely to receive a time-share in the Alps for a skiing holiday, or a night out at the Ritz, as mission families I know do. Many times I have stood by when couples received a gift of a night out or a romantic weekend away.

I believe (and I may be prejudiced) that it is easier to justify financial needs for families than for singles, and so families can find it easier to raise support. We accept that families need to save for a house, or for an annual holiday. Single people are somehow not seen to have the same financial needs – a better car, life insurance, investments, or money to spend on regular relaxation.

Engagements, weddings, births – but when do we celebrate singles?
The next issue can be painful for many single women (I can't speak for men). *Married people are celebrated, but single people are not often*

publicly celebrated. On their engagement, and much more on their wedding day, couples are showered with good wishes, blessings, prayers and car-loads of gifts. The same happens with childbirth, when mother and baby are showered with beautiful words, appreciation and gifts, and perhaps new furniture and a bigger house and… and… and. They are the centre of attention and intentionally loved by friends and family.

Single people usually have to buy the basic household things themselves gradually over time. Sheets one year, towels another, a good Teflon pan for Christmas. Or they might inherit used items. Single people lack the public affirmation and celebration of their lives which is given at marriages and births. If singles are severely introverted (as I am), or socially insecure, they will lack the courage to throw big birthday parties for themselves. I long for single people to receive verbal appreciation, hugs and kisses (as appropriate to the culture), and even gifts, so that they know that they are loved. It is about valuing the individual. I think widows and widowers suffer greatly in this area after their partners die. Birthdays and Christmas can be very painful for them, as they no longer have someone to 'spoil' them at these times, by which I mean to give some personal attention.

I have encouraged a range of single women to make a major celebration of their fortieth birthday. Perhaps a weekend away, a gift list and an extravagant dress, so that they have a special celebration of self. I have encouraged people to show love to singles verbally and openly, especially in public when an occasion arises.

Intimacy
When I say I need intimacy, I mean that I long to be myself with someone, without pretence or careful boundaries. Intimacy is to be known, and to be loved for who we are. Intimate belonging is to be together in silence, but to be understood. To pray together beyond the basic formalities. Intimacy is the place where rawness is acceptable, where joy is held as sacred. Intimacy grows through being together over many years, with shared experiences, the repertoire of lives lived. We long for soul mates (not necessarily only one person), people to share our vacations with, and somebody to buy a house with.

Single people fear the lack of closeness and the lack of memories built up and shared with people we love, who share our lives with us. Many fear a lonely old age. Relationships with married couples have limits.

Often we relate in a more intimate way to one person than his or her spouse.

We can worry about friendships being perceived as becoming *too* close. Close relationships between two singles can easily be seen as unhealthy, emotionally dependant, relationally inseparable, and let's call it by name: sexual. When friends share a budget or a common purse, eyebrows can be raised.

When does a relationship become unhealthy? Is it only when we cross physical lines? When does interdependence become co-dependence? We have to be aware of Biblical principles and what is culturally appropriate, but we should not live in fear of how a friendship might be perceived. Sometimes social pressure can restrict friendships which could have grown into safe, appropriate harbours giving life to both and to society at large.

Celibacy

God has created us in his image. We are first of all spirit, then flesh. God in his grace and wisdom became flesh, and was tempted in each and every way, but never sinned (Hebrews 4:15). In creation God commanded the first humans to multiply and fill the earth. To come together in love and give to each other. To create. Yet Jesus, the Son of Man, never married.

Why is it that so many Christian people are single? Especially women in missions? Part of the answer lies in the fact that we live in an immoral society where dating, love and sex make single people who have integrity afraid to go out with others. What will the expectations be of a date? How much will it take to stand my ground? There are also many other reasons for singleness. One which is not often spoken about by Protestants is that sometimes God calls people specifically to be single, and celibate. A sexless life filled with God.

Throughout church history bishops were seen as married to their diocese. They were to love, cherish and protect the church, and as a result life would flow into the wider community, bringing honour to God and comfort to many souls. Monasteries throughout the ages brought life to the surrounding areas. This life is the inheritance of a celibate priest or layperson.

My experience of being celibate in answer to his call is not that God is punishing me, or testing my love for him. He does not love me more than a married person. He does not jealously want more of me for himself than he wants a married person. A celibate life unto God can bear beautiful fruit that serves God and the church, a fragrant offering to God.

Celibate singles are not necessarily sexually frustrated and depressed. Neither are all those energies suppressed and ready to explode within, a constant wrestling match for purity. The love of God in our hearts transforms something of the flesh, to become again a spiritual union with him. Somehow, mystically, our offering of surrender purifies and ministers to this sex-addicted generation. Celibacy is an act of spiritual warfare for this generation to rule over the powers of perversity and selfishness. Celibacy is worship to God who loves us, who created us for purity and innocence, for passion surrendered, for the flesh submitted. Celibacy is an act of crucifixion. And celibacy is the joy of resurrection as your heart becomes full with satisfaction and intimacy beyond words.

I believe the God who instituted marriage is also the God who calls some to singleness. God sustains us with his love, and opens to us dimensions only known in joyful surrender. May the mystery of celibacy be uncovered also for this generation. The lovely spiritual riches gained by surrendering our lives to God in such a level of trust help us deal with the disappointments and challenges which I described above; the joy far outweighs the pain.

Chapter 13 - Singled out in Cameroon

Marius is a 37-year-old single man, ministering in Cameroon.

The very fact that I am an unmarried man, living alone, singles me out all the more here in Cameroon, besides me being white. People strongly expect that a man my age has married (at least once) and has children; the more the better, so it seems. I have the impression that in this country love is not a very important factor (at least not initially) as a basis for getting married. Traditionally, marriages are arranged by the father, at least in Fulbe culture. People wonder why I don't simply find a wife and get married, especially since being a white man they assume I should have enough money to pay the bride price!

I am also an exception in the mission culture. The Cameroon branch of our mission has included single mission personnel for a long time, so being a single mission worker is at least not an anomaly. However, there are (and have always been) far more single ladies on the mission field than there are single men. In our branch of about 180 adults, I only know a handful of single men, two of whom (my age) are getting married in the near future. Although single men are rare here, I generally feel accepted by my colleagues.

It is no good denying my feelings of loneliness and my unfulfilled longings. It is wholesome to recognize and voice these feelings before God and some trusted people. But I have learned that it is not helpful to spend a lot of time and energy wallowing in self-pity. It is up to me to trust that matters of the heart are with God in good hands. The Lord is indeed my good shepherd and I will lack for nothing, even if I feel I am lacking quite a lot right now.

Practically, I need to take the initiative in organizing the 'togetherness' that I need - for example, by inviting people over to my place to have dinner or to watch a video or something like that. This is not always easy and it would have been great if it just happened automatically by having my own family. But I need to step out and invite others if they don't invite me. There should be a balance between giving and receiving, but sometimes you have to give before you can receive.

VOICE FROM THE MIDDLE EAST

Chapter 14 - A single woman in the Middle East

Melinda *worked as a teacher in Jordan and Yemen. She writes about challenges and opportunities women may experience when ministering in the Middle East.*

I lived in the Middle East for four-and-a-half years as a single woman. The challenges probably were equal to the joys, although most days it felt like the challenges were greater.

I think the greatest challenge for me was the mosque calls. They were intrusive and really sent me into prayer. I felt increasingly negative about them, and I found it hard each day to keep pushing through when the calls from the mosque started. They didn't just come from one direction; the valley was filled with them. As I was single I was living with other girls, and the power of friendship and prayer helped me to walk through those times. I found it very helpful to prayer walk with a friend in the mornings, and to worship with flatmates daily if needed.

Another challenge was the verbal abuse that the men would give in the street to women who had no men to protect them. It made the women feel uncomfortable walking outside, and caused fear. The local women longed to always be with other girls for peer support. Men tend to dominate in this culture. It was hard to see the culture so oppressed by the attitudes of the men, and the hardworking women put down when they were doing their best with the little they had. Perhaps the abuse from the men was worse because they chewed qat, a stimulant drug. Yemeni culture has become dominated by qat, with over 80% of men chewing it. This has led to poverty, unemployment and a shortage of water as so much is used producing the plant. A lot of men choose to chew qat which is expensive and causes the men to become lazy. The men chew the drug for hours every day instead of earning money, which has a detrimental effect on the family. As a single woman, it was hard to know what I could do to help.

It felt overwhelming at times. That is why God gives us community to support each other. When some are down, others are up and vice versa. I found this happened a lot with those around me. Friendships were strengthened and grew deeper through the challenges of daily life. There was no choice about who to be around; the few people on the field became family, as we were all away from home. It forced us to get on with all people from all cultures, and from different denominations and backgrounds.

A lot of expatriates met together for house-church each week, and singles were a large part of that congregation. We were looked after by the families, and some even counted us as part of their families.

The local Muslim families also looked out for us singles, often inviting us for meals or sending food to us. Occasionally, we even had sleepovers at the houses of local girls. This was a rich time to talk, see more of the inside of their lives and discuss matters of importance.

Learning the language was another challenge. As I didn't have children, I was able to commit a lot of time to practising the language. I recommend that new language learners take on a language helper as soon as they arrive, and start making contacts and visiting friends so that they can practice. I also recommend getting involved in the community and cultural events, and asking local people lots of questions about their beliefs, to gain more understanding. Being single can have the advantage of providing more time for all of this.

Being single meant that I had the freedom and time to visit women, often spontaneously. This culture is all about relationships. The customs ensure that building friendships is essential. It is necessary to keep up the routine of regularly visiting these friends, especially during Ramadan and Eid. Time is not relevant here. We must learn to be flexible and ready for anything that could arise. This was easier for me as a single woman, compared to the mothers with children.

This foundation of relationships in the Middle East leads to activities being carried out as a group. Yemenis seldom like time alone, but instead like to be constantly surrounded by people. Single expatriates learn to be with other people, or else they stand out. One of our teachers resigned from his job last term, and so his Yemeni friend also resigned, deciding that as they had both started together it seemed fitting for them to resign together. From the strong group orientation comes the ability to accept all people and not exclude those who are different. On many occasions Yemenis asked me where my friends were, expecting that they would come with me even though I was the only one invited somewhere. Inclusion of all people is very evident in Yemen.

One of the greatest qualities of the Yemeni people is their hospitality. With the natural group-orientated culture, to have visitors is considered a benefit. Upon entering a Yemeni house you will always be greeted and given a drink. People are very generous if you are new and often give more than necessary, especially to foreigners. The Yemenis always insist that you stay for a meal, and they encourage guests to eat as much as possible. Politely saying "no more" or "I'm full" does not stop the food coming. I have learned that saying "Al humdelulila" (Praise be to God) seems to be an acceptable way to highlight the fact that enough has been eaten and it is time to stop.

With the culture having such a strong relationship base, there is pressure on young women to marry and have children early. Arab marriages tend to be the joining of two families rather than just the two individuals. Arranged marriage is a normal part of Yemeni culture. Marriage is greatly encouraged by Islam, the society and the Arab government. It is believed that love marriages cause affairs and the woman could be promiscuous if she loves, so marriages are based on convenience instead. I have only come across two Yemeni marriages based on love before the marriage. Abu-Lughod wrote about this culture saying that, "Many girls and mothers told me about the dangers of love matches; all valued the protections and support afforded by their families in arranged marriages." [17]

It is easy to see why arranged marriages are necessary in Yemen, as daily life is based on a strict separation of the sexes. A young man has little chance of meeting women, and vice-versa. Instead, they have to rely on the advice of the family. In the past the marriage was arranged by the parents and a daughter had no say, but nowadays the daughter usually has the right to agree or disagree.

The separation of men and women and the disapproval of dating also mean that single mission workers find it difficult to meet a potential marriage partner. Romantic messages are not impossible though. One of my funniest experiences occurred in a restaurant. The hummus was brought to us accompanied by cucumbers shaped as love hearts, while the waiters grinned!

The biggest challenges which I faced in the Middle East were not due to being single. The mosque calls and language difficulties would still have been there if I had been married. Living with other single people provided the support I needed to face the challenges. Being single gave me more time to study the language, and more opportunities to spend unrestricted time with the women.

The greatest joys of my years in the Middle East were the time spent with the women, the amazing hospitality, and the family togetherness that takes place in Arab societies (which I feel the West has lost). Being single meant that I was free to fully engage with all of this. I enjoyed the culture and being able to share with people and pray for them. It was a joy to bring touches of truth and life into their lives because of Jesus in my life.

My advice to single people going to countries like this is to always go with confirmation from God, and to always put intimacy with God first.

VOICE FROM EASTERN EUROPE

Chapter 15 - Single parent: is mission impossible? Fostering children as a single mission worker

Paula has served for 20 years in Eastern Europe. She has established house-churches, trained people in mission and provided support for refugees and others who have experienced trauma. She has fostered four children as a single mission worker.

When I went to Eastern Europe in 1993 I was 22, single and determined to change the world for Jesus. I assumed that on the mission field I would find a suitable guy with a similar passion, fall in love and get married and that we would change the world together. I already had a handful of marriage proposals under my belt at that point. All my potential suitors were unsuitable: they weren't my type, or they were not on fire enough for Jesus, or they didn't have a heart for missions. My vision was to have a Healing Home, welcoming children and grown-ups who needed a home and a family, and to see them transformed by the love of the Father.

That was 20 years ago. So far I have not got married, nor had children of my own, but I have opened up my home to those who were hurting. Our home has become a Healing Community, welcoming people with loving arms. Daddy God is the Father in our home; his love is the only love that can truly heal broken hearts. In the past ten years thousands of people have spent time in our community, many meeting with God and receiving his healing.

I have had the privilege of being a surrogate mum to four children. Although she never lived with me, Deena was the first child to really win my heart. She was about two years old and living in an orphanage when I first met her. I used to go there with some girls from church on Sunday afternoons, taking goodies to the children and playing with them. There were about 12 toddlers in Deena's group. Each week when we came in we were greeted by squeals of delight, shouts of "Mummy", and little arms reaching longingly to be picked up. Sometimes when we arrived we found them all propped up on potties against the wall. At that time disposable nappies were not readily available, so from the age of about five months after every meal they would be put together on potties until they had all 'done their business'. Deena's mum, a teenager who had been seduced by a student from Burkina-Faso, had given Deena up at birth. Deena had an ability to win people's hearts immediately, with her inviting brown eyes, her cheeky smile and her lovely curly locks of hair. She was the only black child in the whole orphanage; a great concern in a country where racism was rampant.

I grew to really love this little girl and wanted to take her home with me to a safe place. I struggled with the issue of being single and adopting, knowing it would be better for her to have a father. I had grown up without a father and knew first-hand the pain of that. I spent three days fasting and praying and seeking the Lord about it.

"The choice is up to you", Jesus told me. "You could take her and give her a home if you want to, because to have a mother who loves her and introduces her to a heavenly Father is far better than growing up in an orphanage."

My own mother brought me up alone and introduced me to my Heavenly Father and I turned out okay!

"But if it's too hard for you to be a single mother, you can also decide not to take her," the Lord reassured me. I was shocked by his kindness; it's amazing how the creator of the universe sometimes wants to dialogue with us and give us a choice about important decisions concerning our lives.

I decided to go ahead and try to adopt Deena. I tried for a few years to no avail, only being successful in getting Deena's side of the papers ready. It ended up being too complicated for me to adopt her for a number of reasons: there was no adoption agreement between Deena's country and my passport country, and I didn't have a house in my name, or a job or a regular income. One day when my dear Deena was about eight years old I went to see her and was told that she was being adopted by an American family. The Lord was gracious in allowing me to meet her new mother and say goodbye to Deena. Even though I was pleased she was going to live in a family, it was painful to say goodbye.

Natasha was the first child that the Lord allowed me to bring up. I first heard about Natasha through her cousin Vera who was working with me as a volunteer. Vera had been telling me for a long time about her young cousin who was practically living on the streets. Her mother had died when she was only three and her father was an alcoholic. Vera was unable to help Natasha because of her own difficult circumstances. When I moved from the town we were living in, I invited Vera to come and join me.

"Can I bring my cousin Natasha with me?" was the first thing out of her mouth.

"Yes, of course", I replied immediately without even thinking about it.

I realised the situation with Deena had prepared me to take in children. The first time I saw my precious little Natasha was in the summer of 2000. It was at a conference in a town a few hours from my new home. Having travelled for hours to get there on a stiflingly hot, overcrowded bus, as soon as I was shown to my dormitory room, I raced into the shower. Feeling refreshed, I came out of the shower in my underwear, thinking that I was alone in the room. To my surprise I found a tiny little mite with wide, frightened eyes gawking at me from one of the beds. Grabbing a towel, I threw it round myself.

"You must be Natasha. Nice to meet you, I've heard so much about you. I'm Paula. We've been waiting for you."

Although I spoke her language fluently, the scrawny little girl didn't respond, she just continued silently staring at me. It was days before she spoke or smiled, or let me hold her hand. She didn't know how to use a flushing toilet, and didn't want to take off her old, smelly clothes. She certainly didn't like the idea of having to go to school.

"I'd rather be an alcoholic on the streets than go to school," she declared stubbornly.

A few days after bringing her home, our neighbour's son came and told us Natasha was at the market on the other side of the main road begging for money. We were horrified. When we got her home, we found the coloured pencils she had 'earned' through begging.

"Natasha", Vera and I explained lovingly, "now that you live with us, you don't need to beg for money as we will always make sure you have food and clothes. That's what parents are supposed to do for their children." She looked at us in bewilderment.

"And if you want to go out, you need to ask for permission, as you are a child, and children are not supposed to go outside without an adult's permission. It's dangerous out there and we are responsible for you and we need to know where you are. Do you understand?"

Natasha thought about it and we could see she was not too sure about this business of being looked after. "It's much simpler to just live on the streets, go where you want and do what you want," she said to herself disconcertedly. But soon she got used to living in a home and she blossomed.

Natasha was followed a year and a half later by Ada, a 15-year-old refugee who had been held hostage by terrorists for three months and horrendously abused. Two years later, Andy appeared, a 10-year-old whose parents had been killed in front of him when he was three, and who had been in and out of various institutions and foster homes ever since. He only lived with us for 18 months before he ran away and was forced to go to a state boarding school. Finally Lucia came to live with us, a 15-year-old street kid who had been on drugs since the age of eight.

God gave me the grace as a single parent to bring up my precious children. Jesus was my husband and their Father. I was blessed to have the support of the Healing Community that we are a part of. At the time there were a couple of other single mums living with us. Our team helped with cooking, taking the children to school and spending time with them. Without the support of the Lord and the community of people he gave me, it would have been very hard to bring up my foster children. But with their support it was possible. "Everything is possible for him who believes." (Mark 9:23)

On one occasion our dentist said to me, "I can see that Natasha and Lucia are your daughters, but Ada and Andy must look like their father." I silently nodded my head, not wanting to say anything that would embarrass the children. Although all four of the children had brown hair like me, Natasha and Lucia were thin, as I was, whereas Ada and Andy at that time were both chubby. They found it painful if I explained the family situation in front of them; it caused some awkward comments at times. With Lucia and Natasha having fathers who were still alive, many people who didn't know the situation assumed I had been married to them at one time and was separated.

Being a mission worker living by faith meant that often we didn't know where our next penny was coming from, but the Lord was always faithful. One time we completely ran out of money and the only food we had left was potatoes. The following day was the eighth birthday of the daughter of one of our single mums. We asked the Lord for a special birthday meal. Two members of our team secretly decided to go fishing and came home after a fruitful night with 22 freshly caught fish. What a lovely birthday surprise for Veronica's birthday: a delicious meal of freshly fried fish and chips!

There were many moments which we laugh about now. When he first came to live with us, Andy had no idea about privacy and would barge into everyone's rooms without knocking. My foster daughters were teenagers at the time and very perturbed by a boy walking into their rooms unannounced. I tried time and time again to teach him to knock, seemingly to no avail. I started to think he would never learn. To my relief I realised he had learned on the day I saw him barge into his own empty room and then stop in his tracks and say to himself, "Oh, I forgot." Walking out of his room, he knocked and said "Come in" to himself. Very pleased with himself for getting it right this time, he walked with his head held high back into his own room!

One challenge of being a mission worker, due to the lack of finance, is that when we have had a car, it has been old and needed a lot of maintenance. An added challenge of being a single woman is that mechanics often tried to rip me off, or didn't do a good job of fixing the cars.

Once when Natasha and I were alone in our car, it stalled and refused to start on a busy one-lane highway. As we were on a slow gradient, I told little Natasha, a skinny teenager at the time, to get out and push. I also got out of the car, still holding the steering wheel, and pushed until the car was moving enough to try to jump start it. Somehow the Lord helped us and we managed to get the car going and drive off!

Another difficult thing was that I didn't have a husband who could help with practical jobs in the house. Also as a single woman it was hard to organise the building work. Men in this country generally don't respect women. Often they would not listen to what I was asking them to do, and they did not complete the job thoroughly or clean up properly afterwards. One time I found all the workmen fast asleep on my lovely new sleeping bags, on the dirty floor of the room they were working on. Another time I was enjoying a peaceful lunch when I leisurely looked out of the window, only to see our building project manager doing something up on the neighbour's roof. He was promptly sacked. The Lord gave me wisdom to deal with these situations and often sent men or angels to help us when we really needed them.

When it was time to move into our new house, I couldn't find any men who were able to help us. The pastor's brother offered to lend me his truck, which was slightly bigger than a minibus. It was the biggest thing I had ever driven, but somehow I managed. At the time I had only Natasha and Ada living with me, and Natasha's cousin Vera. The four of us carried all our furniture down two flights of stairs and into the truck. The hardest thing to carry was the fridge, but the Lord helped us and we managed it. At the other end, there were builders, thank the Lord, who helped us to unpack the truck.

The building work took months longer than I had foreseen, and as the lease on the flat we were renting ran out we moved into our new house before it was completely finished. The stairs still had loose planks of wood, as yet unattached, on top of the metal frame. You had to be careful as you walked up and down the stairs not to knock the planks off and fall through. One day Ada slipped and knocked the wooden plank off the stair. I heard a yell. My heart almost jumped out of my chest. I leapt up and ran into the hallway, as did two of the guys. To my horror, I saw Ada's legs dangling through the stairs. One of the guys put up his hands to hold her up and another ran upstairs to pull her back up onto the stairs. Her legs had fallen through the hole, but she had been saved by her elbows which were caught in the metal frame. Although shaken and a bit bruised she was all right. God was looking after his daughter, yet again.

Another difficult thing about bringing the children up on my own was the fact that people would interfere in a way they probably wouldn't have done if I had a husband. It was hard for me to discipline the children on my own, but the Lord always gave me the strength and wisdom to know what to do. One afternoon Andy was so excited to see Sasha, our watchman, arriving in his car that he leapt onto the bonnet and then onto the roof of the car as it was still moving. He managed to dent the roof as he jumped up on it. I was horrified as I watched it happening from the upstairs window and started praying. Angels must have been holding Andy in place and stopped him from falling off. Sasha was furious and started yelling at Andy to jump off, which he did. As Sasha stopped the car he got out yanking his own belt off his trousers and ran after Andy trying to beat him. Andy was shrieking "Mummy, Mummy" as he ran into the house and up the stairs away from the belt and the yelling. I didn't appreciate other people taking the punishment of my children into their own hands. I decided that the little boy had had punishment enough. He came running into my room, shocked and crying. Taking him in my arms, I held him and prayed for him. When he had calmed down I explained to him why it was not sensible to jump onto the roof of a moving car. He never did it again.

There have been many difficult and painful moments in bringing up extremely wounded foster children without the support of a husband. But at the end of the day I am grateful to the Lord for entrusting these precious souls into my life for a time and allowing me to love them and reveal his love to them. It has been a wonderful privilege to be a mum, even though I have never married or given birth to children of my own. There is something really special about having little ones call you "Mum", pouring your life into them and watching them grow and mature. I would not want to have missed that for anything.

I was never able to officially adopt my children, for the reasons I mentioned earlier – it seemed to be legally impossible. This has been hard when I have travelled and have not been able to take my children out of the country with me. But as far my children and I are concerned, I am their mum and I have a long-term commitment to them.

All my children are grown-up now. Given the desperate condition they were once in, they have done well. Lucia has just completed her training as a language teacher. She recently married a lovely young man who also grew up in our community, the son of one of the other single mums living with us. They both love the Lord and want to serve him. The others are not so stable in their relationship with the Lord, but they know where to turn in time of need. Ada is married and Natasha is living with her brother while studying to be a seamstress. Andy is working and is in a government queue to get the apartment due him as an orphan.

In conclusion, I want to say that I have found these words of the Apostle Paul on singleness to be true:

> *Now, to the unmarried and the widows I say: It is good for them to stay unmarried, as I am… But if you do marry, you have not sinned… But those who marry will face many troubles in this life, and I want to spare you this… I would like you to be free from concern… An unmarried man is concerned about the Lord's affairs – how he can please the Lord. But a married man is concerned about the affairs of this world – how he can please his wife – and his interests are divided… So then, he who marries… does right, but he who does not marry… does even better. (1 Corinthians 7: 8-38).*

Even though I am not against getting married, I think I have done better at this point by not marrying. There have been times when it could well have been easier to have a husband, and better for my children if they had had a father. That is of course assuming that I had a godly husband who loved the children like his own, and amongst other things was good at practical jobs, mending and maintaining cars and organising builders. Some people have suggested I am too fussy, and that I am looking for a husband who is perfect like Jesus. I must say that Jesus is hard to beat! He is the best husband and father. But I know there are a lot of good men out there, who are godly, loving husbands and fathers. For those fathers who are reading this book, may the Lord bless you and give you strength and wisdom in your very important task.

There have been lots of good things about being single, just as the Apostle Paul suggests. If I had had a husband and natural children to care for, I think it would have been much harder to do all of the things I have been involved with in the past ten years. These things include setting up and leading our Healing Community where many traumatised by war, terrorism, addiction and abuse have received God's love and healing; starting a couple of simple house-churches; involvement in 24/7 prayer and worship; and training many people in mission and in how to minister to those who are traumatised and how to start simple house-churches. I have been blessed to be a mum and to be able to pour my love into the lives of my four precious children. Being a single parent I had more time to spend with each child individually, as I didn't have a husband or natural children to take up my time and attention. Being single, I was able to give myself fully to the Lord, to serve him and the wounded lambs that he has given me to love, and to train others to do the same. If the Lord brings a husband into my life who has a heart, passion and calling for the Lord and the work that I am involved in, then that is great. But if not, I am more than happy to continue serving the Lord whole-heartedly, walking hand in hand with him as my beloved bridegroom into the fullness of the destiny that he has for me.

VOICES FROM NORTH AMERICA

Chapter 16 - The joy of children and friendship

Eunice Hill, who comes from Canada, was a mission worker in Pakistan for over 40 years. For most of this time she was a house-parent at Murree Christian School (MCS), a boarding school for the children of mission personnel. Now in her seventies, "Aunty Eunice" looks back on a single life which has been rich because of her relationships with God, children and friends. Ministering in Pakistan takes courage, especially for a single woman. In March 2002, there was a grenade attack at her church in Islamabad. Five months later MCS suffered an al-Qaeda terrorist attack. Eunice had the courage, compassion and the calling to serve in the midst of such danger and to help in the follow-up after these attacks.

I took it for granted that I would marry and have children. It is amazing to me that now, in my seventies, I can look back on a single life that has been full of rich relationships, travel, and above all a satisfaction that it was God, who loved me and knew me best, who helped me make those choices.

As a child, I was used to having a lot of people around. My father was a legal advisor to many missions and our home was often filled with either missionaries, or ex-convicts being rehabilitated. My mother gave my life strong foundations. When I was twelve and my sister thirteen, my mother realized that her cancer was terminal. Dad had died suddenly of a heart attack a few months before and my mother had only a short time left to influence a very strong-willed daughter.

It is only in retrospect that I have realized the impact that my mother had on me during that year. We didn't want to talk about death but Mother took opportunities to get her message across. I remember Romans 8:28 being her very strong underpinning: "All things work together for good for those who love God, who are called according to his purpose".[18] She really believed that God could turn all this "together for good" although neither my sister nor I were growing as Christians at that time. I had thought I might be involved in mission someday, but I wanted God to leave me alone right then and let me have my fun with my friends. I wanted my own way.

It can't have been easy for my mother to walk with me through that hard year. I never heard her make threats like, "You'll be sorry when I'm gone". Instead I heard "If God takes me he will care for you. He knows what he is doing". I look back now and am amazed that I wasn't consumed with guilt when Mom died. Somehow she always let me feel she understood, and she left me with a strong sense that God was a Father in a special way to the fatherless. I somehow felt more important to him and as I saw my mother's predictions of his care work out in growing up (not that all the years were easy). I found I could trust him. I remember thinking, "What is really secure in life?" My dad had lost money when the banks crashed. My parents had died and I knew my home could be taken away. It was at fourteen that I decided the only solid future was with God and he was my Father, who would never change and could not be taken away. He planned well for his children and I could trust him. I asked for baptism in my little Brethren church.

My childhood left me with a legacy of faith. I knew if I gave God my future that would be the best choice I could ever make. I spent five years at a Christian boarding school, which helped nurture those decisions. I was with many children of mission workers, known as Mission Kids or MKs. This included some little ones in elementary school who didn't see their parents for four years at a time. A mission worker from Brazil impressed me with the need for teachers for MKs on the mission field. He said, "We desperately need people to teach MKs abroad, so that the MKs can remain in the same country as their parents and see them more often and avoid this separation". I was only 16 but I asked God then to use me with MKs.

I chose education as my field of study. During that time I had a serious relationship with a good-looking young man who was a Christian, but it just didn't seem the right thing. A year of Bible school was followed by two years of teacher training. I started to wonder about this 'call' to missions. It would mean two more years of university and two of Bible school, which seemed impossible. In discussing it with my pastor, he suggested a Christian college in California. "Wouldn't that be very expensive?" I asked. "If God wants you there it won't be a problem", was his reply.

I set off conscious of a desperate need for God to make a difference in my life. I thought I really wasn't mission worker material and I had little money, so I knew only God could sort it out. He did. Three years later I graduated with no debt.

During this time I was chosen to represent my college in a student Missionary Peace Corps program in Pakistan. Murree Christian School (MCS) is a boarding school for the children of mission personnel, and they needed a teacher for a summer. Before I left I was so excited that I told God, "If you'll let me work with MKs I don't mind being single".

Pakistan turned out to be God's perfect choice for me. I arrived there in June 1963, and extended the three months program to fifteen months. I was a teacher, but I also filled in as a house-mother. It was overwhelming. I was responsible for 23 little girls, who were just 6-9 years old and living away from their parents. Since the death of my parents I had felt embarrassed about giving and receiving affection, but the embarrassment soon left when I became a house-mother. On my first night I looked at 23 little girls, all waiting to be kissed goodnight, and I wondered how to handle it. Their little arms came up and quickly taught me how. These children didn't stop to see whether they liked you as older kids might have done - they just wanted someone to love them. Years later an administrator commented on how each group of children seemed to reflect their house-parent. "Yours are always so affectionate", she said. God used the children in my life to bring healing.

In Canada, I was used to having my class in full view when I was in charge of them. Now while in my care they were outside up trees, or in a tin tub in a bathroom with no lights! Bats flew in the rooms as I put the girls to bed. There was snow outside in winter but there was no heating except for a very noisy kerosene heater. The roaring was so scary that we only lit it on Fridays when we had full baths for all in my room. Sad little girls in their nightgowns came to me, homesick and wanting their parents. I gave them my time and comfort. There was something about the job that I loved.

After graduating from college I went to mission candidate school. I could hardly wait to get back to Pakistan. As soon as I could, I went back to MCS as a teacher. It was a mother who challenged me to consider becoming a full-time house-mother instead. She said she felt more concerned about the care in the boarding house than the teaching in school when she had to send her young child away. I switched over from teaching to primarily being a house-parent. I found my vocation in caring for children who had just started boarding.

The role of a house-parent meant being with the children whenever they were out of classes. With 23 children and the bugs of a new country, as well as the usual childhood diseases, there was usually a sick child to look after during the day. I didn't have much privacy. The children were always in and out of my room, and so were staff members and any visiting parents. I was an extreme extravert and loved having people around all day. I formed many wonderful friendships with people serving all over Pakistan. For the first 25 years I lived in one room off the hallway from the children's rooms. My room had large windows so did not feel cramped. I must admit, though, that I was glad when I was given an extra bedroom.

Weekends were a fun challenge: walks in our lovely wooded area with mountains around, game nights and of course the prayer times in the mornings when moms and dads were always remembered. Story times and devotions in the evening created wonderful memories for me. I had one free day each week from 7am until night-time when I was on duty again. It was years before the authorities realized that maybe an overnight off-duty would be good. It was! To sleep knowing that it would be uninterrupted was bliss.

We now know that it is better for this age group to stay with their parents than to be at boarding school, and MCS no longer accepts children under eight years of age. With the troubles in Pakistan these days, it is asking too much to expect very young children to board, knowing the dangers their parents may be in. Much has changed since the 1960s.

One great learning experience was the International Conference on Missionary Kids which began in the 1980s.[19] We had been an isolated school until then and now a world of learning was available. I remember listening to the first lecture on transition by an expert. It was like a huge skeleton over which I could stretch the flesh of all my experiences with MKs. I could have illustrated every point but until then I didn't know any of the terminology about transition, or the theory. We had felt we were doing something desperately wrong when children struggled, but we discovered that transition difficulties were in fact normal. House-parenting is very different now because of what we have learned about MKs.

There were many mistakes and tears on all sides but God was gracious. Children who went through so much still want to meet with the one who was there when it was hard for them. That's grace!

The reason I was willing to be single was to work with MKs, and for a long time it was single people who did that job. The school provided very little accommodation for couples. Nowadays we try to recruit couples.

They can model the life of a mother and father together. It is hard to recruit couples to serve as house-parents for long, as the needs of their family also have to be considered. Some children have a hard time sharing their parents with dozens of other children.

Though I sincerely told God I was happy to remain single, in my thirties I did wonder if God might have someone ahead for me. As I was praying, it was as if I heard a voice saying, "Is that really what you want, more than anything else?" I looked back on God's goodness, the faithful way he had led me and said, "Only if it's your very best, Lord". There was definitely a bit of selfishness there - I wanted God's best but I had to learn that it came from letting him choose. There were times when I struggled with singleness and thought things like, "Am I just not attractive enough"? I would always go back to the truth that I had chosen this lifestyle – or rather, that God had chosen it for me. I would have found it harder to be childless than single but God gave me so many children to bring up that even today I cannot feel childless. They have now grown up, and some of them still live near me. Others are in contact from all over the world. Nothing could have matched this - to see so many following the Lord and doing things I could never have done. I feel very loved.

One of the hardest things for me at MCS was the rapid turnover of staff. Short-termers can fill in well, and we had a wonderful bunch of them during my years at the school. The problem was that it meant a lot of good-byes. Twice I remember praying, "God, every support person I have is leaving this year. I won't make it unless you meet those needs." In one staff meeting I noticed that I would be the only person on the boarding staff to continue the next year. That was scary! I relied on having friends to pray with as well as to get off campus with. It was after twelve years of these changes that God brought a real soul mate, Deb (see chapter 17). We seemed to enjoy the same food, people and the challenges of growth - she really wanted to grow to know God better.

In the past I'd had friends who wanted an exclusive relationship, which I struggled with, but Deb was always inclusive, happy to reach out to others. She had a wonderful loyalty to her high school girls. Meal times around a staff table could get pretty negative if we were tired and frustrated. Deb tended to start off conversations with, "You know that… is a fine young woman." It would lead to other positive observations and instead of criticizing, we were building people up. Deb loved to laugh and her girls loved her and recognized her loyalty to them. I have been privileged to reap the benefit of her friendship for over 35 years.

We both enjoyed travelling and visiting former students, to encourage them. Whether it was in Deb's little Suzuki truck through remote villages in Pakistan or flying to different countries, we have had some amazing adventures. Pakistanis are very hospitable, and men feel they need to protect women, so if we needed to eat at little restaurants on the road, we would ask the proprietor if he had a place for women. We sometimes ate in rooms like storehouses. It sure beat trying to eat in the car surrounded by men and boys, or being misunderstood by entering an all-male restaurant in a remote area.

I started visiting alumni during my first furlough. As I travelled on deputation, I paid a short visit to a student I hadn't even taught. Her response seemed out of proportion as she exclaimed to her friends in tears, "She's from Pakistan! She's from Pakistan!" It made me realize that these visits could be meaningful to our children.

This is where being single made all the difference. Married staff had to put their own children into school and settle down in one place when they went on furlough. They often had more finances to raise and other responsibilities. I had a church which covered my support so faithfully that I was free to travel and follow up MKs during my year of furlough.

I think specifically of Judy (not her real name). She had medical issues and her parents had sent her home to Canada for college. She was staying with relatives, while her parents remained in Pakistan. She had struggled through her first year of college and then dropped out. Because of her medical problems she was unable to drive so her aunt was getting up in the middle of the night to drive her to work. Judy felt worthless. I had last seen her as an outgoing cheerleader and good student. I was shocked. I cried with her and we prayed and spent time together over a few days. I asked if she thought we should encourage her parents to come back to Canada. She was adamant that she didn't want to lose her family home in Pakistan, and she wanted her younger siblings to be able to graduate in Pakistan. The night before I left her I opened my Bible in tears. I found Psalm 27:13 in my King James Version and read, "I had fainted, unless I had believed to see the goodness of the Lord".[20] I cried out to God - I definitely couldn't "see" for Judy. I felt in a way I had failed her—and had God?

Five years later, during my next furlough, I visited Judy and her family who were home from Pakistan. Judy had completed her degree, and kept telling me about how good God had been to her. The family was in transition and trusting God for many needs; again they told me about

God's goodness. We often see that goodness. I can think of some of our MKs for whom classmates and staff have prayed for years and then have seen God's hand lovingly at work. There are also mysteries where in our lifetime we never see the answer to our prayers. God asks some to have that faith which persists without seeing any answer.

Deb and I have met up with many of our former students over the years, including at reunions held in different countries. At one reunion, some of the girls thanked Deb for protecting them. They told me about a time when they had all gone on a Saturday trip to the shops in Murree. Deb stayed in a restaurant where the girls could find her if they needed her. She was catching up on her reading of the magazine *Christianity Today*. Suddenly the girls ran in saying there were lots of awful 'Teddy Boys' on the mall, men who wouldn't leave them alone. Deb went to talk to a shopkeeper about it. Shopkeepers were always willing to help, but this time even he could not control the unruly guys. Murree is a resort area where wealthy Pakistanis go for a break. This brings a sense of anonymity and some men behave badly, knowing that no-one knows them. Deb called for our school bus to take the girls home early, still surrounded by the obnoxious 'Teds'. As the last girls went to step up to the bus a boy's hand went in for a pinch. Deb whacked the offending hand with her magazine and the girls cheered from the bus, "Yay Deb". They told her later how much it meant that she tried to protect them – she never hit people, but was willing to do so if a man was going to pinch them. I've wanted to write the editor of *Christianity Today* to tell him about the impact of his magazine on the Muslim world!

My last few years in Pakistan were event-filled. Deb and I moved to Islamabad. In March 2002 our church there was attacked. Deb and I were in Murree that day, and we came home to find 40 of our congregation in the hospital. There were also five funerals being organized. We had no pastor at the time. We helped in trying to get counsellors to traumatized people, and putting together support groups for people who needed more help long-term. Five months later, Murree Christian School was attacked by five al–Qaeda gunmen. Six Pakistani members of staff were killed while the children hid, wondering whether they were going to die. Deb and I were again involved in the follow-up.

It seemed important to allow the children to stay together as a school, but to move them to a safer location. If the school closed completely, that would be the end of the ministry of their parents in Pakistan. Moreover, the children would be separated from their friends, teachers and patterns which they were accustomed to. Keeping them together meant that they could support each other following the traumatic ordeal of the grenade attack. We helped the school re-locate to Thailand. Deb and I visited each semester, and our home became a launching point for going to serve and visit the re-located school. The pupils coped amazingly well, and many grew spiritually through the life-threatening experience which they had been through. Several chose to be baptised at the end of that year, and they have gone on to do well.

In 2005 I left Pakistan to retire, moving back home to Canada. One of God's great gifts to me is that I was asked to join our mission's member care team, caring for mission personnel and their families. They allow me to include the follow-up of our students under that umbrella. It is a joy to stay in touch with the MKs.

One thrilling thing about MKs is seeing their career choices. Many go on to work in mission agencies, humanitarian Non-Government Organisations (NGOs) or in the diplomatic corps. Deb and I have continued to accept invitations to visit them when we can. Visiting their countries of work has been a tremendous encouragement. We have visited our MKs doing mission work in Bulgaria and Albania, Christian work in Egypt, and aid work in Afghanistan and Cambodia. After the 2006 earthquake in Pakistan, we met up with many of our graduates who were helping with the relief effort. They were with different aid groups and mission organisations, as well as one who was the head of USAID. Most of our children are doing things I could never have accomplished - including being faithful moms and dads at home. I have been blessed, and I feel proud of them.

Now that I have retired, I am sitting in my little apartment in Winnipeg, Canada. My sister is around the corner and Deb is in Pennsylvania. God continues his kindness and I'm learning different lessons. The exciting 'on the edge living' is not the only place to find meaning. I live more dependently and find it takes even more faith to live for God at home. Transition home hasn't been easy but God has been present, and I have plenty in my church to keep me busy.

The phrase "He gives and takes away" comes to me and a fitting response is, "Blessed be the name of the Lord" (Job 1:21). My apartment does have some visitors but nothing like the school life I knew. Loneliness is natural when we leave all the support we have had for years. Although I felt I had made good friends when I had been back in Canada on furlough, many had moved or filled their lives before I got home. People are busy in the west and they already have their close friends. My sister has been very kind but she is an introvert and can't understand anyone wanting more friends - she is too busy for the ones she has. I am adjusting to a life with less contact with people. It has not been easy. Just as I had to trust God for the right support people years ago, I have to learn to trust again now. We can't demand but we can ask God to meet our needs, and that's where I'm at now. That loneliness can be turned to a new hunger for God and time with him. It doesn't sound attractive from a distance - I love being with people - but I think stripping away the company I've loved has been well worth it.

Deb has been a wonderful help. We often speak on the phone. To be able to pray together, though far apart, has been a lifeline. Deb is unable to travel much as her mother is frail, but last year we had a wonderful treat when we visited Germany, Morocco and the UK to see some of 'our kids' (now adults).

My forty-two years in Pakistan can hardly be summed up here but the best image I have is of the little boy who gave Jesus his lunch, and Jesus multiplied it to feed 5000 people. I have given so little in comparison to the way God has multiplied it. I've been able to work with hundreds of children from around the world, and have warm relationships with them and their families. I have seen my mother's faith reflected in many parents who trusted God with their children in difficult separations.

God is faithful. He has worked things together for good in my life, as my mother said he would. "Thus far has the Lord helped us", and he will continue to provide (1 Samuel 7:12).

Chapter 17 - Returning 'home'[21] to care for parents: the pain and the gain, and how we handle times of trouble

__Deb Rupe__ left the USA in 1975 to serve in Pakistan, where she stayed for 30 years. For 25 years she worked at Murree Christian School (MCS). Like many single people, Deb later left her ministry to care for her aging parents. Deb now tries to balance caring for her mother with member care work for her mission. She writes about coping during the times in life when we feel troubled.

The disciples were in the upper room. They couldn't believe their ears. What was Jesus saying? He was leaving? And talking of death and burial? Fear was setting in, and then he said, "Do not let your hearts be troubled" (John 14:1).

Do you find yourself "troubled"? Today, as I write this I am troubled. I am not troubled by my singleness, but by what faces me daily in my care for a beloved aging parent, as I try to balance this care with work.

So I am thinking of trouble and I suspect you too know much about trouble. Perhaps like many single people I talk to, your trouble is centred on being single. Mind you, yesterday I was talking with a married woman who felt troubled, and that trouble would have been lessened if she was not married.

I find that trouble isn't something that can be listed, dealt with for good and then ticked off, like the task list on my computer. I think trouble is more like the waves on the shore. It comes and goes. Trouble is sometimes like a big wave which knocks a person off his feet. Sometimes it is just like a small wave, but nevertheless, like the ocean waves it keeps coming. A trouble is always on its way, so instead of ticking it off, we find ourselves riding it out, day in and day out and in the process getting weary, angry, frustrated, and hopeless. Yet Jesus says, "Do not let your hearts be troubled." It is a command.

Today I got troubled. Maybe you are troubled now. If not, you will be, and you have been. For many people, singleness can be like a big wave that generates many little ones in the back wash: waves of loneliness, childlessness and friendlessness. As a single person, people consider you to be movable, in your housing, on your team, in your family. There may be small but constant waves of feeling not quite complete.

You might feel strange in groups of married couples, and what can you do with vacations? You seem to be waiting. Life now is okay, but something or someone is coming and so life seems like a bus stop and the bus isn't arriving on time.

Early in my life I sensed the Lord saying that I would be single and frankly, that was all right, even good. Coming from a caring and accepting family gave me a place to live where I knew I was loved, and that brought freedom. I am a 'people person' and as a house-parent at Murree Christian School (MCS), God put me in a dormitory filled with children and other adults many of whom were, like me, single. What could be better, at least for me? I loved the children and was shown love by them. I had many friends. I had the gift of a healthy and rich friendship with Eunice (see chapter 16). It was a friendship that drew me to love Jesus and others more. Eunice was a mentor before people called them that.

After I had been at the school for 25 years, Eunice and I moved to Islamabad to begin a new ministry. We established a retreat house called The Shade. It was a place for pupils and staff to get a break from the boarding school, and rest and be cared for. We also used it for training house-parents, and as a place of prayer and refreshment to the larger mission community.

I love being single. However, my singleness meant that at the time of life when such things happen, I was the one who was expected to change the course of my life completely to go and look after my aging parents. My sister and her family were unable to make a transition at that point in their lives, as is true often (although certainly not always) with families. So in 2005 I travelled over 10,000 miles from Pakistan to my hometown in the USA, to care for my parents.

I have often thought, "How did I know when it was the right time to leave Pakistan and return to my parents?" I don't really have an answer for that. There were some specific things happening within our family, mainly my mother's need of knee surgery, but it was more than that. I had a sense that it was the right time. There were some assurances along the way too. From the beginning, we had planned to review The Shade after five years. Those years passed very quickly, as they were filled with opportunities and The Shade was well used. During the five years MCS moved from Pakistan to Thailand and then back to Pakistan. It felt that we had come full circle, and it was time for a change.

Another thing which helped in making my decision was that Eunice felt that it was time to return to her sister. It was a great blessing knowing that at least we would be on the same continent. I had an inner sense that this was the time for me to go home. I knew it was coming and there was a feeling of peace as I moved ahead with the plan. It helped that we didn't do it suddenly. We did some good things to bring closure to our time in Pakistan. I think it's important to say good-bye to people and places. We left knowing that as far as it lay with us, we were in fellowship with our co-workers. Even more, we let them know that we deeply appreciated them.

Even with this good, planned ending, it was still painful to leave Pakistan. I moved away from all my friends and my supports and my life as I knew it to be. Still, it was good to return to my family. At 55 years of age, everything changed: my home, my environment, my friends, my work, my goals and dreams. I love my family and I deeply appreciate my continued (though drastically changed) role in missions. I grieve the loss of my former life and deeply grieve the loss of healthy and strong parents and a fun-filled group of aunts and uncles. I grieve because my father is not with us now, thankful that he is with Jesus. I would put the word 'sad' on much of life right now: not bad, but sad.

What helps when life is sad and I am grieving? Early on in my re-entry I realized that I needed to spend more time with the Lord just listening to him and taking in. I also realized that this would involve some discipline and life decisions. I was good at talking with God, but I needed to learn to *listen* in order to get through my lonely and sad days. It was a natural sadness, related to my parent's aging. I needed to drink more deeply from God's well of living water to help me through this time.

I'm grateful to friends who encouraged me to go to a seminar with others who had gone before me on this journey. I found it helpful to be with these people, listen to their teaching and read books that taught about quiet and reflection. I began to make decisions, like setting a day aside to seek rest and refreshment each week. I made this a 'no screen day' - no computer, work or TV. This has been a great blessing. I have spent more time outside and also reading and doing creative projects, like gardening, bird watching and art. Even more importantly was the fellowship with God that was at the core of that decision. I realized that Sabbath and the times of jubilee were given by the Lord to provide opportunities to trust him. I need to trust him that he will provide enough time for me to do the things he wants me to do, even though I rest one day a week. I also decided to have quiet days or if that isn't possible, quiet parts of days. I don't use these for regular devotions, but instead I go off and have times of evaluation and then listening to God. Calhoun's book *The Spiritual Disciplines Handbook* [22] has been a wonderful help in this.

I added exercise and better eating habits to my lifestyle, so I feel much better about my looks and realize my body is God's gift to me. This journey into his heart of love has been a deep place of comfort, joy and hope.

Although I have not found being single a hardship, singleness has deeply impacted my life. It has impacted it in some very hard ways as well as bringing great joy.

Like I said, today I found myself troubled. That concerned me. What was the core reason? Since arriving back in the USA I have taken a journey. I have travelled the world before, but this journey is different. Starting a new way of life in the USA has been the hardest journey in my life, but also by far the best I have ever taken, and I have had many wonderful journeys. It is one that has taken me deeper into God's heart and there I have found great depths of love and meaning. I have taken this journey primarily though quiet and reflection. Strangely enough, my new life has given me this opportunity as never before. Jesus, his person and his work have become most precious. So, when I get troubled and I know he says not to be, I know that I am entering a dangerous place. I move from a place of peace and rest to a deadening, churning place at the mercy of the waves of trouble.

I had to come face to face with my trouble and what was causing it. I saw that the core of my trouble was *fear*. It looked like this for me: "Mom's needs are so great; I can't handle them and work too. I am not finding any personal time, even to exercise. I can't really make progress on her health needs. How will I meet deadlines, both work and personal? Where will I find space for a breather?" I was swept into the ocean by the wave of fear.

The reason for fear is unbelief. Fortunately there is hope. I will not drown. Jesus is there on the shore saying, "Come! I am trustworthy". And he pulls me to him as I stretch out my hand. "Come to me, all you who are weary and burdened, and I will give you rest" (Matthew 11:28). That rest is found through belief in Jesus and the life of hope he offers.

What is the life that is open to all who trust in Jesus? As I read the Word of God and as I begin to experience it, even today, I find that the life Jesus opens to us does not depend on circumstances for satisfaction. It is a life that is not taken up with ticking troubles off a list or waiting for things to change, like waiting at that bus stop. It is not just a life that works out. It is not about forming that relationship that we have been waiting for, the one we thought we needed to be happy.

It is a life that is satisfied in God, the only one who won't disappoint. It is a life spent enjoying participating in the one relationship that we truly were made to be in. It is a life in which the Lord Jesus is more and more at home. A life of growing in the understanding of who he is and who I am as his child. It is drinking from the water of life (John 4:14). This is a life that is rooted in the cross and the resurrection of Jesus Christ. We are adventurers in the grand plan, the plan to make us holy, partakers of the divine nature (2 Peter 1:4). We are invited into the joy and fellowship of the triune God. For us who know trouble, the truth of this brings restoration and hope.

I also find a life of gratitude, and being grateful makes us more grateful. A person who is satisfied is not striving for more. They have dreams, but they are increasingly aware of who they are becoming in God, and less concerned about what is going to change so that their dreams can come true. Their dreams are about his goodness to them now and his goodness that is ahead. They are dreams that are caught up in the joy of his trustworthiness. They are dreams of a person at rest.

A satisfied person is one who is free to take Jesus' yoke, a yoke that is well-fitted specifically for him or her (Matthew 11:29-30). It doesn't chafe. It is a yoke that includes Christ's work, work through rest. This is the work of a person growing towards wholeness and who brings the heavenly Father joy through a growing confidence in him. It is a work that makes a difference in our troubled world.

Having found this perspective, I don't think that I am still troubled now. What about you? Perhaps today you are troubled. Troubles come and go like waves, but Jesus offers words of comfort, "Do not let your hearts be troubled" (John 14:1). In this passage Jesus comforts his disciples by reminding them that he will come back for them and will be with them. He is with you too.

Singleness and all the issues that arise from it can fill us with fear. But Jesus is greater than our fear and he offers us freedom from it. We can choose to believe the redemptive work of Christ, and experience rest. The fruit of this is satisfaction, grace, and an overflowing life in a fearful world.

Let us not stay troubled. Jesus said, "I have told you these things, so that in me you may have peace. In this world you will have trouble. But take heart! I have overcome the world" (John 16: 33).

VOICE FROM AUSTRALASIA

Chapter 18 - From Papua New Guinea back to Australia: Returning 'home' as a single person

Joy Atkinson *spent 30 years as a literacy specialist in Papua New Guinea where she was involved in a Bible translation project. She writes positively about her time there, where she was part of a mission community including other single people as well as families. Joy discovered that when she returned to her home country, she was the odd one out, not only as she had lived overseas for so long, but also because she was single. She describes how she dealt with this new challenge.*

I have been single all my life, although marriage was an option on several occasions. I have been happy, content with what the Lord has given me.

Over 30 years of my life has been lived in Papua New Guinea where I served with Wycliffe Bible Translators. I was part of a team of four single women from four different countries - USA, England, Switzerland and me, an Australian. In addition to our different cultural backgrounds we were four very different women, but the Lord brought us together. We lived in villages in the Highlands of Papua New Guinea and together we were able to complete the translation of the New Testament into two of the major dialects of the language group.

One factor that was vital in our combining well as a team was *prayer*. We prayed together regularly. We shared and discussed plans and ideas. We never tried to do it alone. We were a team. Our situation was unique, but I do believe that as singles, wherever we are, we need to make it a priority to pray with other singles and with families and our church communities. It can make all the difference.

As a single woman in Papua New Guinea I never felt like the odd one out. The centre of our work consisted of a community of people from many nations and backgrounds. We were all there with a common purpose: to see God's Word made available to the people of Papua New Guinea in their mother tongue. We were a very special community. At our centre in the Highlands there was a large group of single folk. We did things together, like regular weekly nights of fun and fellowship. That was very important. We had a games night for singles every Friday. Everyone brought something for a meal together, and then we played board games. So much fun! There was nowhere we could go out to a restaurant for a meal, but the high school students at our centre put on a 'hamburger night' every Friday - a scaled down version of McDonalds! Our group of single people often ate there together and then went to someone's home for coffee and games. We made the most of what we had. We were all away from home and family, and we made sure that all birthdays were times of real celebration. Those memories will never fade.

In addition, most of us singles were informally linked to families at the centre. I became friends with a woman from the USA. She would invite me to her home for meals. I got to know her family. Her children were my adopted nephew and nieces. I watched them grow up. When I was in the village she would talk to me via the two-way radio – there were no mobile phones in those days. When I returned to the centre after having been in the village for months, she would always have a meal ready for me. In a very real sense they were family. This was not only my experience; many other singles there had similar experiences.

I feel that it is vital for singles to stay connected to families - not only our own, but other families in our church or organisation. If we stay on our own or spend all our time in a singles group there is a tendency to focus only on other singles. I do not believe that is healthy. Singles, couples and families are part of a community together. We need to love everyone in the community. We are all members of one body, contributing something to the others.

Returning to Australia to live after over 30 years in Papua New Guinea was not easy. Leaving the very caring and supportive community in Papua New Guinea was one of the hardest things that I have had to do in my life. Re-entry after such a long time is difficult anyway[23], because you are in some ways a foreigner, having got used to a different culture. It can feel like bereavement, as you leave your home, friends, and the country you have grown to love. Other people have described their experiences like this:

> *The feeling of hollowness and absolutely gutted loss when returning just doesn't bear thinking about. Quite literally the worst experiences of my life were leaving [the country I had been working in].*

> *For some of us it is not a home coming but the beginning of exile. We become displaced persons.* [24]

> *When I got back, I found I was no longer a round peg in a round hole, but a square peg trying to find a hole that didn't seem to be there at all.* [25]

Part of the difficulty for me was that I didn't fit not only because I had lived in a foreign country, but also because I was single. I came back to a culture where being single meant being the odd one out. I was no longer part of a large group of singles, but one of only a few. Marriage and family were the norm. For most families, life is full and very busy with work, family activities and church events. Most families have little time for anything else. It would have been easy to feel sorry for myself, and I did several times. However, the Lord showed me another way.

I was reminded of an excellent book that I had read in Papua New Guinea, *Wide my world, Narrow my bed: Living and Loving the Single Life* by Luci Swindoll. [26] When I came back to Australia and encountered many changes, I read it again. I was blessed and encouraged right from the first page. I had read many other books on the single life. Most concentrated on showing from Scripture that being single is okay; it is an option. None had given a positive approach; it was more a case of 'grin and bear it'. Luci Swindoll emphasises the importance of a positive approach to being single - living and loving the single life, not just grudgingly accepting life, but really enjoying it. She encourages the reader to *celebrate* life rather than just endure it. I feel that is the key thing. This made all the difference to me.

I have re-read the book many times, and I try to continue celebrating life now that I am back in Australia, whether I am with singles or with families. The Lord has provided good friends here. It helped that I was able to come back to a caring church community who had known me and supported me for many years. I did not have to start all over again getting to know people. Many years ago this church had the idea that all the home groups should adopt one of the mission workers that the church supported. One group adopted me. They faithfully prayed for me when I was in Papua New Guinea and they kept in touch and were a real encouragement. On my return I was able to join that group. We meet every fortnight. We pray and share and study God's Word together. It has been a real blessing.

The Lord has brought other special friends into my life as well, and we pray together too. I can celebrate life with them - going out for coffee, lunch or to concerts, and enjoying many of the activities that were not available in Papua New Guinea. If no-one else initiates this, I can. We even have McDonalds here!

Many of the friends I had in Papua New Guinea are now back in their home countries too. Today we are blessed with the wonders of modern technology. The internet provides a means of keeping in touch. I email people. I chat via Skype to my friends all over the world. Facebook has reconnected me with many who I had lost contact with - I am a Facebook fan! We may be apart but we can still celebrate life together.

Part 2: Sexuality

Chapter 19 – Scantily-clad temptation in Burundi

The title of this chapter might suggest that it is about scantily-clad people in traditional dress, or women showing their breasts as they feed babies. That can be an issue, but that is not what this chapter is about. Even the holiest and strongest people can struggle with sexual temptation. The following was written by leading evangelist **Simon Guillebaud** [27], *in his diary, while he was a single mission worker in Burundi. He has shared this in the hope that it might help others to recognize temptation early on, and avoid dangerous situations (or at least jump out before it's too late).*

In the midst of all the stress, I attended a party for friends who were celebrating their second anniversary in the diplomatic corps. Kate was there, representing the United Nations, and she looked gorgeous in a figure-hugging scarlet outfit. She invited me round to her apartment later. I went back home to make a few calls, and then headed to where she was staying.

This is humbling to write, but I was dangerously near stumbling hugely. I wanted her so much. We sat on the same sofa and I found her tanned shapely body almost irresistible. I alternated between wanting to tenderly peel or violently tear off her dress, and allowed myself to dwell on the idea constantly. There was so much for both of us to lose, that I think each was waiting for a blatant enough sign from the other. My heart was beating so fast that my voice trembled. There was a fierce battle going on in me. "Hold back, Simon, behave yourself". "No way, come on, what a great opportunity!"

It was five minutes to the curfew. Was I going to stay the night? I so badly wanted to. "Get out Simon, go home now", I told myself. I pecked her hurriedly on the cheek to say goodbye and, thankfully, didn't linger. I exploded in frustration when I got home, wanting to release the pent-up energy within me. I felt drained, dizzy, disappointed that I hadn't gone for it, further disappointed that I had considered going for it, but in all honesty regretting that my faith and conscience wouldn't allow me follow my natural carnal instincts.

I don't think I've ever experienced such strength of emotion. I found the whole thing a depressing scenario, and it led to a night of dreams where my imagination was unleashed to accomplish all that had been staved off in the conscious realm. Aaaargh! It has underlined to me the fact that maybe I really do need a wife. But who would be willing to live this kind of life?[28]

Simon made the right choices, stayed pure and is now happily married to Lizzie. They continue to serve in Burundi as a family.

Chapter 20 - Single in South-East Asia

If you travel or live in South-East Asia, consider how you will be affected by the sex industry. **Dr Glenn Miles**, *who works for LOVE146[29] in Cambodia, joins* **Dr Debbie Hawker** *in discussing the issues.*

We love being in South-East Asia, but we have learned that in some countries you need to be careful and prepared, especially if you are a man. There can be all the usual scams and pick-pocketing which can happen in any culture, but there are also other issues to consider.

In countries like Cambodia, Thailand, Malaysia and the Philippines you may receive frequent offers of a massage. This can seem innocent and appealing, especially if you have back pain or problems with stress and have found massage helpful in the past. However, many of these young masseurs earn a low income and rely on tips from those who are willing to pay for additional sexual services. They often progress from traditional massage to what can easily become erotic massage. A survey of more than 80 expatriate Christian men working in Cambodia asked "Have you had a 'traditional' massage where the masseur touched you sexually?" 32% of the men reported that this had happened to them, and a further 12% declined to answer the question.[30]

In the same survey, 11% of these Christian men admitted they had had sexual intercourse with a prostitute, and 15% declined to answer. In countries where prostitution is common, the dangers may seem obvious. A man may be continually approached by women seeking 'business', and by 'tuk tuk' drivers and men with photos of scantily clad women trying to draw him into their massage parlour. How many can you ignore or say "no" to before you feel agitated, or are tempted? I know a man who hired a local woman as an escort to walk with him and protect him from being bothered. This may help when you are out, but it might destroy your good reputation, as people who see you with the escort may assume that you are using her as a prostitute, not to avoid prostitution. Some men avoid walking or else travel in mixed groups to reduce the risk of being approached. You can still be approached in a group, and prostitutes may still knock on your door, especially if you are staying in a hotel.

Women as well as men can be affected by the sight of many prostitutes. Seeing many beautiful, seductive women can have an effect on your thoughts. Not all prostitutes are women. Girls, boys and young men are also vulnerable to exploitation. Seeing an Asian child holding hands with a middle-aged, white 'sex tourist' can arouse strong emotions. We may feel angry about the ill-treatment of children, and helpless because we feel unable to rescue them.

The solution is not to avoid going to such regions, or to describe them as 'evil'. Every culture has its own injustices and wrongdoing. Children are trafficked throughout Europe every day, but it is more hidden. Rather than avoiding a country or ignoring the problem, a better solution is to plan how to respond to the situation. What part can you play in supporting those who help change the situation and free people from prostitution?[31]

Because sex tourism is rife, men travelling alone to South-East Asia are sometimes suspected of engaging in it, even if this is far from true. It is worth carrying documents which show what you have been doing (such as letters about your ministry), in case you are arrested on suspicion of sexually exploiting children. This may seem far-fetched, but unfortunately when a man travels alone to South-East Asia, it is often assumed that he is going there for sex.

Here is one true example. A British man who I'll call Adam travelled to Cambodia to spend two weeks training Christian leaders there. He was shown round a Christian orphanage as part of his visit, and given a business card from the people who ran the orphanage. When he arrived back at the airport in London, a border agency officer asked routine questions about where he had begun his journey. When Adam said "Cambodia", the officer asked to check his bags.

Adam complied. The officer found the card with the address of the orphanage. He then took Adam's computer datasticks (containing hundreds of powerpoint presentations) away to check them. He disappeared for an hour, then said that he was unable to access the files (although they were basic microsoft documents).

The officer confiscated Adam's datasticks, camera and laptop computer. He refused to give a reason or to allow Adam to speak to a senior officer. Adam's property was taken to the forensic unit for investigation, and Adam was told it would be kept for 8-12 weeks. We can assume that because Adam was travelling alone back from Cambodia, and had the address of an orphanage with him, he was suspected of sexually exploiting children.

His property was detained for two weeks, and searched for any indecent images or other evidence of crime. Nothing was found, as all the documents were for Adam's teaching and charitable activities. Although nothing was found, Adam suffered great inconvenience. A lot of time was taken up trying to get his property back. Adam had been working on an application for a grant. Because he was without his files for two weeks, he missed the deadline and lost out on a large sum of money for his charity. People who were dependent on bank transfers couldn't receive them, as all the bank details were in the detained files.

When Adam told his Foundation, they asked him, "What do they suspect you of?", as if he might indeed be guilty of something. Adam realised that people think 'there is no smoke without fire', and he wondered whether people assumed he really had done something wrong. Just being questioned might make him seem questionable. Adam felt that he couldn't tell supporters what had happened to him, because being regarded as suspicious could tarnish his reputation. It can be impossible to prove innocence.

Adam had been a frequent traveller in his ministry, but this episode meant that he became more anxious about travelling. This experience caused emotional frustration, loss of sleep, fatigue and a sense of vulnerability. Even though his property was later returned, the experienced troubled Adam deeply.

What can we learn from such experiences? Men travelling alone in South-East Asia are vulnerable. You may be viewed with suspicion. Be prepared to show documents or letters of invitation explaining why you are in this region. Consider backing up computer documents on-line, so that you have a copy if your equipment is seized. Be aware of how visits to orphanages or other childcare facilities might be viewed. If you are treated with suspicion perhaps the best attitude to take is to think, "I'm glad I'm innocent. Jesus was falsely accused too and he knows what it is like. He is with me now. I'm glad that people care enough about sexual exploitation to detain me".

We are prepared to face the inconvenience of being detained for a while, knowing that some offenders might also be detained and then convicted and prevented from perpetrating further abuse. We don't want people to stop caring about exploited children – we need to care more. But in future, we will try to be careful and prepared.

Chapter 21 - Why cross-cultural mission is high-risk for sexual challenges

Dr Rhonda ("Roni") Pruitt is a single mission worker. She served for 15 years in China, Japan, Hungary, and Germany. She opened a Mission Care Centre in Berlin, serving all Protestant mission personnel in the region. In 2001 she established Single Vision, a retreat programme for single mission workers[32]. Roni trained in Biblical Studies and Missions, and then in Counselling Psychology. Her contribution has helped pioneer the field of mission worker care in North America, Europe, and Asia. She is the founder of the first degree course in member care, through Columbia International University, which has programmes in Asia and the USA.[33]

While attending a mission training event I was puzzled when the schedule for the day was read. The leader stated, "The married male staff will meet in room 256 and all other staff will meet in room 308". Later I discovered that the men discussed relationships in a ministry setting and covered sexual ethics. When I inquired why the leader did not open the session to single people he replied, "Because they are not sexual". He limited the understanding of sexuality to acts of genital sexuality, and did not see the person in light of their whole personhood. This was perplexing. Of course single people can have sexual feelings. Many churches and mission organisations fail to discuss sexual issues with single workers, so there can be a lack of teaching and support.

It is risky to assume that we are immune to sexual feelings. We need to be aware of our feelings, and to face the challenges with appropriate responses instead of ignoring or denying them. Cross-cultural mission can be a high-risk environment for sexual challenges, for the following reasons.

1. Increased sexual temptation

The previous two chapters gave examples of types of sexual temptation which the expatriate may encounter. Prostitutes may beckon or approach you on the street, in hotels, at airports and train stations (see chapter 7). You may be touched sexually during a massage. In some countries pornography is posted at bus stops and in shops. Local people may look attractive to you, because of their skin colour, body shape or style of dress. You may spend a lot of time with someone you feel attracted to, such as a colleague or a local contact. People around you (for example, workers with secular NGOs, or local people) may be openly having sexual relationships outside marriage – so much so, that the term 'sex-patriate' is sometimes used for the expatriate community. The expectation might be that you will behave in the same way. It is easy to yield to temptation in a moment of weakness.

2. Anonymity, different standards, and living a double-life
Living abroad often comes with anonymity, especially in a city or for people who frequently travel. This makes a double life possible.

As someone becomes part of a new culture, not only does their behaviour change, but their thoughts, beliefs and standards are challenged through exposure to different views. Black and white thinking is difficult to maintain when integrating into a new culture, because the grey category of life gets larger. There seem to be fewer absolutes.

Individuals who cannot tolerate 'grey' factors are at risk of creating a double life. They might rigidly hold to being person A in select settings and in other settings they become a totally separate person, B. For example, person A might appear to be a Christian mission worker with high moral standards, but in some settings he might become person B, behaving in ways not in keeping with Christian teaching.

3. Stress
Mission personnel often report a high level of stress.[34] Stress can reduce sex drive. But stress or boredom can also lead to feelings of frustration, and some people feel that sexual activity is the way to reduce their frustration. Three United Nations workers wrote a book called *Emergency Sex (and other desperate measures)*, which illustrates such behaviour.[35] However, sex does not solve the problem of stress.

4. Isolation
Cross-cultural workers can feel isolated and lonely in a foreign culture, far from their support network of family and friends. Even after a number of years in the culture, local people will still view them an outsider. The mission worker is not fully at home in the host country, or in their country of origin. Mobility and frequent good-byes create challenges for building deep long-term relationships.

5. Misunderstandings about friendships with the opposite sex
Expectations of communication between men and women differ greatly between cultures. In Western cultures men and women are used to talking together, providing different perspectives and variety to life. However, in most cultures such friendship does not exist. If you are alone with someone of the opposite sex, people may believe that this is a sexual relationship. Your new friend might also assume that this is going to be a sexual relationship, and might start to touch you sexually at which point it can become difficult to stop the situation.

6. Sexual advances due to dress
Western culture has attached an individualistic application to dress; it reflects personality and personal taste. A Westerner may take it as a personal critique of their personality if asked to modify their dress. In many cultures dress is a uniform that states a person's role, status and position in society.

Sometimes women are propositioned just because they are foreigners. Other times they are propositioned because their dress suggests that they have loose morals. Numerous cultures hold the position that a man has the right to take sexual advantage of a woman who states by her dress she has low sexual standards. In many cultures legal action would not take place if a woman was raped.

The best way for female cross-cultural workers to protect themselves is to reflect culturally appropriate dress, for example covering arms and legs. Over the years several national leaders have approached me and requested, "Please would you encourage the women to be cautious in their dress". They said what they found most offensive was low cut tops, tight trousers and tops, and shorts. Leaders feared having these women as guests for even a short term, because of the risk they would be raped.

7. Transition: seasons of heightened vulnerability
There are seasons when a cross-cultural worker is more vulnerable than usual. These include times of major transition, such as initial arrival at a new location. These are times when thoughts work with partial information and there may be an emotional imbalance. Feeling isolated and vulnerable, it can be easy to move too quickly into a sexual relationship.

Having covered some of the reasons for sexual challenges, in the next chapter we will suggest possible ways of responding to the challenges.

Chapter 22 - Sexual desire

Dr Roni Pruitt [36] and **Dr Debbie Hawker** *suggest some ways to respond to sexual desire.*

Many single people long for sexual fulfilment, especially when isolated, lonely, stressed or tired. Feelings may be intensified if other people dress revealingly or act in a more sexually provocative way than you are used to. An anonymous mission partner wrote the following:

> *As a single man I was never very interested in pornography or masturbation. But I often fantasised sexually. I had two types of fantasies, which I call explicit and romantic. My explicit fantasies involved full-blown sexual activity with imaginary women, including (as a teenager) complicated and weird sex in an alien world. My romantic fantasies involved real single women I knew and was attracted to. I would admire their bodies and imagine us kissing, cuddling, starting a romantic relationship, getting married, and so on. My romantic fantasies did not extend to explicit sex scenes, but just thinking about these women could sexually excite me just as much as the explicit fantasies did. Either fantasy, if it came back to me in my sleep, could make my dreams wet.*
>
> *Are these fantasies the kind of thoughts that the Bible describes as impure? Is one worse than the other, and if so, which: explicit fantasies involving imaginary people, or romantic fantasies involving real people? Could either or both of them be healthy, controlled ways for single people to express sexual longing? Does the focus of the fantasy not matter as much as the duration and intensity? Are fantasies about real people safer if they are single and potential marriage partners? Are fantasies about imaginary people safer because they are not? What*

happens if you try not to allow space for either type of fantasy? Are sexual fantasies sin, temptation to sin, or a consequence of God's creation of us as sexual beings, or more than one of these? Did Jesus have sexual fantasies? What did he do about them?

We don't have all the answers, but we offer some thoughts for those who have questions like these. An anonymous chaplain wrote that sexual life is primarily about "what's going on between my ears, not between my legs". Our thought life is very important. Jesus classified lustful looks as adultery (Matthew 5:28). This can seem to place us in an impossible position, unless we understand what lust means. The problem is not the first glance, but the second look and prolonged staring and the thoughts that go with it. Automatic thoughts may come into our heads, but we decide whether or not we will dwell on them. Lust is not the same as looking at someone and thinking that they are beautiful. That is just an appreciation of beauty.

In the book *Celibate Sex,* a pastor wrote:

> *Lust is often confused with sexual desire. Sexual desire isn't lust any more than hunger is gluttony. Lust, in its biblical sense, is predatory; it seeks to entrap and use another person for one's own pleasure. This is when it becomes wrong.*[37]

C.S. Lewis distinguished between sexual desire alone (which we might call lust), and *Eros*, the state which we call 'being in love'. Lewis wrote,

> *Sexual desire, without Eros, wants it, the thing in itself; Eros wants the Beloved. The thing is a sensory pleasure; that is, an event occurring within one's own body. We use a most unfortunate idiom when we say, of a lustful man prowling the streets, that he 'wants a woman.' Strictly speaking, a woman is just what he does not want. He wants a pleasure for which a woman happens to be the necessary piece of apparatus. How much he cares about the woman as such may be gauged by his attitude to her five minutes after fruition (one does not keep the carton*

> *after one has smoked the cigarettes). Now Eros makes a man really want, not a woman, but one particular woman. In some mysterious but quite indisputable fashion the lover desires the Beloved herself, not the pleasure she can give.*[38]

Lust (desiring someone just for our own pleasure) is different from feeling in love with someone and caring about them as a person. The Song of Songs demonstrates the connection between love and sex. Had it been about sex without love it would have been a song of lust instead of a beautiful love-song.

It is normal for teenagers to experience lustful thoughts as a response to their hormones – they might imagine sex with anyone or anything, even aliens or vampires. What thoughts and fantasies are acceptable for Christian adults? Should we suppress all sexual thoughts, or does suppressing them cause more problems? Is it all right to imagine developing a romantic relationship with another single person whom you care about, or with someone imaginary?

Some activities seem to be in a grey area, regarded by some Christians as acceptable but by others as unacceptable. There are grey areas regarding what is acceptable to imagine, and also what films to watch, music to listen to, and what to read.

There may be fifty shades of pornography, ranging from romantic novels and films to hardcore porn. Some people find it best to avoid all romantic or erotic material, if it might lead to sexual tension or viewing people as sex objects. If you are unsure whether a certain activity, film, song, book or fantasy is okay for you or not, think about what effect it has on your thought life, your concentration and your relationship with God and with others. Does it heighten or reduce feelings of sexual tension? Does it leave you feeling content or discontent with your life? Does it cause you to feel shame and would you hide it from others? If the people you minister to or represent knew about it, what impact would that have on your ministry? Are there better ways you should spend your time?

Many people in churches have thoughts about inheriting wealth or making a lot of money. We don't tend to condemn them for greedy thoughts. Some people have suicidal thoughts. We respond by offering help, rather than condemning the thoughts. In the same way, if someone has thoughts related to sexual desire, we can respond by helping rather than condemning.

What can you do if you are single and have strong sexual feelings? The apostle Paul wrote, "It is better to marry than to burn with passion" (1 Corinthians 7:9). That is all very well, but what about people who have not found a marriage partner (which was less common in Paul's day)? You might be looking for a marriage partner, or you might not plan to marry. Here are twelve positive steps, some of which relate to the question of "What did Jesus do?"

1. Maintain a vibrant spiritual life
Dietrich Bonhoeffer said, "The pursuit of purity is not about the suppression of lust, but about the reorientation of one's life to a larger goal."[39] Father Keith Clark wrote,

> *I know in my heart that a committed celibate life cannot be sustained without regular and prolonged prayer because the relational void of not knowing experientially that I belong to somebody will erode even my most dogged efforts at fidelity.*[40]

It is harder to give in to sexual temptation if you are close to God. Feed your mind with what is pure and true (Philippians 4:8). Pray as Jesus taught us, "Lead us not into temptation" (Matthew 6: 13). Learn Bible verses. Have regular times of prayer and fellowship with others. Speak with a mentor, pastor or spiritual director who can help you find intimacy with God. Remind yourself that "God is faithful; he will not let you be tempted beyond what you can bear. But when you are tempted, he will also provide a way out so that you can stand up under it" (1 Corinthians 10:13). Choose not to act sinfully or to dwell on lustful thoughts, so that you avoid sexual immorality[41] (Hebrews 13:4).

2. Acknowledge your feelings and thoughts, and bring them to God
Admit to yourself that you have these feelings and thoughts, and remind yourself that it is normal to have sexual feelings and physiological arousal. If we were never allowed to think about kissing, romance, breasts or passion then we would need to avoid reading one of the books of the Bible, as the Song of Songs is full of these – and portrays them positively. As Eugene Peterson points out, the Song of Songs is "very explicit sexually".[42] You don't need to condemn yourself if you find yourself wondering what it would be like to be kissed, or having romantic

thoughts. Pray that God will help you save your longings for the right time and the right person, and do not dwell on romantic thoughts about someone who is not available.

Writing about your feelings in a journal and praying about them may help. In *Celibate Sex,* Abbie Smith says,

> *I once heard it said that finding the humility and strength to take God into our lust would free us from the sins of lust. In other words, while in the pursuit of God, even lust – something typically assumed as unquestionably and utterly disgusting – has the potential to be offered as a means of holiness. Even lust has the grace-drenched capacity to be used for something good… To relearn love is a lifelong process of tethering our affections to the One for whom they were originally and most fully intended.*[43]

3. Build friendships
God created us to be relational beings, and sex is only one way to relate. If we concentrate too much on sex, it downplays the other valuable ways we have of relating to others. We need to have healthy, open, honest, safe, accountable relationships with a variety of people who may be single or married, the same or the opposite sex, young or old. If we can achieve this, sex becomes less significant as a short-term bolster for our self-esteem.

Developing local friendships is important. Cross-cultural workers often feel, "There is no one here who I fully connect with as a person". It is nearly impossible for one friend to know all parts of your life and understand you deeply. The solution is to build a network of friends, each of whom you connect with in one area (e.g. a shared interest). Also seek one or two friends you are not leading or ministering to, who you can share openly with about your life and any struggles, in a reciprocal relationship.

4. When struggling, contact a friend
At the moment when you are struggling with sexual temptation, if you are alone, try to call a friend, or better still, meet up with someone who is a good role model to you. Many who have tried this have found that their sex drive immediately decreased.

5. Tackle stress, and take exercise

The human body, mind and emotions are intertwined. Your body might be telling you that you need sexual activity, but the real need might be relational, emotional or physical. If sexual desire is stress-induced, then a good way to respond is to reduce the stress. Try to solve problems early, before they grow. If stress leads to tiredness which decreases the ability to resist temptation, the solution may be to ensure that you get enough sleep and rest. Also try stress management strategies such as physical activity. Walk, jog or dance. Exercise is a natural tension release, and a tired body will be more likely to want to sleep than find sexual fulfilment. Do relaxing things which you enjoy (for example watch a DVD, read, play music or do something creative or fun).

6. Find healthy ways to meet your needs

When we feel tired, unwell, lonely, fatigued or low, we often want a 'shot in the arm' to raise our spirits. Some people turn to sexual activity to boost their mood. Others use drugs, alcohol, food, shopping or the internet as a short-term fix. Try to find healthy and pure ways to meet your needs, and to channel your energy. Sugar, shopping or a drink might help in the short-term, but try to solve the underlying issue (for example resting if you are fatigued; improving friendships if you feel lonely; resolving problems, or campaigning for justice when you feel angry about the state of the world).

7. Reduce risk

Avoid situations where you are vulnerable to temptation, whether that is visiting night clubs or gay bars, spending excessive time at your computer, watching indecent films or going through red-light districts where prostitutes are active. Instead of spending time alone with someone you feel attracted to, meet with two or more people. Be careful with alcohol as it can reduce your inhibitions. Chapter 24 discusses ways to reduce the risk of accessing pornography.

8. Value intimacy more than sex

Sex is sometimes portrayed as the ultimate satisfaction in life. People who are not in a sexual relationship might think that their life is incomplete. Try not to give in to self-pity, or the false idea that you are missing the best part of life. A documentary was filmed about a young man who was dying in a hospice. It was a sad but revealing true story.

The young man said his final wish before he died was to have sex. He had no partner, so he went to a prostitute. Afterwards he said it had been interesting to find out what sex was like, but it was rather disappointing and he wouldn't bother again. And that was with a professional! Sex without intimacy is just a mechanical act, and an odd one at that. If I had to choose between sex or intimacy, I would choose intimacy every time. The great thing is that intimacy on some level is open to all of us, married or single: intimacy with God, and with close friends and family members. It is worth pursuing. People who abstain from sexual activity can love in other ways. Grow in your love for God, yourself, and others. C.S. Lewis observed,

> It would seem that Our Lord finds our desires not too strong, but too weak. We are half-hearted creatures, fooling about with drink and sex and ambition when infinite joy is offered us, like an ignorant child who wants to go on making mud pies in a slum because he cannot imagine what is meant by the offer of a holiday at the sea. We are far too easily pleased.[44]

9. Have a hug
Sometimes our real need is for touch, and to feel that someone cares. Try to find ways to receive appropriate touch. This might be a hug from a friend, a massage, or cuddling a pet or baby.

10. Enjoy other pleasures in life
Seek enjoyable sensations such as sights, sounds, tastes and movements (see chapter 26). There are many pleasures in life, and none of us achieve all of them. I doubt that I will ever experience the high of completing a marathon, or reaching the top of Mount Everest, but I don't waste my time thinking about what I'm missing. If you are not in a sexual relationship, instead of imagining what you are missing, why not spend time enjoying other pleasures which are available to you?

What do you want to do before you die? What will you seek out soon, and what will you plan for the future? Eating delicious food; climbing a mountain; white-water rafting; a parachute jump; swimming with dolphins; skiing in the Alps; visiting a beautiful place; sitting on a beach in the sunshine; extreme sport; funfair rides; bungee jumping; driving a train; flying a plane; dancing; a silent retreat; watching a sports-game; beautiful music; creating something special; writing a book; watching the birth of a child; playing the harp; going shopping; meditating; a sauna; seeing a famous piece of art; visiting some of the wonders of the world, or playing golf?

If you don't have time for all that at the moment you could go for a run, as exercise releases endorphins (natural chemicals in the brain which make you feel better). If you don't like running, you might prefer eating chocolate, which contains the mood-lifting hormone serotonin and the 'love hormone' phenylethylamine. No wonder some chocolates have names like 'kisses'. One survey reported that 52% of women would rather choose chocolate than sex anyway.[45]

11. Seek help from others, have an accountability partner, and remember this is a battle for nearly everyone

Remember, it is not just single people who have to cope with sexual temptation. Married people can also be tempted to lust after someone other than their own partner, and they can feel that their partner does not want the same sexual experiences (or as many of them) as they do. We are all called to be pure, and it's a battle for many people. Fight on, and if necessary seek an accountability partner who can encourage you, pray for you, and ask tough questions about how you are getting on in this area, such as, "On a scale of 1-10 how are you doing in the area of sexual challenges?" Choose someone you will be honest with. If you don't want to confide in someone you know, consider speaking to a Christian counsellor. These problems are common, and counsellors are not shocked by them. Secrecy leads to shame. Talking removes the secrecy and can free you from shame, and help you take the first step towards breaking the habit. See the resources below for further help.

12. Receive forgiveness if you sin

For those who have sinned sexually, the wonderful news is that when we repent, we can be forgiven. Counselling may help you to leave you past behind and move forwards.

For those who don't relate to this

Here is a quick thought for those who are not particularly interested in sex: don't worry, that doesn't mean you are abnormal. There are people around who aren't interested, despite what is portrayed in the media. There is probably more interest in chocolate!

For further help
- Stoeker, F. & Artenburn, S. (2009) *Every Single Man's Battle*. Colorado Springs: WaterBrook Press.
- Shannon, E. (2009). *Every Woman's Battle.* Colorado Springs: WaterBrook Press.
- Podcasts on sexual wholeness available at http://www.membercaremedia.com/

Chapter 23 - Masturbation

Is it common? Is it sinful? When is it a problem, and what can help reduce it? **Dr Debbie Hawker** *addresses these questions.*

Masturbation can cause feelings of shame and guilt. Christians who masturbate may feel that this is their shameful secret. Masturbation was condemned officially in 1054 by Pope Leo IX.[46] Myths have existed for centuries about masturbation causing health problems (such as blindness or insanity). In fact, the medical consensus is that masturbation is generally a psychologically normal and medically healthy habit[47] (although there are risks if an object gets stuck).

Masturbation is common among both men and women, single and married, across the lifespan and probably across the world, although it is an unstudied, taboo topic in some cultures. Masturbation is a normal part of childhood development and self-exploration. It has also been observed among many species of animals. Studies in the USA[48] and the UK[49] have found that 92-95% of men and 62-85% of women report having masturbated at some point. 73% of men and 37% of women reported masturbating in the four weeks before their interview. 80% of "religiously active" men admitted to masturbating.

Many people, including some Christians, view masturbation as a normal act of tension release. Sperm build up in men's seminal vesicles every four or five days.[50] These are released either during sex, by masturbating, or in nocturnal emissions ('wet dreams').

The book *Celibate Sex* quotes a pastor who used to advocate against masturbation, but who after much reflection changed his mind and decided it probably was not wrong. He said,

> *The intensity of male desire peaks after three days and remains so high-pitched that a guy feels like he wants to crawl out of his skin. This lasts for about seven days. If a man does not have sex (if married) or relieve himself, he can hardly concentrate on much else. It is simply the way God wired us. Furthermore, if a man does not have some kind of release, his body does it automatically ... In his sleep, so it is completely involuntary, a man will dream that he is making love to someone and will have an orgasm.*[51]

The intensity of sexual desire varies from person to person and with age. Some men don't feel such a high intensity of sexual tension, or remember any sexual dreams, but many men and women do. With women, sexual interest tends to increase at certain points in the menstrual cycle (the follicular and ovulatory phases).[52]

Some people masturbate to help them get to sleep. Some masturbate during their sleep and are not even aware of it. Is masturbation sinful? Some Christians assume it is, but can it be a sin if it is done without awareness? What about during times of awareness? A Christian college professor quoted in *Celibate Sex* reflected,

> *Some have stated that masturbation is simply selfish sex and therefore wrong. I do not think the issue is as simple as all that. It may be that my bodily desire allows me to hardly think about anything else but sex. If I am really hungry, or thirsty, or tired, I can hardly think about anything else but food or drink or sleep. There is nothing self-serving about taking the edge off these desires so I can concentrate on serving others with limited distraction. So, too, with sexual desire and the single person... to relieve oneself takes the edge off the desire and doesn't take advantage of others... it might also make it possible to keep oneself out of an illicit sexual union.* [53]

John White, a Christian psychiatrist, wrote "Masturbation is not, in and of itself, sin at all. Yet many people are convinced that it is sin and feel guilty when they masturbate." [54]

For every Christian who feels masturbation is not sinful, we could probably find another who says that it is a sin because sexual activity should be reserved for man and wife, and anything else belittles the sexual union. Yet some married Christians masturbate, while thinking of their partner, in an attempt to remain faithful to their spouse during times of separation or when their spouse is unavailable or unable to meet their sexual desire, for example if one partner wants more sex than the other. The couple may feel that masturbation benefits their relationship and enables them to draw closer together. Without it the sexual tension might cause them to feel dissatisfied. Some couples engage in mutual masturbation, to give each other pleasure. The respected Christian writer Dr James Dobson stated,

> *It is my opinion that masturbation is not much of an issue with God. ... I'm not telling you to masturbate, and I hope you won't feel the need for it. The best thing I can do is suggest that you talk to God personally about this matter and decide what He wants you to do.*[55]

In trying to find out what God wants, we should consider what the Bible says. The Bible does not refer to masturbation by name. Some Christians refer to the story of Onan (Genesis 38:8-10) to support their view that masturbation is a sin. Onanism and masturbation erroneously become synonymous. However, this story is not about masturbation. It is about Onan agreeing to have sexual intercourse with his brother's wife while refusing to let her become pregnant because he selfishly did not want his brother to have offspring. He broke the Hebraic marriage law (Deuteronomy 25: 5-10).

Leviticus 15:16 states that a man who has "an emission of semen" will be unclean until evening. The same chapter states that a woman who has a monthly period will be unclean for seven days (Leviticus 15:19), so the emission of semen seems to be regarded as less "unclean" than menstruation.

The Bible has a lot to say about thoughts, including lustful thoughts (see Matthew 5:28). If sexual fantasy or sinful thoughts accompany masturbation, the thoughts are more of a problem than the action. When someone asked the theologian Dr Leslie Weatherhead "Is masturbation a sin or not?" he replied,

> *It depends whether the picture on the screen of the mind at the time could be shown to our Lord without shame. If there is no picture on the wall, refuse to be weighed down by guilt. Too many Christians known to me wallow in unnecessary guilt about masturbation and forget that God may be wanting them to deal with other problems in their lives. But of course if the picture on the wall is of someone else's partner or a person to whom you are not married... then a way out of the problem must be found.*[56]

If pornography is viewed to assist masturbation, that is also a problem. Pornography feeds an industry in which people are exploited (see chapter 24).

I have been asked by one mission worker to comment on the use of sex toys. I will not to go into detail here, to avoid creating unhelpful thoughts or images. If sex toys are used purely for tension release, they may do little harm, and the comments on masturbation may also apply to using sex toys in this way. However, some items may not be safe to use, or are only safe for a short period of time. Some cause problems if they are not properly designed or used. They can lead to wanting more and more of them (like an addiction), creating unnecessary preoccupation with sex. It can be hard to buy sex toys (in a shop, on-line or through a catalogue) without being exposed to objectionable products and pornography. Buying them may help fund pornography. If sex toys are accompanied by impure thoughts, that creates problems for a Christian. On the whole, it is probably better to stay away from them, and instead to seek to improve intimate, wholesome relationships.

The important thing is to aim for pure thoughts (Philippians 4:8). We can break routines associated with impure thoughts, and set up positive, new routines. We can try to stay clear of situations which arouse us sexually. If taking a cold shower or going for a run helps to chase off impure thoughts, then let's get cold, wet and fit!

Earlier, we suggested that masturbation may be due to sexual tension related to the build up of seminal fluid, or (for women) hormonal changes. But there is more to sexual arousal than this. As Cusick (2012) puts it,

> *A man's sexual appetite is a barometer for what's going on inside his heart. Your sex drive consists of more than testosterone and the buildup of seminal fluid pressing for biological release, more than being visually stimulated and feeling aroused. Sexual arousal is an accumulation of your experiences, deep needs, and unconscious beliefs.*[57]

Masturbation (and sexual fantasy) may be related to loneliness, isolation, stress, a lack of fulfilling relationships, low self-esteem or a lack of excitement in life. If this is the case, it is important to try to identify the real problem and address that. If masturbation becomes compulsive (taking up too much time and mental space, and it is not possible to stop) or it involves impure thoughts, or is done at the wrong time or place or it leads to consuming guilt, then it is wise to seek counselling.

Here are some tips, provided by Dr Pruitt[58], for people who want to reduce their habit of masturbating.

1. Don't be too harsh with yourself – it is a common practice.
2. Expect to fail multiple times before you have more freedom in this area. Focus on your progress, not on the failures – we are not perfect.
3. Realise that God can still use us even when we are imperfect. God is most concerned about our heart and our desire to do his will.
4. Review when and where the temptation comes, then break patterns of behaviour. For example, arrange to connect with someone at the time you are often tempted.
5. When tempted, stand up and call a friend, or go out for a walk or make a cup of tea.
6. The number one treatment for sexual tension and depression is exercise.
7. Address any issues related to stress.
8. Find one or two trusted people you can tell about your struggles and draw support from. Admitting a secret reduces its power over you.

For further information see
www.missionarycare.com/singles/masturbation.htm

Chapter 24 – Pornography

John Steley *is a psychologist who has worked at InterHealth,[59] and also with the prison service of England and Wales. He now has a private practice in London.* [60]

Definition of pornography
Pornography is defined as "printed or visual material containing the explicit description or display of sexual organs or activity, intended to stimulate sexual excitement".[61] Pornography depicts acts in a sensational manner, to arouse quick, intense reactions.[62] Pornography can be 'softcore' (suggestive) or 'hardcore' (explicit).

Pornography can come in various forms, including pictures (e.g. magazines), books, films, cartoons, sound recordings, video and video games. Nowadays most pornography is accessed via the internet.

Who uses pornography?
Pornography is a problem for many men and women. Anyone who is old enough to know what they are seeing can become addicted, regardless of ethnic group, profession, education, age, marital status, sex, past or current sexual behaviour, religious beliefs or role in the church.

It is easy to turn to pornography. David's[63] story might help illustrate this.

> *David was brought-up in a Christian home. He attended church with his family and enjoyed being part of the youth group as a teenager. David worked well at school, obtained fairly good grades and was reasonably popular. He used the internet, quite legitimately, for study and research. Late in the evening, when other family members were asleep, David sometimes accessed sites that offered pornographic material. He was a committed Christian and felt guilty about this. He sometimes prayed that God would help him stop but he did not tell anyone. Most of the boys at his school did this and he did not think it anything unusual.*
>
> *At university David's use of pornography increased. He had less time in class and more time working on his own. Loneliness and occasional periods of depression*

worsened the problem. He was still active in the Christian Union and attended a local church every Sunday. At times he felt guilty about his 'dirty secret' but still did not share it with anyone. His fellow students and the members of his church thought of him as a fine young Christian man.

In his final year David became interested in short-term mission work. It sounded exciting, his pastor and friends encouraged him and maybe, he thought to himself, it would be the end of him viewing pornography.

David applied to a mission society that worked among street children in poor urban areas. He was questioned about his beliefs and his Christian commitment. The people who assessed him were reassured when David passed his Criminal Records Bureau check, indicating that he had no criminal convictions. They did not ask him about his use of the internet. They assumed that Christians who want to do mission work would not be using pornography, and asking such a question would be very difficult.

After some training and orientation David was sent to a facility for street children in an overseas country. The work was challenging and occasionally rewarding, but at times he felt isolated. The early afternoon heat could be stifling. Other people slept after lunch but David found this difficult. Instead he went to his computer. He felt slightly superior in that while others were taking a siesta he was at work. Again, however, he found himself looking at pornography. Being a mission worker afforded him no protection from this temptation. Still, he thought that as long as nobody knew no harm would be done. The early afternoon was his time for himself, a time for some simple, forbidden pleasures that would end as soon as others woke from their nap. He felt guilty but reassured himself that the rest of the time he and his colleagues were doing good work.

One day David was asked to report to his team leader's office. He had not been expecting this and was given no explanation as to why he had to attend. The team leader looked at David sternly and asked, "Have you heard the rumours? The children are saying you look at *rather degrading stuff on your computer." David was stunned. His secret was out. He confessed to years of misusing the internet. It was the first time he had admitted this to anyone. "But how did anyone know?" he asked. The team leader gave him a long, knowing look and replied, "Never underestimate children's ability to be where you do not expect them or to see what you don't want them to see."*

David's contract with the mission society was terminated. He was told to leave immediately. Somehow he would have to explain to his parents, his friends and his church why he had come home early. The mission agency's reputation had been severely damaged. Everyone in the area seemed to know what the children were saying. David would now have to live with the knowledge that instead of assisting the church in that place he had caused it to be ridiculed and humiliated.

Why is it wrong to view pornography?

Viewing pornography can waste your time and possibly your money. It can cause mental images and thoughts which may be upsetting and distract you from other activities. Pornography can cause you to view people as sex objects, who do not live up to your unrealistic ideal image. It may cause difficulties in future relationships. It can become addictive, and you may want more and more extreme pornography to satisfy you. Viewing pornography may lead to other sexual temptation. It is illegal to view pornography in some countries, and it is also a disciplinary issue in some companies and mission organisations. Seeing pornography can lead you to feel distant from God. It encourages an industry that exploits the poor and the vulnerable.

Initial steps to overcoming a problem with pornography

These steps apply to overcoming the use of internet pornography but many of them apply to other forms of pornography as well.

1. Acknowledge that you have a problem.
2. Tell a trusted person. This may be your pastor, home group leader, another mature Christian or a Christian counsellor. Ask them to enquire regularly about your internet/pornography use.

3. Limit computer use and install filters on your computer to block pornography.
4. In addition to filters, use an internet accountability programme, such as www.covenanteyes.com.[64] You will be asked to name some people who will receive regular emails reporting all the websites you have accessed. Think carefully about the people you choose. Ideally, they should be people with whom you have regular contact and who you respect. Tell them the problem and ask whether they are willing to help by checking your website use. Make sure you have an accountability programme operating on every computer to which you have access.
5. If possible, place your computer where others can see the screen (unless dealing with confidential matters), or can see you.
6. List reasons why you want to stop looking at pornography. For example, your reasons might include feelings of guilt and shame; the amount of time it takes up; the fact that God does not want you to do this; a fear of being caught; not wanting to fund the exploitation which the pornography industry causes (including the abuse of children); not wanting to see people as sex objects or to devalue relationships, and other reasons. If you view pornographic images of children, remember that this is a criminal offence in many countries, and you could face severe punishment. When you feel tempted, look at your list of reasons you want to stop using pornography.
7. Take good self-care. Self-control tends to be more difficult when we feel hungry or tired. Try to eat and sleep well and avoid the computer when you feel vulnerable.
8. If you feel you are going to give in to the urge to use pornography, try putting it off until later. You may find that by then the urge has gone or is at a level you can resist. In the meantime, contact your accountability partner or go out, away from computers. Leave your phone at home if you use it to access the internet. Perhaps go for a run or do some other form of exercise (to get rid of the tension).
9. Be aware that if you use a company computer to access pornography, you may have broken the code of conduct of your organisation. Some companies will dismiss any employee who does this. Check the policy of your company. Information technology staff can access your history of internet use.

10. Ask yourself what need pornography is filling in your life. Is there a need for greater intimacy? More excitement or adventure? Do you have too much idle time? Are you depressed? Do you use a fantasy site because you want to escape from reality? Try to meet the deeper need. Replace the pornography with something better in your life, such as intimate relationships with God and others, and exciting leisure activities.
11. If you go for even a short time without viewing pornography, reward yourself.
12. Even if you have taken all of these steps it may still be worth asking a counsellor to help you.

You may find yourself thinking things like:

"Just a little bit will not do any harm."
"I need to know what is out there, and learn more about sex."
"Everyone does something wrong. This is just my particular failing."
"This is not what I find most titillating."
"Looking at this might help me resist the temptation to have sex with someone".

These are rationalizations. Dismiss them, and focus on something else (Philippians 4:8). If you give in to temptation, do not punish yourself. Ask God's forgiveness. Tell a trusted friend, and go and do something useful. Consider what triggered you, and learn from the situation so that you will be able to avoid it next time. Most addictive problems do not go away easily. You will probably need to persevere for some time, until not using pornography becomes a lifestyle. Give yourself regular encouragement and remind yourself that the goal is worth it.

For further information, see chapter 22 and:
- Cusuck, M. J. (2012). *Surfing for God*. Nashville: Thomas Nelson
- Struthers, W. (2010). *Wired for intimacy: How pornography hijacks the male brain*. Nottingham: IVP.
- www.missionarycare.com/marriage/computer_sex_or_me.htm
- www.interhealth.org.uk (search for information about "internet pornography").
- Clark, D. (2012). *You, your family and the internet: What every Christian in the digital age ought to know*. Leominster: Day One.

Chapter 25 - Same-sex attraction, homosexuality and bisexuality

Can someone who is attracted to people of the same sex be effective in ministry? **Dr Debbie Hawker** *presents thoughts from a number of anonymous contributors.*

Some evangelicals believe that anyone who is attracted to people of the same sex should not be accepted into Christian ministry. Keith Ward writes,

> The growing levels of intolerance of homosexual identity (quite apart from the question of sexual expression) have made the mission vocation very uncomfortable for single people, and particularly for those who might wish to be honest about their sexuality. The result is likely to be that homosexuals will increasingly feel excluded from missionary service.[65]

There are a number of problems with excluding people based on sexual orientation. It does not work, it does not seem to be the right thing to do, and it leads to secrecy instead of support, as discussed below.

1. We might not know someone's sexual orientation
Sexual orientation is not usually obvious, and people do not generally volunteer this information as part of an application. In some countries it is illegal to ask about sexual orientation as part of a job interview (including an application for mission), or to discriminate because of it.

2. Sexual orientation exists on a continuum, and can change
Many people experience, at some point in their life, feelings of attraction towards someone of the same sex. There appears to be a continuum from exclusive heterosexuality, through bisexuality, to exclusive homosexuality. Where you are on the continuum may change.[66] Some people who previously identified themselves as homosexuals later shifted to being attracted to someone of the opposite sex, and have been happily married for years. Others move in the opposite direction, or fluctuate, while many never change their orientation.

3. Anyone can potentially fall in love with a person of either gender

I have met single mission workers who have been concerned that they might be homosexual because they have developed a very close friendship with a single colleague of the same sex, perhaps a housemate. The feelings were not necessarily of a sexual nature, but they worried about the strength of their love. Heterosexual people can 'fall in love' with people of the same sex. Dr Pruitt explains,

> *Dr Lisa Diamond, an expert on attachment, suggests that the system of love in the brain is the same system as the attachment between an infant and a caregiver. It is not based on gender. Romantic love is governed by attachment and care-giving.[67] Many single mission workers share housing and have close relationships with colleagues. It is common to provide care for a co-worker and share responsibilities for meals, errands, and general needs. As daily life is closely shared, it would be normal to become emotionally attached, and the mission setting creates an intense relational dynamic. Emotional attachment and care-giving is common in close friendships.*
>
> *Sometimes a mission worker might feel 'in love' with a same-sex colleague because of their emotional attachment, and assume that this means that they are gay. Diamond (p. 173) writes, "individuals can develop novel sexual desires – even desires that contradict their sexual orientation – as a result of falling in love" in this way.*
>
> *A worker might think, "I have never had these types of same-sex thoughts, and suddenly I find myself attracted to my co-worker. What has happened to me?" Often, all that is happening is that the sexual system has been activated by care-giving and the development of emotional attachment. This is perfectly normal, and simply reflects same-sex feelings of affection. Usually this is not an indication of homosexuality.[68]*

It is not sinful to have loving feelings for a member of the same sex, and it does not make you a homosexual. The Bible demonstrates no disapproval for the friendship between David and Jonathan: "Jonathan became one in spirit with David, and he loved him as himself... And Jonathan made a covenant with David because he loved him as himself" (1 Samuel 18:1, 3). After Jonathan's death, David grieved, "Your love for me was wonderful, more wonderful than that of women" (2 Samuel 1:26). The disciple John refers to himself as "the disciple whom Jesus loved" (John 21:7). We are told that Jesus loved Lazarus (John 11:3, 36). Love is good, not bad!

4. We may have little choice about sexual orientation, but we can choose to be celibate

Some people acknowledge that they have (unwanted) feelings of same-sex attraction which *are* of a sexual nature, but they choose to abstain from homosexual activities. They might not identify themselves with the gay community. They may prefer to use the term same-sex attraction, rather than homosexual. Same-sex attraction (or, for that matter, homosexual attraction) simply describes a feeling, not behaviour or identity.

Many Christians experience same-sex attraction, and choose to remain celibate. There appear to be important biological factors involved in sexual orientation, as well as some environmental factors and human agency.[69] Sexual orientation appears unaffected by an active faith, although sexual behaviour is. Although the Bible teaches that sexual intercourse should be within marriage, a biologically-influenced sexual *orientation* which is not acted on is not something to condemn. Sadly, lesbian and gay Christians often feel condemned for the orientation which they have no choice about, and like Job they feel judged by critical friends who do not understand.

We may have little control over the feelings of attraction, but we can control our actions. Same sex thoughts and desires can arise, just as heterosexual thoughts and desires can. Chapter 22 refers to ways of dealing with sexual desire, whether that is heterosexual or homosexual.

If a heterosexual person, whether married or single, sometimes feels attracted to members of the opposite sex to whom they are not married, we don't say that they cannot be useful in ministry. We don't even ask about it. If someone has same-sex attraction but is committed to celibacy, why should we think they are any less suitable for ministry than the person with heterosexual attraction? Like any single person, they can choose to live a life of celibacy.

5. Putting too much attention on sexual orientation detracts from the main message of the gospel

When selecting people for mission, why do we pay more attention to sexual orientation than to pride, greed or selfish ambition? What message does that send? Many people in society have watched in puzzlement a church publicly tear itself apart over its response to homosexuality. Many outsiders end up with the impression that the church's prime message is hatred of gays, a message they hear so loud that it deafens them to the gospel.

The Bible says much more about justice, love and caring for the poor than about homosexuality. Jesus did not teach specifically about homosexuality. It is not the centre of the gospel. There are only about seven references to homosexuality in the Bible (scholars argue about the exact number which really refer to homosexuality). These are all about sexual behaviour, not sexual orientation. Steve Chalke (evangelical founder of Oasis Global) writes in a controversial article,

> A growing number of scholars, including evangelicals, argue that what the New Testament writers have in mind when they refer to homosexual practice could not have been the loving and stable same-sex unions of the sort that exist today, of which they knew nothing. Not only did the concepts of being either *"homosexual"* or *"heterosexual"* not form the primary axis of Roman thinking about sexuality, no Latin words for these two ideas exist.
>
> Instead, the New Testament references to homosexuality refer to the kind of wild, same-sex, extra-marital promiscuity which we now know was common in Roman culture and also formed an integral part of much of their popular religious practice.[70]

The Bible condemns promiscuity, but has little to say about sexual orientation. In contrast, there are hundreds of references to justice, love, caring for the poor, and reconciliation with God through Christ. We should focus on these things and not let sexual orientation detract from the main message.

6. There is a lack of evidence that therapy to change sexual orientation works

Some lesbian and gay people have been recommended to have therapy to change their sexual orientation. But we don't recommend that heterosexual people have therapy to remove all feelings of attraction to people they are not married to. At the moment, there is no evidence that therapy to change sexual orientation works, due to a lack of high quality research.[71] Sexual orientation cannot be easily changed. Some celibate Christians have a homosexual orientation. They are called to serve, as we all are, and so some of them are in ministry.

7. Some evangelical alliances accept celibate clergy with a homosexual orientation, and mission agencies are beginning to do the same

The Evangelical Alliance of the United Kingdom affirms,

> *We commend and encourage all those who experience same-sex attraction and have committed themselves to chastity by refraining from homoerotic sexual practice. We believe they should be eligible for ordination and leadership within the church, recognising that they can bring invaluable insights and experience to the sphere of Christian pastoral ministry*[72].

Mission agencies and churches are beginning to follow this lead, in accepting celibate mission partners who are known to experience same sex attraction.

8. An atmosphere of acceptance facilitates accountability and support instead of secrecy and shame

Whatever our view, there *will* be people in ministry who are attracted to people of the same sex, whether or not we know who they are. Promoting the view that this is sinful leads to secrecy[73], shame and problems. If we have an attitude of openness, people feel able to be honest about their orientation and seek support and accountability.

Single people can benefit from support related to their decision to be celibate, whether they are homosexual or heterosexual. As an example of the importance of support and accountability, one former mission worker wrote the following, and has given permission for us to use it:

> During the past ten years there have been some personal issues that I have had to deal with, related to same-sex attraction and pornography. This covers the period I was working as a mission worker. I have tried to be open and transparent about my personal life. I believe that effective accountability is very important for standing firm and walking more consistently as a single person who seeks to honour the Lord in my life.
>
> Various accountability structures were put in place for me at different levels, and in later years I met with a counsellor. Some of the support I was offered by my sending church was amazingly useful and pastorally sensitive. A system was derived whereby I had weekly contact (by phone or Skype) with a member of a support team. In addition I spoke to the vicar of my sending church every three or four weeks about ministry matters. I also had regular work supervision sessions.
>
> I am very involved with church, and I have lots of friends. I am better when I am in a community setting and know my neighbours, rather than feeling isolated. I am now a member of the True Freedom Trust[74], and have attended four annual conferences. This has been helpful. The other para-church organisation I've been linked to is Bible Study Fellowship[75]. In my last couple of years overseas this was a great input to my life, and enabled me to have a more structured and disciplined devotional time, which has helped me to move forward in my faith.
>
> In summary, I have been helped by accountability structures, support, friendships, True Freedom Trust, and help with my devotional life. God helps me in my weakness, as I seek to follow Biblical teaching.

9. If people are able to be open about their sexual orientation, we are more able to provide a suitable placement and relevant briefing

Knowing that a person has a homosexual orientation can help when considering a suitable location for service. For example, despite not conducting homosexual activity themselves, some people might feel uneasy in countries where homosexual acts are illegal and punishable by death, or in a team which is intolerant of homosexuality. Some might feel uncomfortable in places where men walk down the street holding hands.

Accommodation arrangements should also be considered. Sometimes workers are expected to share a bed with someone of the same gender, for example while on a short-term placement or living with a local family. Other options should be discussed. A mission worker may appreciate being placed in a team where they have an accountability partner who is accepting of their orientation and can ask them how they are getting on, and support them. During briefing, they can be assured that they do not need to tell everyone in their team about their same-sex attraction, as not everyone would understand.

Conclusion

Can we accept mission personnel with a homosexual (or bisexual) orientation if they choose to be celibate? Yes. People with same-sex attraction can be used by God in mission. I have met many who are. Keith Ward reports,

> There is a growing body of evidence in private papers and in the memories of those who have worked as missionaries, particularly in the latter half of the 20thcentury, that gay people have made a significant contribution to the communities among whom they worked and to the furtherance of Christian mission.[76]

God calls us to be orientated towards Christ and faithful to his call, whatever our sexual orientation or our gender (including people who are intersex).[77]

More information is available in chapters 22-24 of this book, and the websites http://www.truefreedomtrust.co.uk and http://www.themarinfoundation.org.

The following books contain further information
- Marin, A. (2009) *Love is an orientation.* Downers Grove: IVP.
- Roberts, V. (2007) *Battles Christians Face.* Milton Keynes: Authentic lifestyle.

- Tylee, A. (2007) *Walking with gay friends: A journey of informed compassion.* Nottingham: IVP.
- Yarhouse, M.A. (2010) *Homosexuality and the Christian: A guide for parents, pastors, and friends.* Ada, MI: Baker.

For those who want to further explore what the Bible says about homosexuality, two opposing points of view are presented in the following articles
- Chalke, S. (2013) The bible and homosexuality – part 1. *Christianity*, January 22 2013. At www.christianitymagazine.co.uk/sexuality/stevechalkeextended.aspx
- Downes, G. (2013) The bible and homosexuality – part 2. *Christianity*, January 22 2013. At www.christianitymagazine.co.uk/sexuality/gregdownes2.aspx

Chapter 26 - Sacred sexuality: A positive view of single sexuality

*The preceding chapters in this section on sexuality have focused on challenges. To provide some balance, **Dr Roni Pruitt**[78] presents a positive view of single sexuality.*

A theology of sexuality
Many single cross-cultural workers describe sexuality as a foe to be fought and tamed. They battle with their sexuality, wanting to be victors over it. They see it as a burden to bear. Others dismiss sexuality as having no role in their life. They may sense that they miss something and there is potential for bitterness to appear. The assumption is that sexuality means sexual intercourse, which belongs within a marriage relationship and so single Christians must abstain.

It is not my intent to minimize the role of sexual intercourse. However, that is only one part of human sexuality. It is over-emphasized by secular sources to the neglect of a comprehensive view of sexuality.

A positive perspective for single people begins by viewing sexuality as a God-created component of every human being. The Bible has a lot to say about sexuality. It is a sacred part of life that is to be cherished, as it has spiritual implications. A whole and healthy sexuality is possible for single people. Spirituality and sexuality are closely related and both can be tools of worship. This chapter explores sexuality through the eyes of God's creative design noted in scripture.

When God created the first humans, sexuality came into being. God looked at his creation and "it was very good" (Genesis 1:31). Every person can receive this gift from God and hopefully agree with God in saying "it is good". Satan has tainted sexuality in modern society and it appears to reflect the opposite of the nature of God. Therefore, one must look beyond the image of the stain to see what God's original design reveals.

Sexuality models the relationship that God wants to have with us, his creation. Relational intimacy and sexuality are close in nature and flow from the same part of a person. There is a fine line of division between having a deep relationship with a person and the potential to develop sexual feelings for them. For some people if they pray with others there is a danger of creating intimate sexual feelings for their prayer partner. Deep sharing and trust is the foundation of sexuality. The Christian walk is a process of God pressing toward a deeper intimacy with us. Spiritual growth takes places when we in return press toward intimacy with God. We are known fully by God and there is no part of us that is hidden from him. He knows us better than any human. We were created for intimacy with God.

God's final creative touch was to make men and women. God has both male and female characteristics. You need to view both sexes to see a complete picture of God's nature. For this purpose, the Creator brought male and female into existence: to establish an eternal reflection of his whole being.[79] Both sexes are blessed by God. As a young person I used to ponder why God chose to be a man instead of a woman. Does God think men are best? But God is neither male nor female. Though God is frequently imaged in scripture as a male (king, father, warrior), he is also at times pictured as a female (mother, Lady of Wisdom). God is no more a male or female than he is a 'rock' or a 'shield' (Psalm 18:2)[80]. Assigning gender to God is a construct that we have created to fit a divine God into our human thinking. Some women need to hear that both genders are equally blessed and embraced by God as his wonderful creation.

Some think of male as being the opposite of female, but this is not true. Phyllis Trible casts a picture of how they relate as being in likeness to each other:

> In the very act of distinguishing female from male, the earth creature describes her as 'bone of my bones and flesh of my flesh' in Genesis 2:23. These words speak unity, solidarity, mutuality, and equality. Man does not depict himself as either prior to or superior to the woman. His sexual identity depends upon her even as hers depends upon him. For both of them sexuality originates in the one flesh of humanity.[81]

There is a unity in difference between the genders which reflects God's divine spirit. The unity displayed in mutual submission in a relationship is a radical idea born of God, which stands in contrast to the domination and subjugation of the world. God's love is without manipulation.

Sexuality shows how the internal nature of God relates within the Trinity, because each member of the Trinity gives preference to the others. Christ came to do the work of the Father, and to foretell the coming of the Holy Spirit. The Holy Spirit came to do the ministry of Christ and bring glory to the Father. There is a 'oneness' in these relationships. Likewise, in marriage both partners are to prefer the other over themselves (Ephesians 5:21-33).

The body is essential in each of these examples. Christ gave over his physical body for his bride, the Church. We are Christ's body as Christian believers (1 Corinthians 12:12). This means the Holy Spirit is within us (1 Corinthians 6:19). Christ lives through us, and walks among the people in our shoes - we are his body.

God who resides in holy community—three in one— creates humans in the image of the Trinity.

Scripture uses the analogy of marriage to describe our union with Christ (Ephesians 5:22-28). The Christian life is an experience of connecting the personal identity of the individual with the nature and character of Christ to the extent that "I no longer live, but Christ lives in me" (Galatians 2:20). This connection leads to a complete union of physical body and spirit in Christ.

Traditionally in the Church we have had single ministers who gave their sexuality in worship to God. Celibacy was practiced by the Desert Fathers and early Christians to give them a special level of communion with God, a deep intimacy. This is still true in some traditional churches like the Catholic Church. Single ministers give their whole body in worship to God. The writings of St. John of the Cross and St. Teresa of Avila describe worship as being almost sexual in nature. They experienced God with their whole being and body, which included ecstasy. Although most single mission workers are not living a monastic life, devoted to continual worship, the spiritual implications of celibacy are available to them. A deep level of spiritual intimacy is open to them. Embracing celibacy as a sacrifice to God glorifies God. Depending on God to meet our longings draws us closer to God, as we allow God to have us all to himself.

The nature of God reflected in sexual expression is a prophetic visualization of what is to come in heavenly union. Oneness exists in holy union as expressed in the Song of Solomon. Much of this song consists of the woman's voice, showing her joy in her beloved. Christians, in their relationship with Christ, also experience intimacy. There is a deep longing for the day when we will be one with the beloved never to part again. Sexuality is only a foreshadowing of how wonderful is perfect communion with God.

Sensuality and intimacy
Some people feel that they are not experiencing life fully because they have never known sexual intimacy. However, there are other ways to feel fully alive. One way is to look forward to the future and perfect communion with God, as has just been discussed. There are also ways in which we can enjoy sensuality – being in tune with our senses. This can play a key role in our ability to derive pleasure from life as a whole.

Over the years I have asked people "When do you feel masculine or feminine?" or "What events give you the feeling of being a man or woman?" I have never heard a dull answer. Usually the person's eyes light up and they tell me about what they enjoy in life. They tell me about when they feel fully themselves. When you feel fully alive you usually find sensuality expressed.

Experiences which tap sensuality will differ from person to person. Below is a list of experiences that single people have reported which make them feel like a man or woman. Take a moment to examine this list. Maybe an item will open a new way to fully express who God has made you to be.

Examples of experiences that can tap sensuality and intimacy

Touch
Affection received and given to pets
Visiting a sauna or tanning bed
Shaving and putting on after shave
Hugs from friend, family, and church community
Swimming and feeling the water touch your skin
Putting on make-up and pampering yourself
The touch of the wind, sun, rain, or snow
Walking barefoot on grass or sand
Getting a massage or manicure
Someone washing and cutting your hair
Contact sports where touch is appropriate

Taste / Smell / Hear/ See
A special meal that tastes delicious
Fine chocolates that are eaten slowly
The fragrance of a nice perfume
The beauty and scent of flowers

Fine music that is enjoyed and creates emotion in you
Watching a live musical performance

Atmosphere
Walk or hike in the forest or mountains
Candlelit dinner with a friend on a balcony
Sports event where you cheer for your team
A picnic in a scenic location with friends
Going to the theatre, opera or a concert dressed in nice clothes
Sitting and gazing at the sea as the waves come in
Having décor to your liking (a 'man cave' or 'elegance')

Appreciation /Respect
Gifts given and received that reflect care
Time a person invests to be with you
Compliments given and received
Dressing-up in fine clothes and feeling good about yourself
Nonverbal manners shown to denote respect (movements, mannerisms)

Conversation
Shared interests or hobbies that are discussed or enjoyed together
Finding common topics to explore in conversation
Sensing you are understood and accepted as a person
Revealing your true self and receiving unconditional love

Intimacy
Sexuality centres on a basic human need to connect with another person. Without connection with others, people can lose hope in life, become depressed, and lose the will to live. Intimacy is a deep sharing and exchange between two people which creates a sense of being known, accepted and understood. The foundation of human sexuality includes sharing openly and honestly about your self. The true self is expressed, seen and known. Unconditional acceptance and listening create a sense of being known and understood.

A common issue many people face is that they do not know how to share themselves with another person, or they are afraid to expose themselves and be emotionally naked. People need to effectively share themselves with others to maintain health and balance in life. Whether we are married or single, we can all strive for intimate relationships.

Conclusion

In conclusion, single people can embrace sexuality as a positive aspect of life, because it was created by God, and is a picture of our relationship with him. We can look forward to the time when we will be united with Christ, the bridegroom. God is glorified through our sacrifice of sexual purity. We can seek intimacy with God and others, which is one facet of sexuality. We can find ways to enjoy our senses, and so feel fully alive.

Part 3: The journey from singleness to marriage (and, for some, back to singleness)

Chapter 27 - Waiting, dating, or stating that you are called to be single

Am I meant to accept that I have the 'gift of singleness', or am called to be single? Or should I keep waiting for marriage to happen, trusting God for it? Should I actively try to find a partner? **Dr Debbie Hawker** *and* **Rev Tim Herbert** *discuss these issues.*

People go through different stages in their attitude towards marriage.[82] Most single people did not start out deciding to be single. Most children grow up assuming that one day they will marry and have children of their own. As single mission workers move through Bible college or language school and settle in a new culture, their hope of marriage may turn into doubt, disappointment, pain and loss if marriage does not occur. They might go back and forth in stages of urgently wanting to get married, hoping for it, and accepting being single. Some always hope for marriage. Some remain open to marriage but move into an acceptance of the reality that at the moment they are single. Some come to grasp the benefits of being single as well as some limitations of being married, and decide they are happily single and don't want to marry. They can relax and enjoy life. Personality, hormones and personal experience contribute to the fact that some people are content being single, while others have a deep longing to get married and perhaps have children.

There is a group of single people who feel specifically called to a life of celibacy to glorify God. They may refer to singleness as a gift (see 1 Corinthians 7: 7), and this gift can be celebrated and honoured (as in the case of nuns, monks and priests). While for some people singleness is a cross to carry daily, for others it is a privilege to be grateful for, although even people who feel called to singleness can find it difficult at times. There are other books which focus on the vocation of celibacy [83] (and see chapter 12), so we will not concentrate on that here – we will focus on single people who would like to get married.

Should single people who want a partner just wait until the right person comes along? Should they take the initiative and actively seek a partner out? Or should they try to accept the gift of singleness, even if it is an unwanted gift?

There is no right or wrong in this. Some people are called to be single for life, but others are not (see Matthew 19:11-12). If you don't find terms such as 'calling' or 'gift of singleness' helpful, then don't worry about them. Our primary calling is to follow Christ. It is not helpful for married people to keep debating whether they have the 'gift of marriage'. They should just do their best to live well in their marriage. Likewise, single people can seek to make the best of their place in life, and to serve God, without worrying about whether they have a 'calling' to singleness. You don't have to know at this stage whether God has planned for you to be single for life, or whether you will marry. We can live with uncertainty.

I know a five-year-old boy who has autistic spectrum disorder. One aspect of this is a desire for certainty. He asks me "When will you die? When will Grandma die? When will I die? Can I die with you? Will we be walking when we die?" I can't tell him. We live with uncertainty about some of the biggest issues in life – when and how we and those we love will die. Surely we can also live with the uncertainty of whether or not we will get married. We can trust God to provide what we need for today.

We are called to be content but also to seek out what God wants for us and to live life in its fullness. There is a balance to be struck between enjoying what we have been given, while not passively waiting for God to bring us what we think we need or desire. We can be content and stay as we are. Or, if we desire marriage, we can be content but also play our part in trying to increase the likelihood of getting married, by actively looking for a partner. As Paul wrote, "It is better to marry than to burn with passion" (1 Corinthians 7:9).

Trying to find a partner doesn't mean you are not trusting God. I can trust God to help me find a job or ministry, while I actively find out what is available, meet the people involved and fill in application forms. Similarly, I can trust God to guide me concerning marriage, and still look around for a partner, praying that God will shut the door if I'm going the wrong direction. God is not trying to make things hard for us, but sometimes he lets us have a choice. We can play our part in trying to find a partner, without letting this consume the whole of our life and prevent us from doing other things. Even in the days of arranged marriages which were the cultural context of the Bible, Abraham did not passively wait for God to provide a wife for his son, but sent his servant on a journey with that purpose in mind (Genesis 24).

One male single mission worker wrote, "At one level I desire marriage (because that's part of who God created me to be), at a deeper level I desire singleness (for the sake of the cause, as in Jesus' and Paul's teaching), but at the deepest level I desire whichever one God desires for me, since that is really the crucial issue in this as well as other aspects of life".[84]

Mission worker Elizabeth Goldsmith described the time when as a young, unmarried woman in college she dreaded the prospect of becoming a severe-looking middle-aged spinster on the mission field. A visiting speaker set her straight. God knew her through and through, the visitor said. "He knows what you need and what you don't need. If he has made you for marriage he will see that you will get a husband; if he has planned for you to remain single, he has a plentiful supply of all the extra grace that you will need".[85]

Dr John Stott, a single man and a widely respected preacher, gave this advice to people who would like to marry one day, but don't currently have a partner,

> First, don't be in too great a hurry to get married... be patient. Pray daily that God will guide you to your life partner or show you if he wants you to remain single. Second, lead a normal social life. Develop many friendships. Third, if God calls you to singleness, don't fight it. Remember the key text: "Each person has his or her own gift of God's grace" (*cf. 1 Corinthians 7:7).*[86]

Stott recommended developing many friendships. Good marriages often begin as good friendships. Married people are advised to prioritise time with their spouse and family, nurturing their relationships. Similarly, single people are advised to prioritise time building friendships. There should be no sense of guilt about this, as we need friendships.

If you want to find a marriage partner, it is worth investing in things that increase your chances. Some people feel it is important to make the most of your physical appearance. It is even more important to invest in your spiritual life, personality, character and contentment. This is likely to draw people towards you, and increase the likelihood of you having rich friendships and finding a marriage partner. Spend time in God's presence learning to see life his way. Also ensure you make time for relationships, rest and relaxation, to reduce your stress level. To live well, love God, love others and love yourself.

In some cultures, marriages are arranged (formally, or informally, through some sort of match-maker). But in many cultures it is down to you to find a partner and there is nothing wrong with putting effort into finding a suitable person. Asking for help can be a good idea. One of the most touching features of the film *Notting Hill* is the way Hugh Grant's friends rally round (albeit ineptly) to try to find the right woman for him. I (Tim) have sometimes wished I had friends who would do that for me. Single mission workers (and those who have recently left the mission field) sometimes have limited opportunities to meet like-minded singles of the opposite sex. When we do, some of us need to take care that we don't rush into a relationship too quickly when all we really have in common is that we are single and perhaps speak the same language. It is easy to rush into a relationship when we are missing people at home and feeling lonely, but it is helpful to take time to get to know each other.

There might seem to be more chance of meeting a partner in your home culture. You may decide to leave the mission field and return home to pursue a relationship. That might be the right decision for one person, and not for another. Pray for guidance. Dr Ritchey wrote:

> I know of a missionary colleague who was several years away from retirement when a widower back in her home country began to pursue her. She allowed the friendship to move forward, but with the firm stipulation that she would complete her tenure on the field and only marry

him upon retirement. Others have left the field after a while to marry and continued ministry back in their home countries. Some of my colleagues dated men back home who eventually joined them on the field. Others met and married colleagues while on the field. Others have remained single throughout a lifetime of service. Others became widows on the field and chose to stay and continue serving. The bottom line is that these decisions are the result of personal commitments and prayer between each of these women and the God they serve. The decisions will be different for each one but they deserve our respect and support as full-fledged colleagues as we work together.[87]

If you decide to date, are you aware of which dating options are available and culturally acceptable where you live (see chapter 30)? In some areas there are special social events and holidays for Christian singles. Speed dating takes place in some cultures (where you get to spend a few minutes with a 'date', in a public place, and then you move on to the next person). 'Lock and key' events are popular in some locations. These are parties where every woman wears a lock, and every man is given a key and tries to open the locks – the purpose is to help make conversation. These can have their place, but we do well to remember Paul's words in 2 Corinthians 6:14: "Do not be yoked [or locked] together with unbelievers". Marriage works best where the couple have shared values, beliefs and priorities.

Where can you meet single Christians? Internet dating can be an option, using a Christian dating website. This will be discussed in the next chapter.

It's okay to wait, it's okay to date, and it's okay, to celebrate your single state.

Chapter 28: Love on-line

Are dating websites a valid way for a Christian to find a spouse? **Jo Swinney** [88] and **Dr Debbie Hawker** *discuss the pros and cons of internet dating.*

The internet is a useful invention, especially if you are a mission worker far from home. It allows you to communicate with friends, family and supporters, and buy things you can't get where you are living. You might not have many exercise options, but you can go surfing on-line. If security restrictions limit your freedom, you can use the internet to escape to another world. You can check the weather forecast for where you are, where you are travelling to, and where you wish you were. The internet is useful for translations, calculations, booking travel and diagnosing your own illnesses. You can download recipes, sermons, music or movies. If you want a laugh you can search for 'world's weirdest dating website profiles'.

Which brings us to the next point. You can use the internet to find a marriage partner. However did we live without it?

The book *Love at the speed of email* by Lisa McKay[89] tells the true story of how two Christian humanitarian workers, who had some mutual friends, met each other through essays on a website. They pursued their relationship over the internet as they both continued to fly all over the world, before they met face-to-face, and eventually married. This couple had to slog at a blog. Couples who meet through an on-line dating agency can cut out the essay writing, and don't need any mutual friends to help with match-making. Thank goodness for that!

While surfing for a spouse might have once seemed a bit desperate, dating websites have seen a surge in uptake over the past few years. Using them is now regarded as normal, not weird; in fact, some people think that single people who never try them are the unusual ones. It is claimed that in the USA, 17% of couples who married in 2010 met on-line.[90] The internet has become as common a way to meet someone as through a mutual friend or at work. Christians are in on the game too.

There are a number of dating websites specifically targeted at those for whom shared faith is vital.

What are the pros and cons of internet dating?

The Pros

It can be difficult to meet single Christians of the opposite gender who share your interests and priorities. This is especially the case if you are working outside your own country and want to meet someone who understands your culture and speaks your language. Finding a date can also be difficult for someone who has returned home after completing a ministry assignment and discovered that most people their age have already married and there are few like-minded single people in their church. Even if you meet a single person you like of the opposite sex, how can you tell whether they are happily single or interested in a relationship? It can be embarrassing to ask.

Christian dating websites make the process easier. When you sign up as a member you can announce that you are available and would like to be in a relationship. There is nothing wrong with declaring this. You are all on the same level. You might find a 'match' nearby, or they might be far away, but distance doesn't make it impossible to get to know someone if you use the internet.

Most of us have some idea of the qualities we find attractive, and things that we couldn't tolerate for long. Dating sites allow members to upload a photo, and more importantly to provide a profile of likes, dislikes and interests. This helps you to quickly sift through people, cutting down on the time wasted communicating with those who are obviously incompatible with you. While it might seem a bit consumerist to scan a site looking for the closest person to your ideal, unless you have an arranged marriage that is what most of us do anyway when looking for a partner, just in a less efficient manner. It is a modernisation of age-old matchmaking, with the internet acting as a matchmaker.

Some Christian dating websites encourage members to include issues related to faith on their profile. For example, the Christian Connection website[91] encourages members to share the importance of their faith, their church involvement, their favourite Bible verses and other aspects of their Christian beliefs. This can help in finding a soul-mate who is good for your soul.

Even when on-line dating doesn't lead to marriage, many people say they found the experience fun and made friends through it.

Starting a relationship through the internet can have advantages, compared to meeting in person straight away. The author of *Love at the speed of email* writes,

> Having nothing to build our relationship on but words for the following three months forced us to cover a lot of ground… Distance slowed us down, granted us extra time and space to think, and encouraged us to be deliberate and thorough in our communication".[92]

The temptation to go too far sexually may also be reduced.

In recent years, many Christian couples have met through dating websites and have gone on to have a successful marriage.

Safety issues
Is internet dating safe? Can you really be sure that this person is who they say they are? Might they steal from you or even rape you if you meet them? Might they be looking for marriage purely to help them immigrate, or could they be a fraudster after your money (see chapter 11)?

You should be careful as not everyone is honest and it is possible to be exploited. You could also be exploited by someone you meet at work or through friends or even in church, so danger is not only present on the internet. In every relationship a degree of trust is called for. There are safety guidelines to help protect you when you use a dating website, available at www.christianconnection.co.uk/safety. For example, it is recommended that when you meet you choose a public place, let a friend know where you are, and do not accept a lift home.

The vast majority of people on internet dating sites are genuine, but there are a few criminal characters there. It is recommended that you don't send money to someone you meet on-line, especially if you have not met them in person. Good dating websites have security measures in place to help catch fraudsters (who are known as 'scammers'). Not all dating sites have such systems, due to a lack of resources. Some sites even like scammers because they are active on the site and therefore are good for business.

Every person who has been scammed has bought into a believable story. Here are some tell-tale signs to help you spot a scammer:

- The profile may look perfect (because it has been copied), but emails may be full of language mistakes
- Their photo may look fake. It may look like a model shot, or a soldier in uniform.
- They immediately ask you to contact them via live chat, regular email or Facebook (to avoid leaving evidence of their scamming to the site administrators)
- Meetings do not materialise
- You may receive a message detailing a sudden personal crisis, perhaps asking for money.[93]

The chances are that if you read this far, you won't get scammed, as you will be prepared. Being over-cautious is better than putting yourself in danger.

Other cons of internet dating
Apart from safety concerns, the main disadvantage of internet dating is that it can be time-consuming and disappointing if it doesn't lead to a successful relationship. There may be no-one suitable near your location. Hopes rise if someone shows interest in you, life can seem on hold, and then hopes can be dashed again if it doesn't work out when you meet.

It is disappointing to discover that the great majority of 'Christian' dating sites are not run by Christians at all. Some don't even have many Christian members on them. The majority of internet dating sites are run by very large dating 'platforms'. They simply see having a 'Christian' site as another way for them to take money. Most of these sites have no real Christian ethos. They often have a shared database, and members you meet may not have intended to be classified as Christian daters at all, and may not be committed Christians. With large sites there is often less accountability and a much higher risk of fraudsters looking for people they can trick into handing over money.

Before you sign up to a dating site, look at it carefully. Is it very general or is there something distinctively Christian about it? Some sites believe that popping a Bible quote on the front page will convince you, but a truly Christian site will go deeper than that. Read about their ethos and values – do they have any? Is it easy for you to cancel your membership? Some of these sites make that very hard.

Even if you find a genuinely Christian website, members may not tell the complete truth as they want to portray themselves in the best possible light. They are unlikely to mention undesirable habits, and they might miss out important parts of their past. This can be true in all relationships, but the cover-up can go on for longer if you have an internet relationship rather than meeting in person. You might also discover that you or the person you meet might not want to commit to a relationship in case a better option turns up later – we can look for perfection when there is such a large pool to fish from.

An obvious disadvantage of internet dating is that it relies on the internet. If you hate computers, or have little or no access to the internet, then it's probably not for you.

Some people feel that it is unromantic to meet through a dating website. They would prefer to find love at first sight as their hands accidentally touch while they are pulling a drowning child out of a fast-flowing river, with crocodiles downstream. You can continue to dream, or you can actively look for a real, live partner. You could still make your first date at a crocodile park if you want to have a good story to tell the children!

Conclusion

Internet dating is not right for everyone, but it's not wrong for everyone either. If you think it might be right for you, we recommend that you pray about it and ask around for a recommendation of a trusted, reputable website with a genuinely Christian ethos and good security measures. Remember to put God first, be careful about security, behave with integrity, and pursue the kinds of people who will encourage and strengthen your faith. Realise that it might not lead to marriage, but it could lead to friendship, and it might increase the chances of marriage.

Love on-line can be shortened to LOL. That also stands for 'laugh out loud' and 'lots of love', both of which can be good outcomes.

If dating on-line brings you wedding bells, don't forget to thank God for your computer. You might still need it. We know one mission worker who gave birth during a power-cut, with only the light of her Dell laptop. And she didn't even name the baby Adele!

Recommended Christian sites
www.ChristianCafe.com
www.christianconnection.co.uk

Website for people in long-distance relationships
www.modernlovelongdistance.com

Chapter 29 - Against all odds: How one woman found love over the internet

Lizzie *works for a Dutch mission agency. She met her Ghanaian husband on-line, although she was not seeking a husband. It looked like an impossible match, but it has led to a happy marriage.*

I read an article about on-line dating in a Christian women's magazine called *Eva*. The article described how a Dutch woman met a Ghanaian guy through a dating website, and when she went to Ghana to meet him, he and his family prevented her from going back to Holland. It sounded pretty scary. It also mentioned that some fraudsters say things like, "I love you, I want to marry you" from the first or second chat, and that this is how they try to sweep a woman off her feet, only to get quick access to her money. As soon as the woman is 'hooked' by the overwhelming attention of the guy he will start to ask her to send money, inventing stories about sick relatives or wanting money to come and visit. That article would not tempt anybody to try on-line dating!

I wasn't looking for a partner. I only wanted to connect with Christians from different cultures and ask them about the influence of their culture on their Christian life. So I registered on a free Christian website that was mentioned in the article, not a specific dating site, and I met a lot of Christians from all over the world.

One of them was Danny. He is Ghanaian and when I met him through that site he was living and working in Libya, which was very interesting for my research. Our first contact was through e-mail, but soon we started to chat and later we added a webcam. I had met a lot of people through that website, but with him there was a 'click' from the start. I was very cautious, having the *Eva* article in mind. I had some bad relationships in my past, including failed marriages, as a result of which I had two children. I had been badly hurt. I had moved on and had totally surrendered myself to God and been forgiven, but I wasn't willing to get involved in any new relationship, let alone with somebody far away.

As usual, God's ways were different from mine. First God gave me emotional healing from the past. I read a book called *Redeeming Love*.[94] That book brought me a sparkle of hope that maybe it would be possible in the future to have a marriage like God meant it to be. I said to God, "If it is your will for me to ever get married again, please let it be to someone like Michael Hosea (the main male character in *Redeeming Love*), because only somebody like that could break through the walls around my wounded heart and disarm my distrust for men."

Even after this initial healing process, I did not expect to marry again. Not only did I have a deep distrust of men and an aversion to letting them come near me, but I also have autistic spectrum disorder, meaning that I find social situations difficult. The way Danny and I met, through the internet, was the only way we could have got together.

Soon after we started to chat, Danny told me that God had showed him that I was going to be his wife. Alarm bells started to ring! I told him that if that was what God wanted, God would also have to tell me directly, otherwise I was not going to respond. I started to pray over it. Every time we chatted on-line, Danny would ask me "And has God answered you?" And I would say, "No, nothing yet". Danny would say, "Okay, well, keep praying, he will let you know".

One time Danny's best friend also joined our chat session. He too asked if God had answered my prayers and I said "No". He suggested that we pray over it, the three of us together at that moment on-line. He was leading the prayer. It was evening, and the room I was in was scarcely lit by a lamp. Suddenly the room was full of a bright white light. It felt as if somebody opened up the top of my skull and poured something warm into my head which ran down through my whole body. I heard a voice saying, "This is the love that I give you for Danny. Give it to him". Then the room became dark again. I was speechless and wondered if I had lost my mind! I was a Christian, sincerely looking for God's will for my life, but raised in a conservative church with no charismatic influences. I was not familiar with phenomena such as visions and hearing God's voice. I tried to clarify what had just happened. Maybe it was a dream or maybe my mind had been manipulated?

From that moment on I really did feel love for Danny, but I couldn't believe what had happened so I tried to just go to sleep and forget about it. I expected the feeling of love to be gone by the next day. But it didn't go away. I wondered if it was God answering the prayer, but I decided to wait and see and not tell Danny.

When I noticed that the love I felt for Danny grew stronger day after day, I finally told him what had happened. His response was, "I knew God would show you". He wasn't even surprised. From that time we chatted almost daily and often for hours, so we got to know each other well. I warned Danny that it might take years before I would be able to really love him like he deserved, but he was determined to be patient.

We started to discuss how we could meet each other. Danny was still in Libya and it was not safe for me to travel there as a single woman, but he could not get permission from Dutch immigration to come to the Netherlands.

We prayed and decided that I would send Danny money to travel to his home in Ghana, and I would fly there to meet him. My parents and friends freaked out, but God told me to trust him and that he wanted me to marry this guy. Given my history of bad relationships, it was hard for me to trust somebody that I had only been talking to over the phone and the internet. I would never advise anybody to do that, unless God very clearly tells you to do so.

I bought a plane ticket to Ghana, but then it was my turn to freak out. I became overwhelmed by all the negative reactions of my relatives and friends. I became sick from anxiety, not least my fear of flying. I prayed and prayed, but God didn't take it away. He didn't confirm that it was right for me to go to Ghana, but he did confirm over and over again that he wanted me to marry Danny. One week before I was due to go to Ghana I decided to cancel the flight as I was too anxious. I expected to lose all the money that I had saved for the ticket, because it was non-refundable. Then God spoke again. He said "Don't cancel it, just delay it for one week." I asked, "Why would I do that? I'm not going." God replied, "Just do as I tell you and you will see why." So I rescheduled my ticket. Three days later the travel agency called me to say my rescheduled flight had been cancelled by the company, and I received all my money back!

We applied for a visa for Danny to come to the Netherlands. My family and friends ridiculed me. They all said that it would be impossible to get Danny to Holland. Ghanaians were on an immigration blacklist at the time and it was humanly impossible to get a visa. I told Danny that leaving Holland was not an option for me. I wasn't prepared to leave my children or take them to live in Ghana. I believed that if God wanted us to get married, God would make a way.

God was teaching me to trust him. While almost everybody in my environment tried to convince me that I should quit, God said, "I understand that you're afraid, but you have to do as I say." He showed me the story of the twelve spies who were sent to check out the Promised Land. When they returned and gave a report of what they had seen, almost everybody said, "impossible." But two of them believed that if God said it was possible, they should believe him and move forward (Numbers 13-14). That is only one example of how God convinced me time after time that this was what he wanted. God didn't get angry because I was fearful or give up on me because I started to doubt the whole thing. He was patient, loving, comforting and encouraging.

Danny's visa application was denied. We raised objections but heard nothing. So I told Danny that I would come to meet him in Ghana for a short visit, because my fear of flying should not keep me from trusting God. It felt like total surrender. Just before I was going to book my flight to Ghana, the doorbell rang. It was a recorded delivery from immigration, granting permission for Danny to come to Holland! We were amazed by God's kindness.

Danny was granted a tourist visa for one month. We decided that we would get married during this month so that Danny could then apply for a permanent visa. I wondered what it would be like to finally meet Danny eye to eye. Would it be like meeting a stranger? Would it feel like we had already known each other our whole lives? How would he feel? What if I didn't like his odour? When he arrived it all felt natural, and we knew that we were meant to be together, a match made in heaven as they say.

My parents came to meet Danny. They stayed all day, unable to talk to or understand him because they do not speak English. At the end of the day we fired the big question: "Will you grant permission for us to get married next week?" We knew that God wanted us to respect my parents so we sought their permission, even though I knew they had been against my relationship with Danny all along. We trusted God to overcome this obstacle. They were surprised by our question and asked for time to think about it. After five minutes they told us that God had shown them that they could trust Danny, that he is a child of God and that everything would be well. They could trust their daughter into Danny's hands.

My parents had always said, "How can you say God said this, or God said that? He doesn't send little notes down to us." But now they started to receive their little notes from God too! When they came home that night, God showed them the Bible verse that says that he has good plans for us (Jeremiah 29:11). My father wrote it down and hung it in front of the mirror. Every time he started to panic and doubt, he read this verse and calmed down.

At the end of that week we got married, convinced that this was God's will for us. My father gave me away. He made an emotional speech about what they had gone through all those years and how finally God had shown them that it was okay and they were able to just trust God and believe that it was his plan and that it was good.

Three weeks after we got married Danny had to go back to Ghana. We felt sad, but trusted that God would bring him back to Holland. We applied for a permanent visa and he got it, in spite of everybody saying that it would be impossible. Four months later he was in the Netherlands again, this time to stay. For God, nothing is impossible. The immigration office may be in authority over us, but God has authority over them. He reigns, and if he wants it, it will happen. Our part is to trust him. We thank God that Danny has been able to work most of the time, even though he is still struggling with the Dutch language.

God has forgiven us for our pasts, and given us a fresh start. Danny has patiently loved me, like the character in *Redeeming Love*. We have been married since 2004. In 2008 Danny's son was granted permission to come from Ghana to live with us.

There are lots of reasons why our marriage might be predicted to fail: a blended family, very different cultures, bad relationships in the past, meeting on-line, autistic spectrum disorder, and other diagnoses which our children have. But we have a strong and healthy marriage, and we both have a good relationship with our three children. Of course we have had our difficulties as we are not perfect, but we always turn to God and he pulls us through. We stand firm and do not give up, because God gives us the strength, wisdom and love to go on. We are committed to God and to each other, and that is what matters.

Chapter 30 - Dating during cross-cultural ministry

Dr Roni Pruitt [95] and Janet Fraser-Smith [96] explore issues related to dating in a mission context.

Dating in a bubble
Dating in a mission context has been described as 'dating in a bubble', with everyone watching and making comments. You might just be getting to know someone as a friend, but observers might comment on what they think of the 'match'. This can add to the pressure and stress you feel.

It helps if you understand the cultural expectations regarding dating in the place where you are living, as well as the expectations of the person you want to date. There may be local restrictions on being seen in public as an unmarried couple. Perceived questionable behaviour might damage any Christian witness and spoil your reputation, and that of your dating partner. Examples of dating in cultures where men and women need to keep some distance are given in chapters 31 and 33.

Some mission organisations have rules or at least expectations about dating. Some forbid dating during the first year or two of ministry. Some team leaders expect you to consult with them before dating. It is worth being clear about any expectations. Even if there are no rules, it can feel as if other people are observing what you would rather keep private.

Dating during transitions
I (Roni) have served in three cultures during my career in missions. A pattern that I noted in myself was that I had a naïve openness toward marrying into the culture during the first year. During the second year I started to question how marriage and family worked in the culture. As I started to learn about the culture I realized how different it was and that caused me to pause. During the third year I moved to a decision that to marry into the culture would present enormous lifestyle changes that conflicted with the type of marriage I desired.

I believe that my experience illustrates that there are seasons when a cross-cultural worker is more vulnerable than usual. I have learned that major decisions such as commitment to marriage should generally not be made during such seasons, as it is better to wait for a time when you have clear thinking and are not on an emotional rollercoaster. This is why some mission organisations have a policy that a worker should not engage in courtship in the first year or two in a new country.

When a person arrives in a new culture there is usually a 'honeymoon stage' when the culture is idealized. As new customs are experienced it is initially fascinating. The worker is entertained and tries all the new experiences. They might say things like "I love this culture!" There is a false sense of knowing and understanding the culture. The honeymoon stage typically lasts for a few months before the low period of culture shock begins. At this point the individual questions cultural meanings and starts to seek more accurate cultural information.

Another season of vulnerability transpires shortly after the worker returns to their home country when they are in reverse culture shock. They may no longer fit easily into their home culture and can struggle to find their new place in society. They long for someone to understand them in the midst of their confusion. Reverse culture shock is often more intensive than the initial adjustment to the new culture. Common questions are "Who am I now?" and "Why do I feel strange here?" This leads to the conclusion, "If I do not fit here then I fit nowhere." The person feels threatened and lost. They want to connect with someone, and to belong. Some conclude the best solution would be to find another person who has a defined life and enter a relationship with them.

It is not uncommon for a returned mission worker to seek a marriage partner who has never been exposed to another culture. An instant relationship occurs with the stages of courtship skipped. Marriage takes place very quickly, but the failure rate is high. A better method is to get settled and let emotions level out before throwing yourself into a deep relationship.

Cross-cultural dating

Have you ever thought about dating someone from another culture – either as a theoretical possibility, or with a particular person in mind? This is much more common than it used to be. If you date while involved with cross-cultural mission, it might be a cross-cultural relationship. Practically every Third Culture Kid[97] who dates has a cross-cultural relationship, as their partner will not have exactly the same combination of cultures as they do.

But how do you begin a cross-cultural relationship? From the moment of falling in love, or sensing a mutual attraction, how do you move to the point of dating, and possibly even engagement and marriage?

A Christian from the west may assume that relationships develop through participating in activities together, going for walks, reading the Bible and praying together, having meals or watching movies together, holding hands and reading books on marriage. If it works out, in the end you make a decision to get married, and you introduce your prospective partner to your family. It is understood that either partner may break the relationship off at any point before marriage.

Dating in a mission context, outside your home culture, may look very different and your partner may not have the same expectations as you.

In some countries there is no concept of friendship with someone of the opposite sex. Staring at, smiling at or talking to a member of the opposite sex sends the message, "I am interested in you as a potential marriage partner." Some people only date if they are seriously intending this to progress to marriage. Some cultures have no concept of dating, moving straight to engagement. In others, dating is seen just a way of getting to know each other, without necessarily expecting it to go any further.

In certain cultures a man will watch a woman from afar until he decides that he would like to marry her. He will seal this by inviting her to a public event, or for a meal. Acceptance of the invitation communicates "Yes, I accept your marriage proposal." After you meet it is too late to say this is all a misunderstanding. People saw you in public together and your intention to marry has been announced to the community.

Arranged marriages in their various forms are the norm in some cultures and the parents are always involved. This can work very well, but seems foreign to people from individualistic cultures.

People also have different views on breaking up. The local community might show delight that you are dating, and be dismayed if the relationship breaks up if they have no concept of temporary relationships. You and your partner may have different ideas about how to break up – for example, talking in person, on the phone, sending a text message or email, or just disappearing without ever formally finishing the relationship. Splitting up while dating might be regarded as a crisis by some, and as normal by others. If the relationship is not going to last, it is better to spilt up before marriage than afterwards. International divorce is a complicated, expensive and often heart-breaking process, especially when children are involved, requiring arrangements about custody and access.

How do we know whether to enter a cross-cultural marriage?
Intercultural relationships can be wonderful celebrations of diversity. Cultural differences can be a source of on-going interest, discovery, fun and laughter. Enjoying foods from both cultures adds spice to life. The couple bring to their relationship a wide range of life experiences and strengths to draw on.

If you are serious about a life-long marriage it is wise to take time to ensure that you have a good foundation on which to build. Where arranged marriages take place, those making the arrangement and those agreeing to it seek a good fit. For the rest, the choice is down to the couple. If it is culturally acceptable, it helps to get to know each other well and understand each other before making a commitment.

Marriages that get off to a good start with thorough preparation are more able to face challenges effectively. If marriage preparation is available (for example a course run by a church), it is worth making use of it. You can also provide your own preparation for a cross-cultural marriage by discussing the topics listed in Appendix 1.

Here are several issues to discuss when considering whether cross-cultural marriage is right for you.

1. How great is the cultural divide between you?

Some inter-cultural couples say that culture doesn't matter to them. Perhaps their backgrounds are so similar that the differences aren't obvious or their personalities are such that they are able to live with dissonance. But others experience tensions caused by cultural differences. According to one experienced cross-cultural counsellor[98], the three key factors that come up most in troubled inter-cultural marriages are as follows. Firstly, views about gender roles primarily as expressed in the family unit but also in their lives in community and in the extended family. Secondly the expectation of extended families to be involved in decisions such as how to bring up the children, what expression of faith there should be, or financial transactions and housing. Thirdly, the ability of each partner to express emotions, especially in communication and conflict resolution. All three could be an issue for a mono-cultural couple, but they all have associated cultural values so are more likely to be problematic for intercultural couples. They can be discussed prior to marriage, and solutions sought.

2. How strong is your ability to communicate?

The success of any relationship depends on communication. In the dating and courtship period the nonverbal communication (such as loving glances and rapid heartbeats) will often outweigh and possibly conceal other factors that in the cold light of day are very important to us.

3. Language

If you have different mother tongues, are you fluent enough in your shared language to be able to communicate with each other at a deep level? Good communication can help to avoid pitfalls and prevent pain.

4. How similar are your expectations of marriage and of each other?
What do you each think marriage is for, and what might lead you to want to end the marriage? Nearly all marriages go through difficult times. Those who expect this don't see it as a disaster; it is just a challenge to be overcome. Couples who are committed to making a marriage work will do so. Those who are not committed to working hard on the marriage will struggle to stay together. Who understands and will support you both?

5. Are you willing to live in each other's countries on a long term basis?
Although this question may not seem important, it might one day be necessary for family, visa or political reasons. Which aspects of life would you find easy or difficult in each of your home countries?

The challenge of all marital relationships is to integrate the personalities, backgrounds and extended families of both husband and wife to forge a new unit. Adding the layers of intercultural patterns, language and citizenship adds to that challenge, as well as bringing many benefits.

Forming a good cross-cultural relationship
The following tips were offered by intercultural couples on how to form and maintain a satisfying cross-cultural relationship.
1. The choice of a partner is very important, so take as much time as possible to be sure it is right for you both.
2. Take time to explore your own background.
3. Find out what you both share. Learn about and enjoy your traditions.
4. Understand and respect your differences. Recognise that cultural differences are not a problem in themselves but a means of enrichment.
5. Develop your communication skills. Learn each other's language if at all possible, including body language.
6. Never lose respect for your partner.
7. Develop a sense of humour that you both understand.
8. Develop skills in sensitivity, listening, flexibility and forgiveness.

9. Love yourself and each other, love each other's cultures and love the Lord.
10. Discover ways to enjoy each other's company.
11. Strengthen your faith, rely on God and draw on grace.
12. If you feel you are in trouble, get help sooner rather than later.

Useful book for those in long distance relationships
McKay, L. & Wolfe, M. (2012) *201 great discussion questions for couples in long distance relationships*. Washington DC: Karinya Publishing

For further information about cross-cultural marriage see Appendix 1.

Chapter 31 - Journeying on

Dr Debbie Hawker *describes some experiences as a single woman ministering in Swaziland, El Salvador and Pakistan. She then talks about the journey from being a single mission worker to being a married one. She reflects on being content in God whatever our marital status, and viewing holiness (rather than happiness) as our goal, seeking to be thankful for what we have.*

"How many cows does your father have?"

"Pardon?" I replied.

I had just turned twenty, and had completed the first year of my degree. I was spending my three-month summer holiday in Swaziland, as a short-term mission worker. Having never flown before, it was a great adventure. Working at a mission school, I was learning a lot. I had stayed for a few nights with a Swazi family in their homestead in the mountains, fetching water from the river with them, and struggling to carry the bucket on my head. It was great. I felt that I was managing to understand most of the people around me, even those (like my Swazi homestead family) who didn't speak English. But this question threw me.

I had been walking down a dusty track on my own, and a young man I hadn't seen before suddenly asked me about my father's cows. I assumed this was just a friendly way to start a conversation, and more interesting than the usual questions about where I was from and what I was doing here. People in Africa are relational and like to ask about family, so why not ask about cows? Slowly it dawned on me. Dowry. How many cows was I worth in bride-price? This was a chat-up line I hadn't heard before!

I laughed, embarrassed. In a way, it was flattering to be noticed. In Britain the only comments I received from strangers tending to be mocking insults. I knew I was only noticed in Swaziland because of the colour of my skin and my passport. Obviously it wasn't a serious question, but how should I respond?

I had plenty of time to practice responses, as several other men asked me similar questions during my three months in Swaziland. Some were more direct, beginning the conversation with "Will you marry me?"

My father had no cows, but my heavenly Father had many cows as "the cattle on a thousand hills are his" (Psalm 50:10). I decided to use humour to respond to such questions. Other single women had their own solutions: ignore it, or wear a ring and say you have a husband (after all, we are the bride of Christ). One even made up stories about being a widow in mourning, with two teenagers. That stopped the conversation.

My experience in Swaziland confirmed my desire to share God's love around the world. The following year I went with a team to El Salvador, where we worked with children in a school and an orphanage. I had tried to learn some Spanish from cassettes before going. When staying with a Salvadorian family who spoke no English, I tried my best to converse. On the first evening, after I had eaten, they asked me if I needed more food. I intended to reply "I'm not hungry" ("No tengo *hambre*"), but instead I said, "I haven't got a man" ("No tengo *hombre*")! The following evening they asked if I needed to go to bed early. I tried to say "I'm not tired" ("No estoy *cansada*"). By mistake, I said instead "I'm not married" ("No estoy *casada*"). As I had turned down offers of food and sleep by saying "I haven't got a man" and "I'm not married", they concluded that I sounded desperate, and brought in their sons to meet me! Thankfully, we all saw the funny side.

I returned to the UK after my time in El Salvador. Although I loved being involved with mission, I felt it wasn't right to move to live overseas full-time as my mother was unwell and needed support. Instead I continued to have short-term experiences of mission, including providing training and consultations in Romania, Nepal, Pakistan and elsewhere. I also remained involved with ministry while at home in the UK, debriefing mission workers. Being single, I was free to come and go as opportunities arose. I continued to make mistakes with languages, and also in understanding accents. Once when I was about to board a plane in Thailand, I was concerned to hear the demand, "Show me your body parts". It was a relief when I discovered that all I really needed to display was my boarding pass!

When I went to Pakistan, I discovered that it wasn't marriage proposals expatriate women had to deal with, so much as stares and even touch by some local men. I dressed in shalwar kameez like the women around me, avoided eye contact, and only went out as part of a group, but I still received unwanted attention. Some women suffered silently. A more confident woman told me she had found the best way to deal with unwanted touch was to shame the man concerned, by shouting out (in Urdu), "Why are you touching me? Get away!" This seemed to work especially well on crowded buses.

I've heard of men who have also had to deal with unwanted touch in foreign lands, such as another man putting his hand in his trouser pocket. Such incidents can happen in my home country too, but they seem more likely to happen in a place where we stand out because of our appearance and we can't read subtle cues so well. It seems to happen more to women than men, especially to single women without a husband's protection.

I found it restrictive that I couldn't go out on my own in Pakistan, as I love having a daily walk. I made friends with three Pakistani sisters. Their mother had died, their father was elderly, and they had no brother to chaperone them. "How do you cope with the restriction of not being able to go out freely?" I asked them. "We go on our roof every evening and walk round it for 30 minutes" they replied. I admired them, and was thankful for my comparative freedom. Even so, it was hard to not feel resentful that teenage boys were allowed to go out alone, while I, an adult, was not. If I'd had a husband to accompany and protect me, things would have been different. As a single woman I was dependent on group outings, even if they weren't going where I wanted to go. I felt disempowered. But I tried to focus on the freedom I had, instead of the restrictions. I had freedom to be educated, play music, make my own decisions, worship, share my faith, travel the world and return to my own country when I wanted to. I had a lot to be thankful for.

Despite occasional frustration about restrictions, most of the time I found it an advantage to be single. I was able to do what I wanted and I wasn't distracted from the work I felt called to do. When I was about seven years old, my mother had said to me, "You should be glad that you're not pretty. You won't be distracted by boys". It took me many years to see her point of view and to be thankful that I had never had a boyfriend to distract me. I could commit myself fully to what I was doing, with undivided attention.

At the same time, it would have been nice to have someone to share special moments with. Beautiful scenes seem enhanced by sharing them, as do funny moments. My solution was to write copious accounts in my personal journal. Computers were rare then and I found it too expensive to phone from abroad, so I wrote long letters as a way to share my experiences and maintain friendships.

I believed God was sharing the experiences with me. I usually didn't feel isolated, apart from brief moments like the time I shut myself in a cupboard while a crowd of teenagers rioted at the door.

At times a husband would have been very helpful, even if only to take on some of the tasks which I was given. The most memorable of these was when I was introduced to a dormitory of teenage boys, the children of mission workers, at Murree Christian School in Pakistan. I had been asked to speak to the boys as some of them had 'issues', and I was a psychologist. "This is Dr Lovell," the boys were told. "She's going to talk to you about masturbation. You don't need to be afraid to ask her anything. She does this sort of thing all the time." With that, the dorm parents left the room! If I had been married, I would gladly have delegated the experience to my husband.

I loved being involved with cross-cultural ministry, even though there were some awkward or difficult situations. It was sad seeing suffering and injustice, and I knew I could only play a tiny part in trying to help a few people, but it still felt meaningful. I met wonderful people and heard about the good being done in different parts of the world. There was a lot to laugh about. Because I enjoyed my work, I had a tendency to work long hours and not to take holidays. I had to learn to make time for God and for other people.

During my times in different countries I generally shared accommodation with at least one other woman. I was glad not to be in a house alone, as I felt safer and more confident with someone nearby who knew the language and the culture better than I did. However, as an introvert, I didn't always find it easy to share a house, especially as we were put together with neither of us having a say in the decision. Sometimes our expectations were very different. On one occasion I lived with a woman who had been looking forward to us cooking together. I have no cooking ability, and I was trying to live as cheaply as possible as I funded my mission trips myself. I was too embarrassed to offer to share my cheap meals with my housemate. I filled myself up three times a day with maize-meal porridge, like the local people (although by mistake I bought and ate the cheaper animal meal, rather than the version intended for humans). My housemate and I didn't talk about our different expectations until the end of our time living together. Although we got on well, and had good times together, I realised afterwards that I could have done much more to develop the friendship.

From my perspective, one advantage of being single was that I could live cheaply. Air fares are much lower when travelling alone, and it is much less stressful to travel without children. Not having children also meant that I could accept requests to go to dangerous places when there was a need, knowing that I might be killed. I am grateful for all these experiences.

Because I grew up expecting to be single, I was generally content with my lifestyle. I felt inspired by my sister, who lived in a Christian community and made a vow of celibacy. I made a private vow of celibacy when I was a student, but I put a time-limit of "until I'm 21" on it, just in case. I renewed it for a year at a time, until I realised I wasn't doing this because God had asked me to, but rather because I was afraid of close relationships and of rejection, and this vow helped me avoid either. Realising that, I stopped renewing the vow, although I still felt single at heart and expected to remain that way.

I had plenty of male friends. I hadn't expected any to develop into more than friendship, and I had never had a boyfriend, but Dave and I became close. While we were considering whether or not to marry, I was invited back to Pakistan, and Dave was also invited to teach there. As well as offering what we could, we wanted to test whether we could minister effectively together. I felt called to mission, and unless Dave shared that call it did not seem right to continue our relationship.

In Pakistan, we encountered a new challenge. How can courting occur between two workers in Pakistan, where single men and women can only be together within a group? Dave and I developed a secret language, giving a few words new meanings. We were able to pass messages to each other without anyone knowing. We just dropped our special words into a conversation, and other people thought we were talking about nature.

We wanted to communicate with each other more than just through our secret words though. A Christian marriage is a lifetime commitment and Dave and I were taking the decision very seriously. We needed time to talk and pray together, to consider the future. That wasn't easy in the Pakistani culture, where being seen alone together would cause suspicion. The headmistress of the mission school helped us out, inviting us both to her house in the evenings. I entered through the back door. A little later, Dave came to her front door. She then moved to the next room, allowing us to speak.

One Saturday, Dave and I went for a walk to Kashmir Point. It sounds very romantic, but was actually a rather busy, smoky road. Walking together was acceptable in such a public place. A long way in to our walk, there was a break in the traffic, and a quiet voice asked "Will you marry me?" I just had time to reply in song before the traffic picked up again. A hug would not be appropriate in this society, so we continued our walk without touching, our lives changed forever. My decade of mission work as a single was over.

In preparation for marriage, Dave and I read a book called *Sacred Marriage*.[99] This book suggests that we should view marriage as a way to make us holy, rather than to make us happy. I found this very helpful.

We can think of singleness in the same way. Those who are single can become more holy through turning to God to meet their deepest needs, and to be their companion throughout life. Those who marry can become more holy through putting their partner (and, if they arrive, children) before themselves, and demonstrating love, forgiveness and commitment even in the most difficult times.

We live in a time when happiness (or emotional wellbeing) is seen as the goal to strive for. As Christians, holiness (and spiritual wellbeing) is a greater goal. Those in ministry are choosing a life of service to others. If you are a mission worker, it's likely that you don't have as much money as you otherwise might, and you accept hardships (such as leaving family and friends) because of the value you place on sharing God's love with others. For some, the cost is high and it might include being single.

I respect those who are willing to pay a price in obedience to God. This includes those (whether heterosexual or homosexual) who remain sexually abstinent as they are not married; those who decide not to accept a partner who doesn't share their faith or their commitment to mission; and those who remain faithful to God, serving as singles, even when that is a lonely or difficult road.

Before I got married, I thought about advantages and disadvantages of both marriage and singleness. Neither option stood out as obviously better than the other. Being single was a lot simpler, and I liked simplicity. Getting married was a risk. I agreed with the saying, "I'd rather be single and want to be married, than married and want to be single." What mattered most to me was being obedient to God and serving him whatever situation I was in. I wanted to be content whatever the circumstances, whether married or single, relying on God to give me strength (see Philippians 4: 11-13). I guessed that marriage might have both higher highs and lower lows than being single. I took the risk, having given Dave ample warning that he was taking the bigger risk, and that life wouldn't be boring!

Dave and I got married a year after our smoky Kashmir Point walk. We were in our thirties, and ready to begin learning how to be involved with mission as a couple. No cows were exchanged at our wedding, although as wedding presents our guests paid for some goats (and toilets, trees and towels) for a counselling centre in Russia. Soon after hitch-hiking to my father's house on honeymoon, we went on our next mission trip, to train the volunteers at the centre in Russia. Dave said every night, "What a strange, long trip this has been." It was an exciting, unpredictable, hilarious time (involving sneaking $35,000 of cash into the country for aid work, handing it over in the middle of the night, being stopped by police, spending a night locked in an orthodox church, having documents detained by the former KGB, preaching at a moment's notice, and much more). My life as a single person, and later as a married woman, has also at times been exciting, unpredictable and hilarious. At other times it has seemed dull, predictable and serious. In our marriage we've been through better and worse, richer and poorer, sickness and health, deaths and births.

During our first year of marriage, when I was missing my single life, I believe God taught me three things: stop complaining, be grateful, and live in love. I started to think of things to be thankful for, instead of things to complain about. That turned our marriage around. We have now been married for 12 years. I'm grateful for these years. I'm also grateful we didn't get married earlier, as I wouldn't have wanted to miss the years as a single mission worker. I thank God for Dave and for our son Jamie, who has taught me much (including that psychological theories about parenting don't always work in practice!) When I'm tempted to complain about life, I remember what I have to be thankful for.

The Bible teaches us to stop complaining, to be grateful, and to love. Perhaps these three lessons which I learned early in my marriage are lessons for *all* of us, married or single. In the light of eternity, most of the things which bother us now are likely to seem insignificant. With God's help we can flourish whether we are single or married.

What matters is our attitude and perspective. When faced with loss in life, including loneliness, singleness and childlessness, we can face the loss and grieve. We can cry, pray, and talk with understanding people. Grief may rise at various times, and not all be worked through on one occasion.

It can also be good to list the things we are grateful for. My son taught me how to be specific, when he was two years old. He prayed thanking God for underground trains (naming each metro line separately), and for brushing teeth, and other things I like but had never thought of thanking God for.

It can help when we think about people who are in worse circumstances than ourselves. It is easy to compare ourselves with people who we think are happier, or have more than we do, or have what we want (e.g. a happy marriage and children). I could easily feel jealous of people who seem to have a better life, but as someone said to me, "You can't have it all". I'm reminded that when Peter thought another disciple was getting a better deal, Jesus said "What is that to you? You must follow me" (John 21: 22).

There are many people in the world in worse circumstances than us. Comparing ourselves with them, instead of with those we envy, can help us become more grateful, compassionate, outward-looking and content about our place in life. I realised this when I wrote the following lines:

A full life

I've had some sorrows in life.
The unspeakable grief when my mother died early.
The loss of friends
And I baby I had carried for several months.
Mis-carried.
Could I have done more?

Bullied as a child,
Spat at and abused,
I nearly starved to death while still at school.
Feeling unloved and unlovable.

Recovered, I wanted to fight injustice.
I travelled the world to listen and to train.

I carried starving children,
and held grieving orphans.
I felt earthquakes, saw volcanoes erupt,
heard bombs, tasted tears and smelt death.
I knew fear, cowering in the dark
as they pounded my door.

And I knew peace.
On my own in the dark, but not alone.
Through suffering, resilience can grow.
And gratitude.

I have so much to be grateful for.
I could have been born an orphan,
My mother dying while I took my first breath.
I might have spent my childhood searching for food,
Never going to school.
I could have sold my body.
Or parts of it.

I might have suffered torture.
Or worse, I might have been made to torture others.
A child soldier.
Killing my brothers and destroying my sisters
to save my own breath.

I could have known true misery.

We have so much to be thankful for.
I have known love and laughter,
Food and clean water,
Health and education,
Friendship and warmth.
I can brush my teeth

and take a shower.
I have somewhere to live.
I can see and hear,
And move freely where I want to go.
I can choose my beliefs
And live by my values.

I can do what I believe in,
To make life meaningful,
Life to the full.

I have had a blessed life.

Chapter 32 - Open doors: Can God use a married woman? Can God use a widow?

Dr Lois Dodds *expected to serve God as a single mission worker. After she met Larry she realized that God can use married woman as well, and they married. They served in Peru until Larry experienced burnout. After he recovered they set up Heartstream, a ministry offering support to cross-cultural workers. Larry then developed three terminal illnesses. After he died, Lois faced the question: can God use a widow? The answer is a resounding "yes". Lois continues to serve as CEO of Heartstream Resources. She has taught in about forty countries, and is author of over one hundred articles and more than a dozen books. She writes here about the doors which open and close throughout life.*

When I was four I met Jesus. He welcomed me and dried my tears. I had wept a puddle of tears, through the slats of the old wooden chair. I passed through the white door of salvation. I knew then I would always love God. Jesus became my best friend, my refuge, my point of reference. At eleven I was as sure that he had called me as that he had called Samuel. I would serve him with all my heart. I lived that year with two single women, 'home missionaries' in the Mojave Desert town of Boron, of the Borax mines. I determined to be like them—single, and fully available to serve God. I admired their life of faith, their education, their open home and their total dedication.

Steadfast in my commitment to serve God, I decided I would prefer to never marry. In my mind I closed that door. The life of the two dear saints seemed far better than my mother's continual suffering as the mother of twelve children and a mostly absent husband. I used every opportunity to serve during my schooldays. Years later I learned that the single missionaries I lived with were investigated by the authorities who thought that perhaps I was being exploited! For me, the chance to serve was a great reward; I was trusted and gaining experience. I turned down a chance to study at Stanford, and chose instead a small Christian college. I wanted to go to Peru on Jesus' behalf as soon as possible, as well prepared as I could be.

It seems paradoxical that my strong desire to be single was upended; so many of my sisters in missions long to be married, yet they are not. Larry came in to my life through *Youth for Christ*. He was unlike any man I had met in my multiple moves and churches. Since the age of eight he had dedicated himself to become another Dr. David Livingston, to go off into the far places of the earth to provide medical care. This musical, athletic man was bursting with enthusiasm for learning and bounding with energy, taking stairs two or three at a time.

After meeting Larry I began to examine my 'vow' of singleness. Was it truly a vow? Would God release me if it was, or would I suffer some Old Testament consequence for breaking a vow? My solution was to make a huge chart of the women in the Bible, listing names, roles, marital status, and answering the question, "Does God use married women?" The answer "Yes" gave me freedom to join my life with the young doctor-in-the-making. Of course, I identified more with Deborah than with Jael (Judges 4).

We married while Larry was in medical school. I went the whole route of training with him, attending anatomy lab for dissection and working in the medical field to share his domain of knowledge. We planned and worked, expecting to be poor for Christ's sake. We raised support to go to Peru with Wycliffe Bible Translators (WBT). It was exhilarating to be rushing towards the open door.

Then God shut the door. Larry was drafted into the U.S. Army. He used to say that by the time his appeal went through he was already wearing a green suit. We had to reassess God's purpose, which turned out to be manifold purposes. God opened a new door of opportunity in those three years—paying off medical school bills, space and aviation training for Larry, learning to fly, becoming President Johnson's flight surgeon, and serving in Vietnam. We lived in six states and attended churches of many denominations—all perfect training for our years to come in missions. At last, after much more training in residency and other points of service we headed off to Peru, six years after we had first bought our tickets.

I was discovering that God does, indeed, use married women, but I never lost my deep respect for my many sisters in the faith who chose to go to the ends of the earth to serve even if it meant going alone. My friends who are apostles were taking the gospel where it had never gone, learning languages never before written and translating the Scriptures for those who had never known of a Saviour. It was awesome. I found I could invite them into our home, now pulsating with a family of five, for respite care, refuge, encouragement and to share a family's love. Our home became a hospital, quite literally, as we served in the Amazon jungle of Peru. I discovered the roles God had for me, beyond my official work. Reaching out and taking in those who lived the single life became a joy.

I saw that God used me, a married woman with children, in unique ways, and that he also used my single sisters in ways I could not serve. Clearly, he blessed us all, whatever our marital status. I found joy in marriage, children, home and my work. And I found joy in sharing all that with my single sisters who often lived in hardship situations in villages or tiny mountain hamlets, taking the Word of God where it had never gone. I say sisters because during our years WBT had over 2,000 single women and only a handful of single men.

I also enjoyed spending time with my widowed sisters. Pat reared two children in an indigenous village in the jungle after losing her husband in a commercial jet crash. To this day she fervently serves God worldwide, writing and consulting on literacy. I was later inspired by Beth, who brought up four children on the field after her husband perished in a crash. These women were often expected to work as many hours in ministry as single women, while at the same time raising children alone. They are truly heroic widows for whom God pledges to be husband and parent. I saw his faithfulness first hand.

I had wanted to be single. Yet I never regretted marriage, or failed to see God's choice for me to be married. What I learned is the beauty of the Body of Christ, and the diversity of gifts and opportunities God creates in his plan. My love of art, decorating, sewing, painting and remodelling were gifts I used for my single sisters. I decorated ugly dorms and barren apartments for their sakes.

We expected to be in Peru forever. That was the strength of our commitment. So it was a shock that after thirteen years Larry was about to die, in a state of depletion which later came to be known as burnout. Being on call 24 hours a day, having a practice area the size of the state of California, and having suffered several of the jungle's diseases was wiping him out. Our commitment had not flagged, but his strength had.

Was the door closing to the ministry we loved and had fully embraced for 'forever'? We scoured the Scriptures for answers. We settled on the truth that God's call is on our lives, not just the place. Just as he chose Moses and placed him first in the palace and later in the desert to lead his people, so God would honour his call on our lives in other places. Just as God's call was not changed by marital status, it was not changed by place of service. He would always honour what he gifted us to do, wherever we happened to be. His gift of hospitality, hospital-ing people and bringing them into a loving family, would still be fruitful.

After almost ten years of my teaching and counselling and Larry working in public health, while educating our children and ourselves, God opened another door. We launched the ministry of Heartstream. It came about due to our experiences in Peru and talking with mission workers around the globe, whose conversations often ended with, "Wouldn't it be wonderful if we had somewhere to go when we are in crisis, or burnout, or depression—*some place where they would understand!*" Over and over we heard that longing for a place of emotional and spiritual safety, where mission personnel could receive medical care, spiritual enlightenment, encouragement, counselling, emotional respite, and relationship help.

We could see how God brought together all the phases of our lives and ministry, and both of our professional careers, going as far back as medical school when we had wished we could take young doctors and their wives by the hand and teach them how to live. As far back as our years of struggle and challenge in the jungle. We found a confluence of our fields of medicine, psychology, counselling and biblical studies; a convergence of our experiences, our gifts and talents. So, Heartstream was born.[100]

God's open door was reflected in our own open door—well, by then it was five doors, as we use five homes at Heartstream's centre in Pennsylvania, all on a cul-de-sac in a rural hamlet. For two decades we have had a continuous flow of guests, most staying for our two-week Intensive Care Programs. Larry and I loved collaborating in the restoration of God's special servants who had lost hope, home, or ministry. It was a wonderful culmination of God's call upon both our lives. We enjoyed seeing God's special servants regaining the light in their eyes as well as a spring in their step. This was not a life of poverty – it was very rich.

We thought it would last a long, long time. In 1999 God opened a different kind of door, this time a black door of suffering we never expected. Larry was diagnosed with ALS (also known as motor neurone disease or Lou Gehrig's disease). His life expectancy suddenly shrunk to two or three years. We sought God earnestly. Would he cut short the fulfilling and effective ministry he had created through us? God seemed to say, "I have a purpose in this. You are not to be healed physically, but trust me." Larry did trust, in the most amazing ways, saying each day, "My role is to watch and see God's goodness in the midst of this." He quickly came to believe, "Whether I live or die, I am with the Lord—I am already in eternal life."

Two years later Larry was diagnosed with cancer. He was still working full time, still vigorous in spite of losing muscle strength. His love for the Lord was vibrant. As his body grew more feeble, his counselling became ever more effective. His witness of God's goodness was irrefutable.

Four more years went by. Then Larry was diagnosed with a third terminal illness. He was often asked, "Why God would let this happen to you, of all people, since you have been serving him?" "Why *not* me?" Larry would ask. Twice he was invited to Hershey Medical School because faculty and students wanted to know how a physician could have three terminal diseases and face death with such calm assurance. Some said hearing his testimony was the most inspiring event of medical school.

After eight years Larry had lost all movement except for his neck and head. He drove his huge motorized wheelchair with precision, using his chin to control a tiny joy-stick about a quarter of an inch long. He said it was the same mental skill that allowed him to balance a helicopter. During the continual loss of muscle strength he always said, "If I can't do something one way, I will do it another." His skill and flexibility were impressive. An 'eye gaze' computer enabled him to still do all his computer work. He continued to teach and consult. The nimble hands which once did surgery, sewed up wounds, flew helicopters, built our furniture, fixed the plumbing, and created code on the computer became hands in repose, up-turned to God. His spirit seemed to soar, a total contrast to his physical immobility.

We laughed more in those years than in any others. Often, at the end of the day when I prepared him for bed Larry would say, "Oh, I forgot I was in a wheelchair today!" That's how positive he was.

Based on the neurologist's word and our evidence that Larry still had great lungs and a strong singing voice, we expected he would go on living a long time like physicist Stephen Hawking, the longest living ALS patient, who had survived almost three decades. Then it seemed the door jammed shut. Larry died very unexpectedly and quickly due to the medication being used to treat his third disease. I was stunned; we had so much more planned.

God had opened a radiant door for Larry, but had he at the same time closed a door for me, the door of ministry we so loved? Once again I went back to the Word to seek God. I was 68 years old, and I was back to being single. I questioned: can God use a once-single, once-married *widow*? What would happen now to God's precious call on my life? What would happen to our ministry?

My grief was like no other. I called it 'good grief' as it was so unlike the complicated grieving of my life, including suicides of friends and relatives. Those were full of ambiguity and regrets, so painful, almost bereft of comfort. This good grief was a healing grief, an energizing grief.

It did not match any pattern I had ever studied. It was filled with loss and sadness, but much more.

The morning after Larry's death I sat with our three children, planning a funeral for my beloved. Unexpected joy filled me. "These are Larry's children", I thought. I could see him in each of them as they discussed the Scriptures (choosing their father's favourites), classical music, liturgy, hymnody of the centuries, and creative ways to celebrate their father's life. The planning would honour him well. This was an awesome grief, filled with gratitude for all that Larry and I had shared, as lovers, as spouses, as parents, and as partners in ministry. I felt grateful that we would be together again. I saw that it gave me more in common with Mary, the beloved mother of our Lord, as she grieved as a widow for her precious son.

Missing Larry came in waves, always born up by a deep sense of gratitude for our life together, and a profound desire to honour him. I never expected that these sentiments were part of grief. I had become who I am because of his ability to pass on God's love to me. The man whose absence I grieved had loved me well, and infused into me strength to live well and to grieve well; grieving for him was a privilege. Many objects, events and conversations prompted my memories of him. I loved to think of him and talk about him. Grief welled up when I heard music, especially listening to his funeral and memorial service, hearing over and over our son playing his violin tributes to his father. There was healing music, healing memories and healing words from our children. There was still laughter, prompted by him.

It seemed I could still easily converse with Larry. As our son Michael said at Larry's service, Larry had "slipped through the veil" but we were all still connected as a ring of five, interlocked with the rings before us and the rings behind us, formed by our children's own families. Larry had moved beyond the veil, but was still very much alive, in eternity already. The sense of Larry's presence in God's presence was a huge comfort. How could so much of life be the same, and he was simply removed from it?

Soon after Larry's death, a woman asked me, in shock, "How could God take Larry when he has done so much good in this world? When he was still so young?" At that moment God gave me words to say: Larry had completed the work God created and ordained for him to do (Ephesians 2:10) and fulfilled his numbered days (Psalm 139:16). There was great comfort in my sudden understanding of those truths. What was Larry's real work? Making God visible through three fatal diseases! What door would open to me then? When I could turn my eyes from my loss, I saw that God had never closed the door. It stood wide open, the green door of opportunity. God beckoned me to pass through this door, once again single in serving him. Yet a widow is never a single self again; rather she is a once-married, half-a-pair-self.

I have worn Larry's ring since his death, along with my engagement and wedding rings. He bought those rings by selling his blood pint-by-pint during college. Forty-seven years of marriage—or, ninety four if we both count. Now what? What does the church do with widows other than expect their mites? Usually, that's not an inspiring picture. Yet, I have the love and support of a wonderful family, a devoted Heartstream team and a host of friends who are faithful to me in my widowhood. Instead of focusing on a widow's mite, we can focus on God's might. God's path for me was clear. Go forward. Honour God and honour Larry by continuing the work to which he had called us.

What more can I say about grief? It has no set pattern for me. Much of it is good, as it prompts memories of precious times, hard times, clinging-to-God times. Some unexpected small thing may bring on a wave of loss, of sadness. Another thing may bring on a wave of gladness, gratitude, and resolve to honour the one I loved. It is not the dreadful scourge I once thought it would be. It is a way of passing through one door to another, being able to look back to the rooms we have passed through and the ones yet ahead. As Paul said, we have that great hope that the mortal will be clothed with immortality, the perishable body with imperishable glory (see 1 Corinthians 15). I have God's promise that "in all (my) distresses he too was distressed" and he sends the "angel of his presence" to be with me (Isaiah 63:9). Presence? Yes, he is my very present help in times of trouble (Psalm 46:1).

When Larry died, my mind was brimming with thoughts as my eyes were with tears. The truths I learned in childhood jumped up in me, "Precious in the sight of the Lord is the death of his saints" (Psalm 116:15). Precious? Death? How so? It must be that God loves to have his children come bounding home to him! I also had irreverent thoughts from our technological age: "Isn't there some way to download Larry's brain, to preserve this awesome mind, to keep the soul of this precious person?"

Most mornings when I walk I stop at Larry's grave. The monument is black marble, with two inter-twining oak trees etched in white, along with a flock of sheep led by a shepherd. Verses from Isaiah tell the story: "The Spirit of the sovereign Lord is on (him)… (We) will be called oaks of righteousness, a planting of the Lord, for the display of his splendour" (Isaiah 61:1-3). God is greater than three terminal diseases. God says to me, "Even to your old age and grey hairs I am he, I am he who will sustain you. I made you and I will carry you; I will sustain you and I will rescue you" (Isaiah 46:4).

My name is on the grave too. It is a good reminder that I too must number my days, and have a heart of wisdom (Psalm 90:12).

This I can say with certainty, God is in our status—single, married or widowed. He still equips us, in whatever state we are. He is still calling you and me to serve him with glad hearts, to give every gift of our singleness or married-ness or widowhood to draw people to his heart.

Chapter 33 - Singleness and widowhood: Married for two weeks

Catherine Bezold left her home in South Africa to serve God as a mission worker. Travelling in dangerous environments, she prayed for a husband to protect her. She met Martin while they were both ministering in South Sudan. He seemed to be the answer to her prayer, and they got engaged. But Martin died within two weeks of their marriage. Catherine describes his death, interwoven with her memories of mission trips and how she met Martin.

> **The doctor looked at me with pained eyes and said that it was the end and that we should say our last words. I saw them preparing the needle for morphine and felt all the energy, vitality, faith, passion, hopes and dreams drain out of me like a fountain spring suddenly running dry. I felt like I was going to faint. The nurses took me to another room to recover. As my head hung between my legs my mind scanned through memories and dreams of the past.**

The past, remembering how I felt at airports when I watched people hugging and holding each other, saying their goodbyes with tears in their eyes, knowing they would be reunited in each others arms some day. Somehow I always felt like something was missing. I had amazing family and friends but I didn't have a beloved to share my adventure with. I was single and alone. But I still pushed forward with faith, believing that God was in control and that loving him and serving him was all that mattered. I entrusted my passionate heart and dreams to him.

Looking out of a plane window, I could see the airport (containing my family and friends), Table Mountain and the sea. Once such a large part of my life, they were now becoming smaller. In my hand I clutched some cards, the words bringing love, comfort and encouragement to be strong and courageous. I felt alone in the plane, leaving everything and everyone I loved and held so dear. I realized how easy it is to be strong and courageous when surrounded by friends and family, and how hard when alone. It was my dream to leave all that I held dear for the sake of the call to follow Jesus Christ as a mission worker.

The first part of this dream began on a mission ship. I was a teacher for the children of those who were ministering elsewhere on the ship. I had a desire not only to teach the children, but to love them and create a joyful environment where they too could discover Jesus in a new and dynamic way.

Life on the ship was at times wonderful and other times frightening. Some days were beautiful and calm, an expanse of blue skies without end, with the occasional visit of a school of dolphins who surfed the wake of the ship's bow. Other days involved making sure everything was tied down and secure. It was hard to keep myself steady or focus on teaching a lesson when all I felt like doing was being sick! One rough day during the school break when the children were playing, a huge wave hit the side and deck of the ship. We were wet through and shocked and came into the safety of the classroom. The bookshelf had been knocked half way across the classroom by the wave and all the books had been flung onto the floor. The ropes used to tie everything down were not strong enough for that big wave.

I sometimes felt like that too, that I was not able to tie down the feelings going around in my heart and mind. There were days filled with deep meaningful conversations with the children about God and Jesus. Early morning prayer meetings and times with my new friends were full of fun, laughter and joy. Life seemed calm and good. But then came a wave of loneliness as some of my friends ended their term on the ship and went home. In my heart I wanted to be strong and courageous, keeping everything nicely tied up and in control. I found it hard to share a small cabin, without space to work through my thoughts. Jesus said, "If anyone would come after me, he must deny himself and take up his cross and follow me" (Mark 8:34). I realized that he said "follow me", come with me. He did not say "be strong and courageous and walk this narrow path alone." He said, "Do not be terrified; do not be discouraged, for the Lord your God will be with wherever you go" (Joshua 1:9). I was single, but not alone.

During my time sailing from port to port I had an overwhelming sense that I was called to walk alongside a people group, teaching and guiding them on better pathways of life, discipling people as Jesus did. The ship had been a great learning curve but it was time to move to the next stepping stone of my life. I wanted to develop more in the area of working among a people group for a longer period of time. Nelson Mandela once said that if you speak to a person you can capture his mind but if you speak his mother tongue you capture his heart. Learning not only a language but a culture became crucial to working with my brothers and sisters in the townships.

> **The nurse came through with a glass of water which I could barely hold. I still wanted to live in the past and was not yet ready for the reality of the present. Memories of my emotions, dreams and feelings during mission trips all came flooding back to me.**

We were a team of eight people from my home church and two local guides from Mozambique rowing two inflatable boats. Our aim was to row up the Zambezi River to a coastal region of Mozambique where the gospel had not been preached. The team consisted of men, me and one other young woman. The sun had set and the jungle seemed to be a mass of moving shadows. All you could hear was our breathing, together with the lapping of water at each stroke of our oars. Suddenly we heard from the boat ahead of us, "Back! Back! Back!" It was pitch dark. There was splashing, yelling and then grunting. In my heart I prayed, "Oh Lord protect them, whatever animal it is, you have power to overcome it." The splashing came closer and closer towards us. We were afraid to put on our torches in case it angered the animal even more. We saw the faces of our friends, ash white with shock. "We hit a hippo", they exclaimed.

I felt numb and wanted to cry, but the men in the team all seemed excited and continued rowing through the night. So, putting on a brave face, I followed their lead and continued to paddle, praying with each stroke that we would not hit a crocodile or hippo. It took all my emotional energy to carve my oar into the dark water. When the tide eventually changed we stopped on the riverbank. Getting out of our boats, we stepped straight into thick, deep mud, and made our way through the squelching mess to a reasonably flat part of riverbank. I had a tent to myself and the guys helped me set it up in the middle of the horse shoe-shaped arrangement of tents. The entire team was exhausted and everyone collapsed into their tents to try to get some sleep.

Our third day of rowing was a race against the tide as we rowed further up the Zambezi and came closer to the ocean. The challenge facing our guide was to get us to the smallest part of the river delta at the point at which the tide was at its highest, allowing us enough water to row to the coast where the tribe was situated. There seemed to be just the right level of water for our boats to pass through. However, our guide soon started to tell us to row faster as it seemed that the tide was running out. It happened quickly, as though someone had pulled a plug from the bathtub. In minutes all the water was gone and we were stuck in the mud.

This was the least of our problems, as we were suddenly attacked by thousands of mosquitoes, all bombarding us like miniature kamikaze pilots. Our arms and faces were transformed into a mass of black, swarming insects, and it appeared that the more we tried to hit them, the more they attacked us. Looking ahead, I saw the tracks left by crocodiles as they slid into the water, as well as traces of many other kinds of animals. Thankfully our team leader chose that moment to revert back to the days he spent in the army, announcing, "Gentlemen, stopping is not an option! Cath you go ahead of the boats and pull out all branches and broken trees to clear the way."

Determined to embrace the challenge, I prayed in Jesus' name and charged ahead, diving into the mud and pulling out branches that could have caused a puncture in the boat. I had the fleeting thought that if I died at least it would be whilst doing the Lord's work. The men pushed our two boats filled with our supplies. It was like pushing a large animal through the mud. We were covered in mud and mosquitoes, with the men pushing so hard that some of them were vomiting. Finally we saw water and this encouraged us to push faster until the boats glided and eventually floated. With the strength of God we made it through to the other side. Our guide was afraid that we would be angry with him, but instead the men were jumping for victory and cracking jokes. I realized that men and women are very different. I thought that if I cried it would dampen their high spirits, so I held my emotions in check.

When we finally reached the banks of the river where the tribe we wanted to visit lived, I was relieved. We set up tents, made a fire, ate and went to bed. I couldn't sleep and I picked up my torch, my Bible and a toilet roll. I walked up the riverbank far away from the team. When I had gone far enough that nobody could hear me, I burst into tears. I needed to release all the emotions that I had experienced throughout the week and I needed God to help me. In that moment I cried out, "God please provide me with a husband, someone who would understand my delicate emotions – someone who would take me in his arms and let me release my feelings". After an hour, with a pile of wet toilet paper and my Bible damp with tears, I returned to my tent. I was surrounded by tents of snoring men but I was too exhausted to care and I managed to sleep well that night. In the morning I felt better and I decided not to tell my team about my struggles.

The following night, after eating, the men made a fire on the beach. Our day had been good. We had made some connections with the people using a translator and had set up a base from where we would run our ministries. We felt we needed time to be refreshed by our Lord before beginning our ministries of preaching, teaching and running children's programs. We sang worship songs and then waited quietly on God. One of the men in his prayer said, "I see Jesus coming towards us. Cath he is coming towards you and just wants to hold you." I felt the presence of

Jesus coming closer to me. In that moment my knees hit the sand and I wept. My team came around me and held me. This made me cry even more. As they prayed for me I felt encouraged and understood. After our prayer time the men chatted to me and said that they finally saw that I was a normal woman and not some kind of superwoman. I explained how I didn't want to let them down. As Jesus stripped away my pride I realized I could just be simply Cath, not "General Cath" as I had become known among the team. These mission trips inspired me to join a team in South Sudan among unreached tribes there.

> The doctor and nurse came to me and said, "Frau Bezold we don't have much time. We will give you and Martin five minutes alone and then we need to inject him with morphine and then he will not know who you are. You need to say your goodbyes".

Martin, I can remember the first time I met him. He was part of a new mission team that I had joined in South Sudan. I was sitting in the back of the Land Rover with some of the other team members, full of excitement for the venture we had all embarked on. Our team was from all over the world. Martin was a German farmer and sat watching us all talking. You couldn't see if he was smiling or not because of his beard.

We approached a large river. Some of our team vehicles and trucks had gone before us and they simply drove through the river. I was petrified and clung to the seat praying. As we hit the river, the water seemed to part and although it rushed past just below the windows, we made it through without incident. The more we travelled the more our journey involved rivers, slipping and sliding in mud and non-existent roads. For the men on the team this was exciting and adventurous; for me it would take some time to get used to. I remembered how I had tried in previous mission trips to be "all tough". This time I reminded myself that I was simply Cath and that it was normal for me, a woman who had grown up in a city, to be overwhelmed by the journey and the rougher terrain I now inhabited. After about six hours we reached a mountainous region, green and lush. We waved at people along the way who were working in their fields. As we drove past we could hear the echo of their greetings. The people seemed open and friendly and I was excited to live amongst them and learn their language and their culture.

Living in a Lopit village in the Eastern Equatoria district of South Sudan meant that we experienced events that were very foreign to my culture. Often, the young girls of the village would make up a song that replayed an incident that had happened and would sing about it and dance under the full moon. These people had no written language. It was only their traditions, song and dance that kept their culture alive. It was through these experiences that I found a key to reaching the hearts of these lovely people. I had the idea of creating a drama with song and dance with different messages from the Bible. I could not do this alone so I shared my idea with the team and asked if any of them were interested in helping me to put on a drama.

This is where Martin made an incredible impression on me and crept into my heart. He seemed a very quiet person. Whenever he shared something with us it was well thought out and significant. He was happy serving each member of the team, and he worked quietly behind the scenes, whether by carrying a gas bottle or washing dishes. On the day that I shared my idea about putting together a drama of Bible stories, he was the first to volunteer. I could not imagine how such a shy and quiet person would manage on a drama team, but I decided to give him a chance. I prepared scripts for each actor and we started putting together the drama for the youth of the church. In the practices this mystery man seemed pretty good and the other actors were also doing well. On the day of the performance Martin swept me off my feet. When he was before an audience he was absolutely brilliant, and funny. I and the other actors were shocked, as we knew him so differently, but the audience were enthralled by him and loved it when he came on stage.

The more I choreographed dramas, the more Martin became one of the main actors in each performance. I was pleasantly surprised when I arrived at each practice that Martin had prepared chairs and got everything ready. He encouraged me a lot in this ministry. I started confiding in Martin more and more and he soon became a good friend.

I had to really discipline myself as my feelings for Martin were growing stronger. I kept praying that the Lord would remove this temptation from me and help me to remain focused on God and the ministry that I was doing in Sudan. Every time I felt tempted to dream about Martin I would grab the journal that I had set aside for my thoughts for my future husband and write asking the Lord if Martin was the one for me. The following is an entry from my dairy to my future husband:

> *I do believe God is opening my eyes… a life partner is more than passion, romance and love… it's about being partners accomplishing things for God. I see Martin as my Boaz and will wait patiently for God to move in us. I am afraid to love at the moment. It's scary for me because I have been rejected so many times. The Lord is the one who has sustained me and kept me a virgin but he knows my heart and the key that fits. I hope that key is you, as I long to be your Ruth!*

I waited and prayed for a month or so and one day I found the following letter from Martin hidden in one of my books:

Dear Cath,

Have you already found your future role in the Lopit community after being a learner? For today I would like to share a parable from the depth of my heart with you.

…One month ago, I discovered during my birthday quiet time in the mountain river, that a planting in my heart had started germinating. I don't know for how

long, but I believe with a lot of prayer you have sown a seed of God's love, affection, interest, and care. When I discovered this germinating seed I rejoiced and tended to see in it another miracle of God's love arising in me. And believe it or not I care and pray about this strange plant daily. I don't know what kind of plant it is and what will it look like at a later stage. Sometimes I'm not sure – is it a weed or a wonderful flower for God's glory and people's joy and blessing? Would you like to help me identify this not yet unfolded plant? For now I would like to share with you three words from our Father which were comforting and directing me during the last days:

Isaiah 43:19 "See, I am doing a new thing!"
Psalm 37:4 "Delight yourself in the Lord and he will give you the desires of your heart."
Hosea 6:1-3 "Come, let us return to the Lord. He has torn us to pieces but he will heal us; he has injured us but he will bind up our wounds. After two days he will revive us; on the third day he will restore us, that we may live in his presence".

Yours Martin

I read the letter over and over again and it brought such joy to my heart. I could understand how the scriptures from Isaiah and Psalms fitted into our future lives together but I could not understand how the Hosea scripture fitted and so I left this one up to God to show me.

> **I had five minutes to say goodbye to my husband. Lord is that what the verse in Hosea was saying to Martin - that we would be torn apart and that you would raise Martin into eternal life in your presence? What about all my dreams about having a husband and a family? Lord are you calling me to be single again, a widow?**

Every letter that Martin wrote to me romanced me and drew me closer to him. I desperately wanted to run into his arms, have him hold me, and have his hands touch my hair and face. I prayed many times for God to help me wait until it was God's timing for us to come together as one.

For 18 months we kept a mutual dairy which we exchanged each week, recording our deepest thoughts, passions and desires. Above our human passions and desires was our love and relationship with Jesus and our hearts were also passionate about loving and reaching out to the Lopit people. In our waiting we wanted to honour God and the Lopit culture and we did not want to become physically involved until after we were married. At the back of the diary we had a page with three columns - for kisses, hugs and back massages. Each time one of us felt the desire to give a back massage or hug or kiss we would write it in our dairy, saving it up to give when we were married.

Martin met my family, and then it was time for me to meet his family in Germany. We packed up our things in South Sudan and prepared for the long journey.

I had a wonderful time getting to know Martin's family and friends. Even though I could not speak much German, love developed between his parents, friends and I. After about two weeks spent with Martin's family, Martin proposed and I accepted. We planned to have a small wedding three months later.

During our time in Germany Martin was not feeling well. At first we thought it could be malaria or a tropical disease that he had picked up in

South Sudan. He saw many different doctors, who conducted various tests in an attempt to diagnose what was wrong. They realized that Martin needed a hernia operation and suggested that he have the operation before our marriage. We planned for him to have the operation on the 10th February 2009. I was with him in the hospital and the doctors told him that it would be a quick routine procedure, lasting approximately 30 minutes. After he was taken into the operating theatre, I waited and waited. I did not know what was wrong.

After waiting for over three hours, Martin was wheeled out of theatre, attached to a number of different drips and machines. He looked in a lot of pain, and I could not help him. I stayed with him, held his hand and prayed. Martin was so unwell he could only speak German at the time and I tried my best to understand him. I tried to ask the nurses and doctors what was going on but they could not speak enough English to explain. They kept taking him for tests and then a CT scan.

A few days later we received the news that they had found cancer in Martin's brain, lungs and stomach. They told us there was no hope and they were not sure how much longer he had to live. We held each other's hands tightly in disbelief. In front of the doctor I told Martin that I loved him and still wanted to marry him until death parted us.

After the doctor left the room Martin looked at me and said; "Cath, I don't want to marry you anymore". I held his hands with tears in my eyes and asked him why. He said he did not want to make me a widow. I told him we had started a love story together and that I wanted to finish it with him. Then with embarrassment and pain he looked at me and said, "Cath, I cannot offer you sex." I held him and replied, "Mein Schatz, I want to marry you because I love you and not because of sex."

The days were full of challenges but with Christ's help we managed. Our wedding took place on 7th April. I had learnt that you normally do not wear your wedding dress to the *Standesamt* (court wedding), so I planned to wear a simple red dress that I had had for years. A friend made me some pearl-like earrings and offered to do my hair in the morning. I had no time to plan any major details but it all felt wonderfully spontaneous and cost us nothing. We walked to the *Standesamt* and picked up the flowers on the way. The ceremony included part of the South African National Anthem in English and it really touched my heart. We were both so gloriously happy, and I had done nothing, except to sign the register making my marriage to Martin legal in the eyes of the German government.

We had agreed that we wanted to have a church marriage ceremony before sleeping together in one room. This was hard for many people to understand but we both felt very strongly about this. Normally people would plan their church wedding a day or two after the official court wedding. However, we wanted to have my parents and grandmother from South Africa at our church wedding and had to wait for them to get their visas. Thus we planned our church wedding for the 2nd May. I had my white wedding dress and shoes ready and our church arranged to have a meeting to plan the decorations on the 20th April.

But God had a different plan for us on the 20th April. On this day, Martin's breathing had become so bad that he could not sleep at all; he also battled to eat and swallow his tablets. This was the first time I had seen Martin in such pain. Our friends had helped me move Martin to my apartment so I could look after him better and we had also organized an oxygen machine. But nothing was helping him. I realized that we needed to bring him to the hospital where they could help give him pain killers through a drip to ease the pain. When we arrived at the hospital the doctor told me it was the end and that we needed to say our last words before they injected Martin with morphine.

At that point Martin realized that I was going to faint and tried to tell them. I managed to find a chair and put my head between my legs. Then I found some strength and came to his bed. He took my head and laid it on his lap and stroked my hair. He remembered that I had said long ago that when I was small and needed comforting my mother would hold me and stroke my hair.

I looked at him with tears in my eyes, amazed that he was still looking after my needs when he was about to die. He looked into my eyes and said; "Cath, will you forgive me for giving you such a hard time in Germany?" I told him that it was not his fault, that it was the cancer. He replied, "Cath, please look into my eyes and tell me you forgive me." He spoke through all the areas where he felt he had failed me and wanted my forgiveness. He knew how much I loved flowers and even asked for forgiveness that he had failed to bring me flowers. I told him I forgave him and loved him very much. We then said the Lord's Prayer together. I realized that Jesus was planning a much better and bigger wedding feast for Martin in heaven.

The next day Martin breathed his last and Jesus took him safely home.

As the small plane came closer to the familiar three peaked mountain, a flood of emotions and memories crossed my mind. This was the place in South Sudan where Martin and I had fallen in love, and pages of love letters had been exchanged. As I walked slowly up the path that for years had been so familiar, it now seemed more dry and barren than ever before. My heart echoed the emptiness and barrenness I saw around me.

Arriving at the door of my mud house, my first instinct was to look across the valley to where Martin's house was. It is strange that I imagined he would somehow still be there as if I was in a dream, although I knew full well that he had died in my arms and I had buried him in Germany. My heart sank as I finally had to embrace the reality that he was gone.

Most of our good memories had been formed in this place in the middle of Africa. As I stood there, I did not know how I would ever manage to go on without him, but I learned to allow myself to feel the pain of my loss and let the tears flow. As the tears streamed down my face I was grateful to have a team with me – people who knew what I had been through. They came and held me and allowed me to weep.

Coming back to this wonderful place, with all the memories it held of Martin, was a good yet very difficult experience. It was good to be back with my mission friends and community. Many people came to my house to pay their condolences and they shared with me that they had danced and mourned for Martin when he died. They asked me if I was pregnant, and I said no. They then asked me if Martin had any brothers. I told them no. They were very sad and I asked why. They explained that in their culture if someone dies the brother takes the widow as his wife to bear children in his brother's name. These women were sad because they felt I had no hope of having children. With tears welling in my eyes I told them that Jesus knows my dreams and my heart and I trusted him to provide.

Through this experience of embracing the death of a loved one I could understand the Lopit people much more. We uttered no words but just looked into each others eyes, and we understood each other on a deeper level. When someone in the village died I joined the people in their mourning and I wept with them as I now knew what it was like to lose someone you love. When I was asked to share, I could tell them I knew part of their pain and that the only person who could carry them through the pain and comfort them was Jesus Christ. I know that Jesus carries my pain and that I am not alone.

"The Lord watches over the alien and sustains the fatherless and the widow" (Psalm 146:9).

If you would like to read more about Catherine's journey and what God continues to do in her life, go to www.cathonamission.com, or http://visionandaffections.wordpress.com.

Chapter 34 - Single again, after separation or divorce

Can someone who is separated or divorced serve in mission? If they do, what challenges might they face? **Dr Debbie Hawker** *explores these issues.*

When we have to tick a box to show our marital status, there is usually one box for "separated or divorced". Just one box, but every tick represents a very different story. We will consider divorce, but the same also applies to long-term separation.

Surveys in the UK and Australia found that 13-32% of single adults who attended church were separated or divorced.[101] Karen Carr's research in 2011 (reported in chapter 37) found that of single mission workers responding, 93% had never married, 2% were widowed, and 5% were divorced. So, while 13-32% of single people in the sending churches were separated or divorced, only 5% of mission workers were in that category[102]. Is this because divorced people are less likely to be accepted as mission workers?

That was certainly the case twenty years ago, when some mission agencies had a policy of not accepting anyone who was divorced. This was because divorce was strongly frowned upon in the cultures (and especially the churches) those organisations worked in. In many mission agencies, the policy has now changed, as opinion has changed. Now people realise that there may be acceptable reasons for divorce, and some divorced people have a lot to offer in ministry.

Moses wrote: "When the woman a man marries becomes displeasing to him because he finds something wrong with her, let him write her a certificate of divorce, give it to her, and send her out of his house" (Deuteronomy 24:1). Jesus did not speak so lightly about divorce, but even he allowed for divorce if a spouse was unfaithful (Matthew 19: 9). These days some Christians appear to be very judgemental of anyone who has been divorced. They do not regard them as suitable people to be in ministry.

Although we don't want to embrace easy divorce, neither should we assume that every divorced person has made an unacceptable decision. Take as an example John Wesley, co-founder of the Methodist movement. Wesley's wife Molly became jealous of women who wrote asking him for guidance. She wrote critical letters to him and spied on him. She sent his private papers directly to his enemies so that they would slander him. She even assaulted him. He sought reconciliation a number of times, but eventually Molly accused him publicly of adultery over a period of twenty years, and she left him. Wesley continued his fruitful ministry throughout this time. He wrote of Molly, "I did not forsake her, I did not dismiss her, I will not recall her".[103]

Wesley is not alone in having been abandoned by a spouse but still being fruitful in ministry. We know people in ministry who have separated or divorced for the following reasons:

1. Their spouse left them, although they didn't want this
2. Their spouse went off with a homosexual partner
3. Their spouse committed adultery
4. Their spouse was violent towards them, and put the children at risk

There are other cases where someone has become a Christian after their divorce, and wants to be involved in ministry. There are cases where the marriage has not worked for other reasons. We all make mistakes and get things wrong, and we all sin. Thankfully, God does not write us off because of this.

Some divorcees choose not to explain the reason for their divorce. It may feel too painful to talk about. Some feel foolish for having married someone who was unfaithful to them. For example, we know of several cross-cultural marriages where the husband committed adultery throughout the marriage and that was accepted as normal in his culture, even among Christians. The wife in each case did not wanted to tell people what happened, or to explain why she eventually separated from her husband. She blamed herself for not realising before the wedding, even though it was not her fault.

Mission workers who are single again after divorce can face some of the same challenges as other single people. They may struggle with sexual temptation (which can be stronger for people who have known sexual intimacy before). Like other single people they may struggle to find the best option for accommodation and holidays, and they may long to experience touch. They may experience loneliness (which can be even more intense after knowing the companionship of marriage).

Divorced people may also face additional challenges. They may receive less respect from colleagues because they are divorced. Nationals may view them as untrustworthy, sinful or cursed. They are less likely to be given leadership roles. Some friends may have taken sides with their former partner and no longer have contact with them, which can leave a sense of loss. Other friends may try to stay neutral to both sides, or not know what to say, which can dilute the friendship.

Family life can be complicated, especially if they have children. It can be difficult to raise children as a single parent (especially when busy). It is also difficult to share children with an estranged partner. Some divorcees remain in touch with their in-laws, while others do not. Some divorcees remain friends with their former spouse, while others do not. Some go on to remarry, which can bring joys and challenges.[104]

Some divorcees have strong feelings towards their ex-partner, and about the divorce. Feelings may include immense grief and sadness over what has been lost, rejection, betrayal, guilt, self-blame for not being able to save the marriage, confusion about why this has happened, anger, and depression. The intensity of feelings may fall and then rise again at times, for example if they discover their "ex" is in a new relationship. Many feel that divorce is a stigma, and that other people will judge them because of it. Will people see them just as a divorcee, and dismiss their gifts, experience, character and personality?

Those who have been through divorce may need to grieve the loss of the partner and the marriage which they had hoped for. They need to forgive and move on. They may have lost friends, family members, a home, shared possessions and money as well as their own reputation. Other people might look down on them, but the important thing is God's opinion. God sees the heart, and understands.

God can use divorced people. In the Bible we see plenty of people who "had a past" but were still used by God. King David committed adultery and arranged a murder, but when he repented God used him mightily, and Jesus was one of his descendants. When Jesus was brought a woman who had been caught in adultery, he said "If any of you is without sin, let him be the first to throw a stone at her" (John 8: 7). Jesus also said, "Do not judge, or you too will be judged" (Matthew 7:1).

Jesus once met a Samaritan woman who had been married five times, and was living with a man she wasn't married to (John 4: 4-26). Jesus spoke to her, although a man would not usually speak to a woman in that culture, especially not a Samaritan woman. He offered her "living water". He did not condemn her. She then went and told the rest of her town. This divorced woman became the first evangelist to the Samaritan people. "Many of the Samaritans from that town believed in [Jesus] because of the woman's testimony… and because of his words many more became believers" (John 4:39, 41). Jesus can use people whose marriages have not been a success.

Divorcees who feel called by God to ministry should feel free to put themselves forward as mission candidates, choosing an organisation and a church willing to take them seriously. If they are not selected, they should be given clear reasons why, so they know whether it is because they are divorced or for other reasons.

Let us not judge people who are divorced. They too may have a useful role in ministry.

> If you get rid of unfair practices,
> quit blaming victims,
> quit gossiping about other people's sins,
> If you are generous with the hungry
> and start giving yourself to the down-and-out,
> Your lives will begin to glow in the darkness,

your shadowed lives will be bathed in sunlight.
I will always show you where to go.
I'll give you a full life in the emptiest of places –
firm muscles, strong bones.
You'll be like a well-watered garden,
A gurgling spring that never runs dry.
You'll use the old rubble of past lives to build anew,
rebuild the foundations from out of your past.
You'll be known as those who can fix anything,
restore old ruins, rebuild and renovate,
make the community livable again.

(Isaiah 58: 10-12, MSG, italics added).

If you have been divorced, or you know someone who has, and you want more help with the issues involved, you might benefit from reading one the following books:

- Retief, F. (2010) *Divorce*. Tain: Christian Focus.
- Smoke, J. (2007) *Growing through divorce*. Eugene, OR: Harvest House Publishers.
- Croly, J. (2004) *Missing being Mrs.* Oxford: Monarch Books

Part 4: What we know about single people in ministry

Chapter 35 - Cold comfort: What not to say to single mission workers

Alison Clarke holds a Masters in Mission Studies from All Nations Christian College. She is currently church planting in the south of Romania, as well as working with Romanian mission senders to develop the area of member care. During her 13 years in Romania she has noticed many unhelpful comments that well-meaning people have made about her singleness. She reflects on these comments.

Once upon a time there lived a wealthy man with a happy, healthy family and a successful business. Life was good. He was a genuinely nice person too: generous, hospitable, God-fearing. Then, without warning, his children were all killed in a freak accident and his business was destroyed by thieves. All in one day. He was understandably upset. To top it all, he got sick. After a while some friends came by to comfort him, but their words just made matters worse – to him it sounded more like judgment than encouragement.

I think you know the man's name: Job.

I don't for a moment claim that the suffering of being unmarried compares to the suffering of Job. But the lessons of Job apply. Neither Job nor his friends had read Chapter 1. They did not know what was really going on. Job's comforters did more harm than good because they were trying to find explanations for something they could not understand.

Some years ago I began keeping a list of things people have said to me by way of comfort or encouragement which actually left me feeling condemned. In some cases I clearly recall the context, in others I don't. Some are things that have been said to me many times over the years. All these statements were made by well-intentioned people – mostly mature Christians – who genuinely wanted to encourage me. If you are married and reading this, I hope it will give you some insight into how your kind sentiments might be interpreted when expressed in phrases which sound nice but are not well thought through. If you are single, I hope you will be encouraged that it's okay to feel what you feel even when it doesn't seem super-spiritual.

I'll give you the entire list of statements first, then group them together under headings to discuss why I found them at best unhelpful.

1. "God wants to teach you something first"
2. "God is perfecting you"
3. "God is preparing you"
4. "A good Father disciplines his children"
5. "I wish I had your freedom"
6. "God is sufficient for you"
7. "The Lord is your husband"
8. "You are so strong"
9. "Your standards are too high"
10. "You don't have enough faith"
11. "You need to be more pro-active"
12. "It will happen when you're not looking"
13. "Good things come to those who wait"
14. "God's timing is perfect"
15. "Wouldn't you rather wait than marry the wrong man?"
16. "One day you will look back on this time and thank God"
17. "Married people have problems too"
18. "Marriage isn't all good – we argue!"
19. "Marriage is hard work"
20. "Marriage has become an idol to you"
21. "When are you going to get married?"

A. **Being Prepared**

"God wants to teach you something first"

"God is perfecting you"

"God is preparing you"

"A good Father disciplines his children"

I can see where people are coming from when they say things like "God is preparing you" or "God wants to teach you something". They want to encourage you with the idea that marriage is a wonderful gift that will come to you one day, and that it will be all the better for the fact that God has spent years working on you, moulding you, transforming you. It does sound like a lovely thought... from where the speaker (usually married) is standing.

But for me, it comes across as criticism and judgment. What I understand when I hear these comments is that I am not yet good enough to be married. I haven't yet passed the test. I look at married people around me and wonder what on earth it is that they have learned but I am too stubborn to grasp, however hard God may be trying to teach me!

I have two issues with this way of explaining singleness: one is experiential, the other theological. Firstly, it simply does not ring true when we observe the world around us. There are a great many people who are unprepared for marriage when it comes. I think the majority of married people would include themselves in that category if they are honest. You do not have to pass a maturity test or an obedience-to-God test in order to get married.

It is true that the good and bad things you do have consequences which may impact on the likelihood of you finding a marriage partner. If you allow God to work on your character you will probably become more attractive to the opposite sex. On the other hand, if you are bitter about being single you may find that you become less attractive. However, there are no guarantees and there are plenty of exceptions.

Theologically speaking, I think this view ultimately confuses God with Santa Claus. It says that God makes good things happen to those who are good, and bad things happen to those who are bad:

> *You better watch out, you better not cry*
> *Better not pout, I'm telling you why*
> *Santa Claus is coming to town.*
> *He's making a list and checking it twice;*
> *Gonna find out who's naughty and nice*
> *Santa Claus is coming to town.*[105]

The conclusion is that if something good (in this case, marriage) is missing from your life, it must mean that you have done something bad – or at least failed to do something good. The root of this kind of thinking is a gospel of works: God will give me what I want if I do what he wants, and will punish me if I don't.

Thankfully we do not live by works but by grace. None of us deserves any of the good things the Lord pours into our lives. We have a love relationship with God which goes beyond the good and bad that happens. God is not a vending machine providing what you ask for if you insert the correct money. You cannot judge a person's walk with the Lord on the basis of whether or not they get what they want. In fact, this is exactly the kind of thinking that God rebukes in Job's comforters.

By the same token, God's discipline does not function this way. When the Lord disciplines me, I know exactly where I have erred. God points it out to me very clearly – painfully so. If I am unaware of what I have done wrong, I have to conclude that what I am experiencing is not the discipline of the Lord. If a parent disciplines a child without the child understanding what they did to deserve punishment, the discipline is meaningless – the child learns nothing.

Whatever the nature of the suffering we experience, God can turn it into an opportunity to build our character. The Lord has taught me much through the struggles of singleness. I believe it has made me a better listener, a better pastor and a better friend. It is true to say that God teaches us valuable lessons through all of life's experiences, but this is not the same as saying that God makes us endure difficult things in order to teach us a lesson.

B. Advantages of singleness
"I wish I had your freedom"

Some people try to put a sticking plaster on singleness by saying, "You should thank God for your freedom." Even if such remarks are true, they fail to comfort when they come from people who have never felt the suffering involved in the single mission life.

I am not going to argue with the idea that single people are 'freer' in that we don't have to structure our lives around school hours and bedtimes. I am very aware that this offers certain advantages in terms of the things we can and can't do. However, many of us would gladly swap this 'freedom' in an instant for the privilege (and the trials) of having a family.

My real gripe with this piece of encouragement is that the speaker is usually someone who married in their early twenties. They are thinking back to the freedom they had in their youth and imagining that it is only having a family that has forced responsibility and structure into their life. It isn't. It's growing up. Single people also have to deal with the responsibilities of life: paying the bills, getting repairs done, shopping, cleaning and running a car. If you are single, there's often nobody to share these tasks with.

In missions single people are frequently expected to work extra hours because they don't have the same responsibilities as families. I have single friends who never find time to shop, cook and clean because their married colleagues (usually married men whose wives run the home) assume that they have nothing to do besides work.

It is true, of course, that I do have more freedom than I would if I had a family. I can live where I like, move when I like, take a pay-cut – *anything!* I can make major life decisions when and how I like. Other people might be affected by what I choose to do, but they'll get over it. It won't change the direction of their lives. Ultimately my decisions only really impact on myself. For me the flip-side of this freedom is a deep sense of loneliness. People may counsel me and support me as I take big decisions, but the consequences will not affect them: my life's course is mine alone.

People who envy my freedom would not want this. What they want is a holiday: a week of not being woken up in the morning and not having to structure their lives around children. Then they would go back to their families refreshed.

Having said that I am free to take absolutely any course in life, I often find that singleness hinders me in my decision-making. When I am faced with something simple like booking flights or a conference six months in advance, I find myself wondering if I might meet someone between now and then who would change my plans! There have been times when every future plan made has been painful because it is a plan to be single when that time comes.

C. **Relationship with God**
   "God is sufficient for you"
   "The Lord is your husband"
   "You are so strong"

I understand what people mean when they say "God is your husband" and I completely agree that God is sufficient for me. I have certainly seen many older single people whose intimacy with the Lord is enviable. Then again, I have seen others who lack that, and I know plenty of married people who have a wonderful walk with God. Being single does not guarantee intimacy with God any more than being married excludes it. Single people can be left feeling condemned because they know their relationship with the Lord is no better than average, despite being told that they are single because God wants them all to himself.

My complaint here is that it seems rather insensitive to make such remarks when I am lonely or struggling to cope with life. I don't doubt that God is sufficient, but you wouldn't say that to someone who is starving. You'd give them bread. God *is* sufficient for our needs, but he usually meets them through people. To be blunt: even if the Lord is meeting my emotional needs, he doesn't change light-bulbs! Sometimes I need the companionship and practical help that only another human being can provide.

We were created for relationship: relationship with God *and* relationship with one another. God himself said that "It is not good for the man to be alone" (Genesis 2:18). I suspect that goes for women too. We are made to be in relationship with other people. Not just the kind of relationship you have with the local shopkeeper or even the people you are ministering to, but real, deep, intimate relationship. Many single people in missions lack this altogether.

We don't have to be super-spiritual and pretend that our relationship with God completely replaces human companionship and intimacy. Nobody condemns you for being hungry when you have not eaten, so nobody should condemn you for feeling the loneliness that comes when you are not truly known. Even if they do judge you, God will not. He understands the loneliness; it's okay to feel it.

D. Finding a mate

"Your standards are too high"
"You don't have enough faith"
"You need to be more pro-active"
"It will happen when you're not looking"

I love the idea that my standards might be too high. It conjures up the image of crowds of men trying to win my approval, while I turn them away one by one because of minor faults. I wish that were true, but it's not. I haven't exactly been overwhelmed by offers.

On the other hand, I have seen people lower their standards considerably. I understand why they did so (and I couldn't say for sure that I wouldn't have done the same in their place) but it does make marriage even more work than usual.

It amuses me when one person tells me I'm trying too hard and simply need to have 'faith', then the next tells me that I'm not trying hard enough and need to be more proactive. I figure that means I've got the balance about right.

I'm not sure how I'm supposed to demonstrate that I have 'faith'. Buy a wedding dress? Book a church? Faith is not evidenced by whether or not God answers your prayers, but by how you respond when he doesn't. Faith is when you keep on following and loving Jesus even though things are tough and he doesn't seem to be hearing your prayers. The Bible praises Abraham for his faith – that's Abraham who complained bitterly to God that a servant would be his heir (Genesis 15:2) and who then tried to fulfil God's promise by himself (Genesis 16).

The reality is that couples get together in thousands of different ways, both intentional and completely unexpected. There are no guarantees. I've come to the conclusion that the best thing to do is to get on with walking with Jesus and stay open to making friends with anyone I happen to meet along the way.

E. Waiting

"Good things come to those who wait"
"God's timing is perfect"
"Wouldn't you rather wait than marry the wrong man?"
"One day you will look back on this time and thank God"

"Good things come to those who wait" is one of those sayings heard so often that many Christians would be shocked to discover that it isn't in the Bible. The reason it isn't in the Bible is that it isn't true. Sometimes good things come very quickly and unexpectedly without any waiting; other times they never come at all. The Bible talks about people who waited all their lives and never saw the fulfilment of promises (Hebrews 11). God's perspective on history is much wider than ours.

"God's timing is perfect" is easy to say in hindsight. Was God's timing perfect when the Israelites entered the Promised Land after a delay of forty years? Those who entered the land might say yes, but those who died in the wilderness would probably disagree. I suspect that I could have said that "God's timing is perfect" had I married at any point in the last fifteen years – just as I might yet say it at any point in the next fifteen years. Looking back I can see good things that might not have happened had I been married, but I can also imagine good things that might have happened and didn't. To say that I would have preferred to have married in my twenties is not to say that I am not thankful, it is simply being honest. I am thankful for much that has happened in my life; I am even grateful for the lessons I have learned during the tough times.

To those people who ask whether I wouldn't rather wait than marry the wrong man, I point out that that is exactly what I am doing and have been doing. My waiting has never been intentional – I have never thought to myself, "No, I think I'll wait!" I don't even really think of myself as waiting; I am busy getting on with living my life. "Waiting" sounds like you are standing at a bus-stop – every so often a bus comes by and a few people get on, but it's never your bus![106] A single person's life doesn't have to be like that – we can lead a full and fulfilling life.

F. Marital Blues

"Married people have problems too"
"Marriage isn't all good – we argue!"
"Marriage is hard work"

It's worrying that people think you'd be encouraged by the thought that marriage isn't a fairy tale. I don't think I am the only single person who has observed enough marriages to have been undeceived on that point long ago. Most of us have also shared a home enough times to know that living with another person is always a challenge.

Somebody once told me, "We spent the first two years of our marriage trying not to kill each other." I retorted, "And I spent the last two years trying not to kill myself"! My point was that the struggles to work out who you are and what your role is in the world have more to do with your stage in life than with your marital status. If you are married as you deal with identity issues, you express what you're going through in arguments with one another. If you are single, you battle it out within yourself. At times I would have loved to have had somebody other than myself to argue with – you get a bit bored of your own arguments after a while.

Sometimes it's the debating (to use a more positive term) that goes on within a relationship that can lead to the best decisions. When there are contrasting points of view they must be examined to find the best way forward. In a marriage the relationship is (hopefully) more important than winning the argument, so a solution must be found that is acceptable to both parties. As a single person, I can choose to 'put up and shut up' for the time being, rather than addressing the issue. Or I can choose to walk away from the relationship.

No single person really believes that marriage will solve all their problems. The older you get, the more realistic you become on that point. I am well aware that married people can get sick, have financial worries and be victims of crime, and that such difficulties can be even harder to bear when you have children to care for. I don't think that being married makes life easy, but I know for sure that being single is not easy. The two options are simply differently difficult.

G. **Idols**
   "Marriage has become an idol to you"

While it's not a great thing to say by way of comfort, I think the person who said this to me had a point at the time. If you define an idol as the thing you think about most often, or the thing you seek in order to meet your emotional needs, then I would admit that there have been times when the dream of marriage was an idol in my life.

However, I don't think that feeling the need for something you lack necessarily means that that thing has become an idol. If an unemployed person is desperately hunting for work, you don't tell them that finding a job has become an idol.

As mission workers, we frequently hear the accepted teaching that our priorities should be God first, family second, ministry next, self last. Married people are encouraged to put their relationship with their spouse and children before their ministry. But for a single person, to prioritise finding a mate is considered selfish. For a single mission worker the order is reduced to: God, ministry, self. Often this leads to overwork and burnout, as well as a failure adequately to meet one's own personal needs such as rest, exercise, friendships, healthy food and fun. Many single mission workers feel that they shouldn't take the time for holidays, social events or even training courses, which would give them an opportunity to widen their circle of acquaintanceship among their single peers.

The root problem of the God-family-ministry-self doctrine is that it compartmentalises life. By putting God 'first', we often try to separate him off into the 'spiritual' segment of life, while in reality he should be at the centre of our family life and our ministry as well as everything else. The Lord does not want to be just one of the things we do, even if he's top of the list. Rather, he wants to be intimately involved in *all* that we do. That means that it is all right for a single person to invest time and money in activities that might help them meet a suitable life-partner, so long as these activities are part of their walk with the Lord, not tucked away in a separate compartment of life where we hope God won't notice.

H. Just plain unhelpful
"When are you going to get married?"

Then there are the people who keep asking, "When are you going to get married?" I always want to respond, "Erm, let me see… I have a free Saturday three weeks from now… would that suit you?" How am I supposed to tell you *when* I'm going to get married when I can't tell you *who* I'm going to marry?

These people seem to think that I am single simply because I haven't yet got round to getting married. I generally ask whom they suggest I marry. If they come up with a name (which usually they can't), I have to then point out that the fact that a person is single and of roughly the right age does not necessarily mean that we are suited in other ways. I am aware that marriage requires people to adapt to one another, but not to change beyond recognition.

This reminds me of the expression 'lifestyle choice' used by many politicians and journalists when talking of the increasing numbers of people living alone. In my experience, it is generally not the case that there is any 'choice' involved. Whether Christians or not, those who have made a conscious choice to remain single are in the minority. Most are simply waiting.

Finding the words

After so many pages of discouraging words, you may be left wondering what you *can* say to encourage people like me. I'm not sure that there are any words that can really help. As with so many types of suffering (illness, bereavement, barrenness, joblessness, etc.), words will never change the situation. However, there are actions and attitudes that can offer encouragement, strength and hope. The starting point is listening rather than speaking; hearing my heart rather than telling me what ought to be in it.

Some single people are struggling with being single; others have reached a place of contentment. Most oscillate between the two. Single people are individuals – we respond differently, struggle in different ways, and express ourselves differently. I am not the same as you were when you were single; I am not the same as that other single mission worker you know. Take the time to get to know me rather than making assumptions about me and you will go a long way toward helping me to flourish as an individual.

Single people are not defined by singleness and it is not the most important thing about us. We have interests, opinions, activities and dreams that are part of who we are, irrespective of whether or not we eventually marry. Our most pressing struggles may be entirely unrelated to singleness: ministry, team, elderly parents, finance or theology. When these are overlooked, we can be left feeling misunderstood and undervalued. Often in the missions world we are grouped together simply as 'singles' regardless of age, ministry involvement or field of service. We may have nothing in common besides our marital status. This has the effect of making singleness an issue even for those who are otherwise fulfilled and content.

What I want from those around me is not sympathy but to be treated as a whole person. I am not simply one half (and the lesser half at that) of some future partnership which may or may not materialise. I am a real person here and now, with real needs, hopes and fears and a real contribution to make in God's world. When it hurts, I don't need suggestions and advice; neither do I need to be told that I'm better off as I am. I just need a friend who will walk with me in my pain without judging and who will allow me to express what I feel without giving me trite answers to impossible questions. And someone to relax with, have some fun with, or share a meal with. Someone who might help out with the practical stuff I simply can't do alone. I need a friend, married or single, who sees beyond the category of 'single' to the person within, and who encourages that 'real me' to grow, blossom and thrive.

Chapter 36 - Isn't it better if single people stay home? How to respond to questions like this

Dr Jessie Ritchey has been a mission leader for four decades. She is based in Ecuador. She believes that one of the strengths of the Latin American mission movement is that generally the churches are directly involved in sending mission workers. The pastor's blessing and support are decisive factors in whether or not a mission worker is sent. Since so much of the decision-making power lies with the church leaders, Dr Ritchey believes it is important to address the spoken and unspoken concerns of pastors. She has encountered many pastors who question the wisdom of sending single women as mission workers. Here she and **Dr Debbie Hawker** *respond to their concerns.*

Shouldn't single people (especially women) stay home to care for relatives?

Within Latin America (and also Africa and Asia) the family is valued highly. We often perceive an unmarried adult as being a member of a larger family rather than as an individual in their own right. They are frequently identified as someone's daughter, son, uncle or aunt and are generally expected to live at home until married. It is often expected that a single woman will be available to help look after nieces and nephews and take care of elderly parents, even though she may have a full time job.

It is good to value the family, but this does not mean that single people should never serve in a different culture. Parents might not need assistance, or siblings might be able to provide all the care that is needed. A single person may be free to serve for many years (with the support of their family) before they are needed at home, if they are needed at all. These days, if there is an urgent need, it is often possible to fly home within a day. It is possible to honour the family and also follow God's call to serve far from home.

Don't single people lack the maturity needed to serve in ministry?

We heard about a mission team whose members were aged between 18 and 35 and who were all single. A church leader said, "They are all good people. Have you got any adults on the team?" What he meant was "Have got any *married* people on your team?"

Because marriage is often seen as a rite of passage into adulthood, a single adult can find themselves living in an ambiguous state as there is no defined cultural way to determine when they have passed into adulthood. They may have the responsibilities of an adult without having the complete autonomy of an adult.[107] The age of majority (legal adulthood) varies around the world from 15 to 21, but if someone is over 21 they should certainly be treated as an adult, whether or not they are married. Marriage does not cause maturity – some single people are more mature than their married peers. We need to remember that Jesus was single, even though most Rabbis at the time were married. He proves that single people can have the maturity to be in ministry.

Aren't single people incomplete?
Even though a single person may be well-educated and have a well-established career, people often perceive them as incomplete because they are not married. Many women feel the pressure to marry simply to escape this perception.

There is a pervasive myth in many cultures that marriage is the ideal state, and that we all have a 'soul mate' somewhere in the world who is 'the one', made for me and me alone. I am incomplete until I find my other half. This goes back to Greek mythology, which states that humans originally had four arms, four legs, and a single head made of two faces. The myth states that Zeus split each person in half, condemning us to spend our lives looking for our lost soul mate or else to feel forever that something is missing.

This myth has found its way into Christian culture in the belief that "God will lead you to the only person who is intended for you." In reality, this is not a Biblical injunction (although it is easy to convince ourselves about a few Biblical examples). We are not incomplete if we don't have 'another half'. We are complete in God. We don't need to believe the Greek myth.

Shouldn't single people concentrate on having a child?
Some people think the status of a single person will rise to 'an adult to be taken seriously' if they become a parent. Many single women have chosen to become pregnant in part for this reason as well as to experience being a mother and having someone to care for them as they age. Various single women have received suggestions from people in their sending churches to marry a local and have a child or simply have a

child without getting married in obtain a network of security. This external pressure is layered upon their own internal desires.

Becoming a single parent is not the answer for a Christian. Above and beyond their desire for marriage and parenthood, single mission workers want to be obedient to God's call on their lives even if it means remaining childless. They realize that they have been given one life and they want to invest it wisely and obediently.

Jesus did not become a parent, and we do not have to either. We can concentrate on raising spiritual children instead.

Isn't it better to wait until singles marry or at least until they gain experience?

Single women have historically had a difficult time being allowed to obey God's call upon their lives. In the early days of mission from North America, single women were often only allowed to go to the mission field if they accompanied a couple or went to care for missionary children. Early single women missionaries went to serve as maids to the missionary couples they accompanied.[108]

Single people today can still face difficulties in being accepted for mission. As I (Jessie) train candidates across Latin America and converse with young women who have a strong sense of God's call on their lives, they tell me of the frustration of hearing over and over again from pastors, "Not yet, you need to be married before we can send you out" or "Who will take care of you? I can't be responsible for sending you out single." Others tell of being required to have ministerial experience before going out, yet not being given the opportunity to gain that experience in their churches because single women are not given leadership roles. This is quite a dilemma. Some of these women have been waiting for over ten years because God's call on their lives will not allow them to marry someone who does not have that same call, and pastors who will not send them if they are single.

Some people assume that every single person is just waiting for marriage. There is even a derogatory expression in Spanish, "Hay que encontrarle alquien para que le haga el favor" ("you need to find yourself someone who will do you the favour"), which is commonly used without thinking about its belittling connotations. Little time is taken for empathetic and realistic assessment of the many ways our society and even our churches communicate that singles are somehow of lesser value or should be sidelined from ministry due to their single status.

Perhaps one of the most public and insulting ways I have seen these attitudes played out is via frequent jokes on the part of pastors as they introduce single female speakers. Recently I was in a large meeting where the pastor introduced a mature and effective cross-cultural worker who is working in a strategic and dangerous location by asking the congregation to raise their hands if they knew of an available husband for her. There was the requisite loud laughter and then she was given the microphone and was expected to launch into sharing about her ministry right after experiencing the humiliation of a very disrespectful introduction. Many of our single cross-cultural workers have shared with me that they get tired of trying to laugh off these well-intentioned but very careless and hurtful remarks which generally come from men in leadership over them. The only relief comes when people finally decide that you are past a marriageable age and come to accept your singleness and leave the topic alone. Perhaps instead of waiting that long, we could begin to rethink some of our rhetoric about the single cross-cultural workers we interact with.

Many of our churches in Latin America (and Africa and Asia) have a historical link to single missionaries who left their homes to bring the Gospel to us and then stayed to disciple, mentor and cheer on the leaders they had trained. Pastors who are reluctant to send single women overseas tend to forget that the Señorita who taught them in seminary was a single woman who travelled here to serve. Without these single women, our churches would not exist in the way they do today.

History shows us that single people can be excellent leaders, and can serve in ministry. Once again, we can look at Jesus as one example.

Don't single mission workers face too many challenges?
There are undoubtedly challenges to serving in cross-cultural ministry. However, challenges should not be deterrents. Rather, we need to be informed about them and discover ways of facing them.

One study of workers from the Ibero American mission movement, found that the biggest challenge reported by singles was solitude or loneliness (37%), followed by gender discrimination (24%), occasional feelings of depression (23%) and harassment (16%). 76% of the workers indicated that their agencies have a preference for married leaders.[109]

Single mission workers at times feel that they are not given freedom to express their opinions and may not be considered fully-fledged adults within a team of married couples. It is interesting to see that some of the attitudes they faced in their home country follow them as they work with Latino team members within another context as well. Single people should be included in decisions.

Many cross-cultural workers find themselves serving on international teams. Team interaction is usually not in their first language, and often takes on the communication and cultural patterns of the majority. Team meetings and group worship times may require a great deal of energy and concentration rather than functioning as a relaxing oasis where they are refuelled. It helps if people are aware of this, and support them.

The ministerial options and effectiveness of the single person depend greatly on the support of the team. Team members might be able to help with logistical hassles, and provide protection when a woman needs to travel or be alone at night.

There is always the danger that some may look at the list of challenges and use them as arguments against sending single people (especially women) to serve in mission. However, I would argue that we should use the understanding that we have gained to help in the preparation and care of the workers that we send out. When we are aware of the challenges, we can take steps to deal with them. It is hoped that the ideas in this book (especially chapter 40) will provide help in dealing with these challenges. We all face challenges in life, and that is not a reason to deny single people the opportunity to serve as mission workers. It is a reason to try to understand and support them as much as possible.

Is singleness ever an advantage in mission?
There are many benefits of singleness for mission workers (see chapter 40). Single workers often have more time to study, travel, visit, seek God and be involved with ministry, and more flexible schedules. They often become accepted as members of local families, and have the opportunity to experience the benefits of extended immersion.

It is not our aim to argue that single people are better cross-cultural workers than married couples. However, it is our aim to stimulate thinking about the assumptions currently in place which prevent single believers from using their spiritual gifts and dedicating their lives to cross-cultural service. The task of the great commission is large, and workers are few. There are not enough married couples volunteering for the task. It is poor stewardship to allow unexamined customs and prejudices to impede us from investing the resources, gifts and lives we have been given. We should send single people as well as married couples.

The track record of the single people that we have sent as mission workers has shown that they are creative and effective in forming friendships, establishing trust, contributing positively to the community and sharing their faith in the midst of it. They are generally very hard workers with a strong network of relationships that greatly strengthen the impact of ministry teams.

Sometimes the prejudices single people (especially women) deal with become a positive tool in God's economy. Single women may seem unthreatening. In many ways these sisters can 'fly under the radar', and be used mightily in the process. However, it is important that they do not fly under the radar within our churches. We should affirm and respect them.

Conclusion
Jesus said we should open our eyes, look at the fields, and see that the harvest is plentiful but the workers are few (Matthew 9:37). Why would anyone look at the huge harvest and the tiny workforce trying to gather it in and seek to eliminate any workers whom God would call? [110]

Single men and women are no more incomplete or immature than the rest of us. They can be hugely effective in cross-cultural ministry. We should respect them, and seek to help prepare and support them for the work God has called them to.

Chapter 37 - Understanding and enhancing the resilience of single mission personnel: Learning from over 800 workers

Dr Nancy Crawford *has served for over 25 years with AIM International (formerly Africa Inland Mission), first as a teacher and counsellor at Rift Valley Academy, then as a clinical psychologist at Tumaini Counselling Centre in Nairobi, and now helping to facilitate students' involvement in cross-cultural ministry.* **Dr. Karen Carr** *lives in Ghana, serving on the Mobile Member Care Team as Clinical Director. She and her team are engaged in a community-based model that is focused on building the member care competencies of mission personnel, developing community relationships, and enhancing the resilience and health of God's servants. Karen has lived in community in West Africa since 2000 with her teammates. She is originally from Virginia, USA where she trained as a clinical psychologist. Nancy and Karen are both single, and conducted research on the resilience of single mission personnel.*

In 2011 over 800 mission workers from 26 passport countries (across six continents) working in 73 different countries completed a confidential questionnaire on resilience and marital status. The primary requirement for participation was that the person was currently living and working in a country different from their passport country. Both single and married mission workers recorded factors which contributed to or reduced their resilience. They completed the *Self care and lifestyle balance inventory*,[111] and also answered a combination of other rating scales and narrative questions (which means that both statistics and narrative themes can be reported below). Full details of the research methodology are available elsewhere.[112] Forty percent of the participants were single; 60% were married. More women than men participated in the survey (70% vs 30%). 91% of the singles were women (reflecting the proportion of single mission workers who are women).[113]

The majority of the singles were content in being single (67%), had the emotional support of family (67%), were part of a loving community (67%), had a close friend who speaks the truth in their lives (76%), and felt they were resilient (84%). These percentages were linked to a dominant theme for both married and singles when asked what contributed most to resilience: having close, supportive relationships.

While both the single and the married mission workers reported a high level of resilience, the self-reported resilience of the married mission workers was slightly higher than that of the singles.[114] In a related finding, 80% of the married mission workers indicated that marriage made it easier to be resilient, while in contrast only 30% of the singles indicated that singleness made it easier to be resilient (and 40% felt that singleness had a negative effect on their resilience).

By far the most frequent reason given by the married mission personnel for their resilience was the consistent companionship and emotional support of their spouse. Many of the married workers wrote that it wasn't marriage *per se* that helped their resilience but rather it was the support of their particular spouse that helped. A representative quote was,

> Marital status by itself does not impact resilience as much as with whom I am married. In other words, my wife is a huge factor in resilience for me.

Likewise, when married respondents indicated that their marriage had a negative effect on their resilience it was because of distress in their marital relationship. As one participant wrote, the effect of marital status on resilience was,

> Negative or positive depending on the season of our marriage. Unresolved conflict/struggles can bring extra stress. There have been times when I have wondered if we should be on the field or if we could survive.

> However, when our marriage is working well, it strengthens my resilience.

Lack of readily available companionship and their host cultures' view of women were the two most cited reasons single people found singleness difficult as a mission worker. As one single woman wrote,

> Being single does make it more difficult to be resilient. The culture I have been in is patriarchal. It is difficult to do things alone, and without the protection of a man, a lot of the times that does wear one down.

Additionally more singles than married respondents indicated that they were likely to be discriminated against because of their marital status. In response to the question about how you (as a single) are viewed by your married colleagues, there were a significant number of comments that indicated that the singles sometimes felt treated as inferior, incomplete, less mature, less adult, to be pitied, or to be matched up.

Although married workers were more likely to have emotional support from family members and be part of a loving community, single respondents were more likely to have a close friend who spoke truth into their lives and to have their self-worth not related to their marital status. The primary ways that singles indicated that their singleness contributed to their resilience were having the freedom to engage in meaningful relationships, in ministry, and to attend to their personal relationship with God. Many singles also mentioned how their singleness helped develop their independence and competence in areas they never expected.

When responding to the question of what contributes most to resilience, a theme that came up more often for singles than married people was a sense of God's call or knowing they were exactly where God wanted them to be. For singles, a personal call or passion is what led them to serve in mission and to persevere through difficult circumstances. This was also true for many married people. However, some married women are in cross-cultural service because of their husband's call.

An earlier study on female mission workers demonstrated that there was a difference in the level of well-being between those who perceive that they are mission employees as opposed to trailing spouses. Women who perceived themselves as mission employees reported lower levels of depression and higher levels of overall well-being than those who perceived that they were in missions because of their husband's employment.[115] Single workers are never trailing spouses!

The theme of the importance of a sense of God's call on and active presence in their lives was also apparent from a noteworthy minority of both singles (15%) and married people (6%) who stated that their resilience was totally dependent on God alone and not related to their marital status. Many of the respondents who viewed their singleness positively mentioned how singleness enhanced a closer, more dependent relationship with God. As one widow wrote, "I imagine I'd feel stronger with a 'help meet' [116] (at least for meeting the daily crises). Yet not having a human 'help meet' presses me to lean more on God." A married mission worker wrote that the effect of her marital status on her resilience was,

> None whatsoever. In fact, the extra toll of caring for a family takes the time away from my being able to spend ample time in the Word and in prayer or with a friend… For me, resilience isn't in having a husband. It is in dwelling in the place (God's presence) that gives you the strength of resilience you need.

Interestingly, what singles enjoyed the most was what married people missed the most, and the reverse was also true. Singles enjoyed freedom and independence and married people missed these. Married people enjoyed having someone to share their lives with and companionship, and single people missed this.

The benefits of freedom and independence were expressed by one participant as, "I am able to make decisions about what I will do, where I will go, and when I will do it without having to consider the needs of a spouse." Another aspect of being independent was, "I think it helps, as I can adapt to the situation, without added stress of a spouse who may be having difficulties." And as one divorced mission worker wrote, "Being single allows me to travel freely without the concern of whether my spouse wants to go too."

Unique perspectives were offered by those who were widowed, divorced, or had served as a single mission worker for a significant amount of time before they married. As one divorced individual wrote, "There are times I wish that I had an intimate partner, but I know too well how difficult marriage is. This keeps me in reality." To quote a widow, "I have experienced both – marriage, and single (or widowed – which is probably different) – in either, I believe the most important thing is still one's relationship with the Lord – either status has its challenges." Someone else who had experienced both singleness and marriage as a mission worker wrote, "Each has pros and cons. Being married is more comfortable, easier, I have more immediate support. But being single I felt my ministry was more effective – I had much more time to offer people."

A divorced mission worker wrote, "I am a team player so being divorced has taken a hit on my resilience in one sense, but I have been compelled to find and develop a new direction." This perspective echoed a dominant theme for many singles, a perspective akin to "what doesn't kill you makes you stronger." Two representative comments were, "Have to be more resilient since I'm single and living alone so I must keep going," and "Singleness improves resilience (out of necessity)."

Several married and single respondents referenced life stages as a factor in the relationship between their marital status and resilience. The importance of life stages was also found in a study which measured cross-cultural adjustment stress.[117] Significant differences were found in levels of cross-cultural adjustment stress when married and single cross-cultural workers were compared by age categories. In their twenties, late thirties and forties married cross-cultural workers had higher stress scores on the CernySmith Assessments (CSA)[118] than did singles. The increased stress of married workers may be due to feeling responsible for the well-being of spouse and children, especially at the critical stages of their children's development. In their early thirties and early fifties single cross-cultural workers had higher stress scores on the CSA than did married workers. In their early thirties, the additional stress for singles may be due to having reached an age where as a single, they are now a minority. In their early fifties, the additional stress for singles may be due to grieving the possibility of bearing children.

Notably, from ages 56-65 the reported cross-cultural adjustment of married and single cross-cultural workers was the same. One participant's journey through her life stages looked like this: "Singleness as the opposite of my dreams undermined resilience until about the time I turned 50, when I had menopause well behind me and began to realize that I am valuable even apart from my marital status, because I was able to make a contribution and be respected through the work I do."

Overall, workers felt their singleness had the most negative effect on their resilience during transitions. Two representative comments on this dynamic were, "One of the hardest times to be resilient as a single is during transition especially when your friends or support system leave or go on furlough and when you change locations or go on furlough and don't really have anyone who understands your situation," and "Being single does make it tough in some situations – especially, having recently moved to a new city, having to build relationships again from the beginning. Not having one life companion is hard then."

Several of the single participants noted they had to be very intentional to do the things they know build resilience: building community, taking vacations, taking a day off, exercise, etc. As one single participant said,

> Resilience can also come from a good balance in life/play/ministry and sometimes this is hard to achieve when you are single. I find that I'm very focused on work and therefore I don't get those times to replenish my batteries to ensure that I am resilient when it is needed.

In conclusion, this study of resilience and marital status found that while both married and single mission workers perceived themselves as resilient, married workers' perceptions of self-resilience were slightly higher. Six of the study's primary themes are: companionship increases resilience; marital stresses decrease resilience; more than marital status, resilience is ultimately related to the individual and the status of their supportive relationships; transitions are particularly vulnerable times for singles; singles may have to work more intentionally at resilience-building activities, and singleness can enhance resilience out of necessity.

The following quotes from one married and one single participant capture the above themes well:

> As a single missionary for my first term, and as a married missionary thereafter, my own experience, as it relates to resilience, has had both pros and cons related to marital status. Overall, however, I think I have had more resilience being married, due to the companionship of my husband and children. That's not to say our marriage or family is perfect, but we have the intimacy and support of each other, which enhances our resilience, which we did not have as a single missionaries. On the other hand, however, marriage and family come with additional responsibilities (and stress), which a single missionary does not have. So, in the end, resilience may be more a part of who a person is (or is meant to be), rather than a marital status.

> Being single continues to be something I wrestle with periodically – particularly at times when other stress factors are at play – e.g. in the middle of challenging transitions, Christmas and holidays and wondering who to holiday with etc. On the other hand having walked the single life as a cross-cultural missionary for so long I am used to *having* to deal with many things by myself,

travelling by myself etc., and so find myself more resilient than some of my married co-workers.

Additional themes not represented in these two quotes were the negative impact that discrimination by the host culture and colleagues had on singles' resilience, and the positive impact of greater freedom to minister and to build relationships with others and God.

Several implications can be drawn from these findings and our wider experience with the mission community. First of all, resilience might be enhanced if all mission personnel have periodic check-ins (perhaps with someone from their church or agency, or a member care provider) where they discuss how they are doing and what support they need in areas such as:

- Current sense of call
- Relationship with the Lord
- Level of contentment
- Identity in Christ (does self-esteem come from who they are in Christ or from what they do?)
- Friendships/community of believers
- Their family
- Need for any practical help
- Perceptions of discrimination or negative judgment
- Vacation plans
- Upcoming or current transitions

Secondly, while most single mission workers were content (67%), the level of contentment with their marital status was higher for married people than singles, and 33% of single mission workers were *not* content. Those who are not content might benefit from talking with friends, leaders or member care personnel, to help to identify and tackle the root of discontent. Some questions to consider are: Is there any fear, hurt or anger? How do they feel they are viewed by God and others? What is the foundation of their sense of acceptance and worth? What is the status of their relationships? How could they be further supported in any areas that are battered — relationship with the Lord, identity in Christ, relationship with family, relationship with friends, sense of call or satisfaction in their ministry? What changes should be made?

Finally, we can all encourage leaders and decision makers to take a fresh look at their policies and practices regarding housing, finances, retirement, home assignment expectations, leadership structure and decision making. Some questions for mission leaders to consider are: Is there anything that is making it harder for singles to do well on the field? Is there a subtle or not so subtle bias? Are they in any way considered second class members?

We close with words from one of the single participants: "I imagine that the freedom of singleness, coupled with a strong sense of belonging on my team, has enabled me to remain longer in cross-cultural ministry."

Chapter 38 - Singularly significant: The value of single people in ministry

*Some single mission workers are overlooked and do not feel valued. They are less likely to be given leadership responsibility than their married colleagues. Even those who play a major role overseas may be sidelined when they return home, especially single women. They are sometimes regarded as less mature than married people (see chapter 36). In this chapter **Dr Debbie Hawker** affirms the value of single people in mission.*

Single people have been the bedrock of the modern mission movement. They include such pioneers as Gladys Aylward, Amy Carmichael, Mary Slessor, Corrie ten Boom, Mother Teresa, Helen Roseveare and Jackie Pullinger (who has been single for most of her ministry). Among the notable single men in mission are David Brainerd (American missionary to the native Americans), Sadhu Sundar Singh (Indian missionary), Robert Murray McCheyne (mission to the Jews) and John Stott (who preached worldwide). There are thousands of less well known single mission personnel whose lives have had an eternal impact. They are greatly valued by God and by those they have worked among.

The Bible clearly shows that God values those who are single, and can use them in ministry. Jesus was single, and no ministry comes near to being as significant as his. At that time single people were regarded as odd and treated with little respect, so it is remarkable that God chose for his Son to be single. Jesus chose some single friends, such as Mary, Martha and Lazarus.

The apostle Paul, another single mission worker, wrote,

> It is good for a man [we could add "or woman"] not to marry… Now to the unmarried and the widows I say: It is good for them to stay unmarried, as I am… I would like you to be free from concern. An unmarried man is concerned about the Lord's affairs – how he can please

the Lord. But a married man is concerned about the affairs of this world – how he can please his wife – and his interests are divided. An unmarried woman or virgin is concerned about the Lord's affairs: her aim is to be devoted to the Lord in both body and spirit. But a married woman is concerned about the affairs of this world – how she can please her husband. I am saying this for your own good, not to restrict you, but that you might live in a right way in undivided devotion to the Lord. (1 Corinthians 7: 1; 8; 32-35)

Related to this passage, Rob Bell (2007) states,

It's not just that you're fine single. The premise of the Scriptures is that you are able to connect with God and serve God in ways that those who are married can't. The tilt is *towards* being single, not away from it. [119]

God considered an Ethiopian eunuch (a single man) so valuable that he sent Philip to the him, so that Philip could explain the scriptures to the eunuch, tell him about Jesus, and baptise him (Acts 8:26-39). Tradition tells us that it was the eunuch who then brought the gospel to Ethiopia.

God told Jeremiah not to marry (Jeremiah 16:2), so that his life of singleness could be a prophetic statement. It is likely that John the Baptist, Elijah, and Daniel were also single. Ezekiel, Ruth and Naomi were widowed. Many Bible passages teach us that God cares about those who have been widowed.

It is remarkable that a significant part of the New Testament was written or spoken by single men, even though most men (and certainly leaders) at the time were married.[120] Single people can sometimes achieve things which married people cannot, as Richard Foster observed:

A single person can venture into forms of simplicity that are closed to the rest of us. By word and deed the

> Church should encourage these faithful servants of Christ. They should never be looked down upon or viewed as somehow odd. We should do all that we can to be with those who have chosen the single life, because they need our friendship and we need their wisdom... The life of St Francis gives us a healthy model of celibacy... To be quite blunt about it, celibacy is necessary for some forms of simplicity. Francis could not have done what he did if he had not been single. Nor could Jesus... The single person can concentrate with abandon on the advancement of the Kingdom of God. [121]

God's original blessing on Adam and Eve, coupled with the commandment to "Go forth and multiply" (Genesis 1:28) is sometimes mistakenly understood to imply that marriage and parenting are necessary to be obedient to God and receive blessing. In his book *Redeeming singleness: How the storytelling of Scripture affirms the single life,*[122] Barry Danylak points out that in the ancient biblical world people had little concept of an afterlife, so they 'lived on' in the memories of their descendants, and in the land which they passed on. In this context it became important to them to marry and have children. However, the prophets started to refocus this, and Isaiah in particular (56:4-5) promises the childless (eunuchs) who are obedient an even better inheritance than having descendants, and a perpetual memorial.

In the New Testament we find Jesus promising a reward to those who have given up family to serve him (Matthew 19:29). Danylak reminds us that the Old Testament mandate to "Go forth and multiply" is not repeated in the New Testament, where the mandate becomes "Go and make disciples of all nations" (Matthew 28:19). In a world full of people who do not yet know God, the imperative to increase the size of *his* family takes precedence over creating our own.

Church history demonstrates the value of single (and childless) people. Hsu observes, "In the early church, singleness was viewed as a truly freeing and liberating opportunity." [123] Over the centuries many monks, nuns and priests have taken a vow of celibacy, and committed themselves whole-heartedly to serving God. The majority of the well-known saints were single. For further reports of remarkable single people, see *A Singular Devotion: 366 Portraits of Singles Who Have Changed the World*.[124]

Pope John Paul II reflected,

> In virginity or celibacy, the human being is awaiting, also in a bodily way, the eschatological marriage of Christ with the Church... The celibate person thus anticipates in his or her flesh the new world of the future resurrection... Virginity or celibacy, by liberating the human heart in a unique way, 'so as to make it burn with greater love for God and all humanity,' bears witness that the Kingdom of God and His justice is that pearl of great price which is preferred to every other value... It is for this reason that the Church, throughout her history, has always defended the superiority of this charism to that of marriage by reason of the wholly singular link which it has with the Kingdom of God. [125]

Single people have value because they are created by God and loved by him. Single people, as well as married people, should be considered for leadership roles and should not be overlooked. Singleness is of value, just as marriage is, in pointing towards our need for Christ, the true bridegroom. Neither position should be elevated above the other. Whether married or single, we are all of equal value.

Chapter 39 - Issues to consider prior to starting cross-cultural ministry (or changing team)

Dr Debbie Hawker lists some issues for single people to consider when choosing an organisation, location or team to serve in, and when preparing for cross-cultural ministry.

When someone is applying to serve in cross-cultural ministry, there are many issues to consider. How can they find a good fit with a suitable sending organisation, location and team? What preparation and training is necessary to help them be effective and resilient? General information on placement and preparation is available elsewhere.[126] In this chapter we focus on particular issues to consider when the applicant is single. We assume that everyone involved in the decision will be seeking God's guidance during the process.

Consider the following questions and preparation points:

Finding a suitable organisation to serve with
- Does the organisation show suitable support for single people, for example in terms of assisting with appropriate housing while serving and when on home assignment?
- Do they have a reasonable view of the finances needed by single people?
- Is there good member care for single people? Some agencies encourage supporters to send 'care packages' of gifts to families but forget that single people would appreciate these too.
- Is a sense of close community important to you? If so, does the organisation help foster this? [127]
- Is personal time encouraged, or does the organisation nurture a culture of over-work?
- Are retreats recommended and budgeted for?

Is the location appropriate?
- Is this a location where you can feel reasonably safe and supported (especially if you are a single woman living alone)?
- Are you likely to be harassed if you go out alone?
- What possibilities are there for friendships (with local people and expatriates)?
- Will there be someone who can assist if you need practical help?
- How would you feel in a culture with intense sexual challenges (such as prostitutes propositioning you, or adverts for pornography in public places)?

Is there a suitable team to serve in?
Some organisations send single people in pairs, and others ensure that singles are welcomed into healthy teams. It can be difficult being the only single person in a team, surrounded by families who are busy with their own children. It can be even harder to be placed where there is no team at all.
- What sort of team is available, and what opportunities will there be to form healthy friendships?
- What are the other team members like?
- Would your views be listened to, especially if you are a woman and the team is dominated by men (who might listen to their wives but not hear the views of single women)?
- Are there people around who would treat you like a family member, inviting you to share celebrations with them?
- Are there people who would offer protection and practical help if you needed it?

Are you happy with the living arrangements?
Some Christian agencies have a team house for all their personnel in the area. Men and women share the house. While this is considered acceptable by Christians in some cultures, in other cultures this is viewed as inappropriate. Try to find out what your living situation will be, and ensure that it is appropriate for you.
- What are the living arrangements, and do you feel comfortable with these?

- Will you be able to choose whether to share a house or to live alone?

Preparation: learning about the culture
- Learn about how men and women relate to each other
- Learn about the place of married and unmarried people
- Is the culture accepting of single people, or does it treat them as if there is something wrong with them?
- What are the expectations, assumptions, usual roles, and restrictions? How do you feel about these?
- Will you be free to travel alone as a single person, or will you need to be accompanied?
- What are the options for holidays?
- What cultural issues should you be aware of regarding dating (see chapter 30)?

Ken Williams wrote, "Be sure to discover the sexual cues and mores in that culture. As a man or a woman you need to know how to avoid signalling a 'come on' and how to show that you are not interested in having a sexual encounter. Learn what behaviours indicate sexual looseness, how to recognize sexual advances, and how to deal with them effectively." [128]

Preparation: self-awareness
- Have you received help for any issues which you have been struggling with such as depression, anxiety, eating disorders, addictions or pornography? (If you have been abused, see Appendix 4).
- How will you build strong relationships?
- What strategies do you have for dealing with loneliness? [129]
- How satisfied are you with being single? [130]
- What brings you joy, and what do you find difficult? Be aware that difficulties can be increased when working in a stressful environment far from home.
- Do you hope to marry at some point?
- How will you respond if you feel attracted to a local person where you are working?

- How will you resist sexual temptation? It can be harder when you feel lonely, isolated, stressed or longing to be loved because you are far from those who love you.
- To be effective and avoid burnout it is important that you have time off to listen to God, rest and relax. Will you be supported in doing this?
- What will you do to relax? Pack any equipment you might need (e.g. to exercise or play music or games).
- Consider asking friends to send you DVDs or reading materials.
- Will you wear a ring so that strangers assume you are married?
- Do you have an accountability person who can ask how you are doing, and who you feel able to be honest with?
- Do you have enough support (prayer, emotional, practical and financial)?
- Consider putting filters on computers to screen out harmful sites.

As part of your preparation, we recommend reading the following chapter which lists common challenges faced by single people in missions, and possible responses.

Chapter 40 - Conclusion: Responding to the challenges and reaping the benefits of being a single person in ministry

*This concluding chapter by **Drs Debbie and David Hawker** lists ten challenges to being a single person in ministry with responses to each, and also some benefits.*

What do you think are the top ten challenges faced by single mission workers, and what might help in response to these? We will present our list later in this chapter. You might have noticed from the previous chapters that across different cultures, ages and genders some similar themes emerge, as well as some differences.

A poll of 1039 single people in Britain found that 56% of single women were very happy with their lives as they were and had no desire to be married. 46% of single men felt the same. Almost half of single men questioned said the biggest downside of living alone was a lack of sex. For women, the biggest concern was that people always assumed they wanted to be in a relationship.[131]

When considering what to include in this book, we sent an email out through the Global Member Care Network, asking single mission personnel around the world what they would like us to cover. We also asked what they have found helpful, and what suggestions they would like to offer other singles involved in mission. This chapter is based on their responses. We list the ten main challenges reported by single mission personnel who responded. Unsurprisingly, most respondents were women, so this list does not include some of the challenges which apply mainly to men (such as the suspicion of single men, discussed in chapters 7 and 20).

Just listing challenges seems somewhat negative, so alongside the challenges we have offered possible responses, based on ideas that other people have found useful. These are not the only options. You may find better alternatives. We offer these humbly as a starting point from ideas that other single mission personnel have found helpful.

If you support people who are single, you might get some ideas from these pages about issues you could talk to them about. Don't assume that any of the challenges listed here, or the responses, will necessarily be relevant for a particular person. Everyone is different. Listen to people as individuals, and ask what the challenges are for *them*. Their challenges might or might not be the same as those listed here. Often people want to be listened to and understood. But they don't want you to offer them a quick fix.

Some single people don't struggle with any of these issues. We don't want to give the impression that singleness is a problem to be solved. We hope the preceding chapters show that single people can be happy and fulfilled. However, just as married couples face some challenges, so can single people. Marriage books tend to focus on how to improve a marriage, and this chapter focuses on ideas for improving the experience of singleness. We begin with what appears to be the biggest challenge for many people, and so this is the one we have the most to say about.

Challenge 1: Loneliness, or wanting to be someone's 'special person'
Living far from family and long-term friends can be especially difficult for single people. No-one nearby knows your history; at least couples have each other. There can be a deep sense of rootlessness, and the loneliness of the long-distance worker. There may be limited opportunities for developing friendships, due to location, lack of time, and frequent moves for you and your friends. Frequent mobility leads some to stop trying to invest in friendships, as it seems too painful to keep saying goodbye. There can be an intense longing for a partner to share all of life with, and be appreciated by. Being on your own is especially hard during times of trouble such as danger, illness, bereavement, sorrow, stress or conflict, with no partner to stand with you. Questions about faith can arise when confronting different religions, suffering and injustice. It is difficult when there is no-one to share these questions with.

Response:
Three aspects to consider are increasing intimacy, building community, and finding ways to cope with the loneliness itself.

Increasing intimacy (deep relationships): We all need intimacy. There are different dimensions of intimacy, including spiritual intimacy, friendships, family and colleagues. Married couples are advised to prioritise time for each other. In a similar way, *single people are advised to prioritise time with their friends, forming deep, rich relationships.* It is good to make time for friendships (see Genesis 2:18). Don't feel guilty about saying no to requests in order to spend time with friends. Do you find it helpful to use technology (e.g. the internet, or the phone) to maintain contact with friends and family members? Or does reading about friends on social networking sites add to the pain, as you are faced with a constant barrage of information about how other people are enjoying themselves? Find out what works best for you. People are worth investing in even if you will need to say goodbye to them sooner than you would like. You may be able to stay in touch, and perhaps even meet again.

Are there people from home that you want to visit, or to invite to visit you? Could you travel home (or to see friends elsewhere) more frequently if that helps you be effective in the long-term? Your travel costs are less expensive than those of a couple or family, so maybe your supporters can contribute extra so that you can travel more often. You might find it helpful to list the people who are currently in your life (friends, family, colleagues and acquaintances). Which relationships do you want to invest more in and how can you do this? Do you want to make new friends and how could you do that?

Friendships with local people can be deeply rewarding. It is often helpful to also have contact with other expatriates, even if they are not Christians, because they might understand your culture, language and the transition which you are going through.

Building community (sense of belonging): Psychological research suggests that human need is not so much for one partner as a need to belong, which could be satisfied in various ways.[132]

Throughout church history, single people have lived as part of communities (such as monasteries and convents). The community benefits from each single person, and the single person benefits from being part of a community where they can find support and friendship. We all want to belong. Many of us express this longing through collecting 'friends' on Facebook or other online communities. There are many forms of community, such as extended family, friends, church, colleagues, village, or a group who share an interest. Conferences, seminars and retreats can help establish connections with other people who are doing similar work. Consider the pros and cons of developing a community on-line.

Karen Carr[133] offers the following suggestions for intentionally building a supportive community with team members, colleagues or friends.

Attitudes
- Yielding my preference for the sake of another
- Sharing concern for each other
- Generosity
- Inclusiveness
- Speaking the truth with grace

Practices
- Prayer (both planned and spontaneous)
- Regular time to refocus time and review: What went well? What didn't go well? What do I want? What do I need (for the coming week)?
- Having fun: laugh and play together
- Care for those who are unwell
- Touch (if appropriate) e.g. hugs or handshakes
- Service: helping each other with practical things

- Acts of kindness
- Reading Scripture together
- Farewell and welcome: e.g. songs of blessing when someone leaves or returns
- Spending vacation together (if wanted)
- Exercising together
- Forgiveness
- Hospitality

Handling loneliness: It is understandable that single people can have an intense desire to have someone who is willing to, as is said in a traditional marriage ceremony, "forsaking all others, be faithful to you as long as you both shall live." There is nothing wrong with desiring this. But marriage is not a perfect answer to loneliness. It is possible to be lonely in a marriage too. Some mission couples spend much of their time separated, with one of them travelling for months at a time. Couples can go separate ways in their thoughts, work and beliefs, or have little time to share with each other. Don't assume that marriage is the only answer to loneliness.

Ruth Ann Graybill writes:

> In contrast to married women, a single woman does not arrive on the mission field with a 'built-in' companion or an already established support system. Rather, she goes as a unit of one. She has no guaranteed intimate partner, no primary committed person with whom to share her joys and sorrows, with whom to build a future. She enters the mission field alone, likely with no one there knowing or sharing her history. Over time, this sense of 'going it alone' can lead to a real feeling of isolation and loneliness if good, solid relationships are not eventually established.[134]

The same could be said of single men. Graybill continues,

> Recognize that loneliness is not caused by isolation or singleness per se, but by the mindset that says, "Someone ought to be here." Loneliness has been described as being alone with one's self while solitude is being alone with God. Loneliness is simply part of the human experience and is part of what drives us to a deeper relationship with God and other people. Ask God to teach you how to spend time with Him as a friend. Remember that you always have the freedom to choose your own attitude.

We don't have an innate *right* to be married. Jesus wasn't married, so why should we expect to have more than our Master? We might or might not find someone to marry. Either way we can make the best of what we have at the moment. It can help if we stop comparing ourselves with those who have what we want, and instead compare ourselves with those who want what we have (i.e. people who are less well off than us). When we look to God to satisfy us, we can turn our attention to loving, trusting and serving him, and can find our fulfilment in him, whatever our situation.

Nearly everyone feels lonely at times. It is part of life. Yet it is possible to be alone and not feel lonely, instead enjoying solitude.

Father Keith Clark writes,

> Loneliness is not a problem, whereas attempts to avoid experiencing and looking at it have caused me some real problems... loneliness is a privilege experience because it prepares us for intimacy. [135]

Clark believes that it is important to name our feeling of loneliness, and to realise that it is okay to feel lonely. Prayer and intimacy with God can help us through the lonely times. Loneliness can move us to deeper intimacy with the Lord, as we share our feelings with him. Jesus understands. He too went to weddings without a partner. Moreover, Jesus knows what it is likely to feel totally alone and rejected. He was betrayed by friends, and cried out from the cross, "My God, my God, why have you forsaken me?" (Matthew 27:46). We can express our deepest feelings to Jesus, because he understands.

Journaling can help as you put your feelings into words. A journal can become your friend, and can help you express yourself to God. Consider seeking a mentor, spiritual director, coach or confidante who you can be honest with, and discuss your spiritual journey with them. Perhaps your church or agency can provide one for you.

When we have recognised that we are lonely or sad, and told God about it, then we might choose to do things which help us feel better. It is okay to feel lonely, but it is also not a bad thing to plan activities to help you feel better. For example, you might read, play music, exercise, watch a DVD or go somewhere you enjoy. You could treat yourself to something you like, or visit someone. Another option is to plan celebrations, such as parties or pizza nights. See Appendix 3 for more ideas of things to do when you feel lonely or sad. If necessary, speak with a pastoral carer, Christian leader or counsellor about your loneliness. You may find it helpful to read the book *Freedom from Loneliness: 52 Ways to Stop Feeling Lonely*.[136] That book contains some good ideas, but we should also remember that it is part of being human to feel lonely at times, and we don't have to seek to be free from that experience forever. Our life can be a balance of times with friends, ministry, and times of solitude with God, as described by Clark:

> My friends are important because they have formed me and they sustain and support me in my celibate life. The ministry which I have been given is also important, and it helps me know I belong uniquely to God. Most of my life is spent in the company of friends or in the exercise of the gifts I've been given in ministry. But my celibate life needs something more. It requires that I allow God to have me from time to time himself. [137]

I might not be someone's 'special person', but I have something much better. I know that I am special to God, and he wants me to spend the rest of my life with him.

Challenge 2: Pressure to marry, and assumptions people make
There may be pressure to marry, especially from parents. Even if this is unspoken, you may feel that people wonder what is 'wrong with you' because you are not married. In some cultures it is rare to be an unmarried adult. Single people might be viewed as 'not grown up yet' and expected to sit with the children. You may be given less responsibility. If you are a woman as well as single, both of these may mean that you are given less authority. You might be perceived as odd, mentally ill, worthless, or even cursed. Alternatively, you might be assumed to be homosexual. People may treat you with less respect than a married person receives.

Response:
Pressure to marry can be very painful, especially when it comes from loved ones. A common mistake is for people to say "I'm praying that God will give you a partner." It can help to realise they are doing it because they want the best for you – although they don't know what *is* best.

Maybe you can gently inform them that the pressure only makes it more painful for you, and that you would like them to accept you as you are. Or use humour to deflect comments. Funny comments I've heard include "I'm a sad and sorry man-child", "My husband died at birth" and "I prefer giraffes!" When told that "There are many more fish in the sea", you could reply, "Oh yes – I've always wanted to marry a fish!" Or perhaps if a married person asks why you are single, the reply could be "Why are you married? Why have you settled for him/her? Why don't you want freedom?" We need to be careful not to offend, but perhaps it could help the speaker realise how their questions come across, and that not everyone wants to marry – some people are content to be single.

It is frustrating to be treated with less respect because of your marital status. You may have gone from being highly respected as a professional in your home culture, to being treated like a child in the host culture because you are unmarried. Such a change is not easy. Remind yourself that you have worth because God made you, regardless of marital status or anything else. If your mission agency doesn't seem to respect your status as a single person, challenge them about this. If the culture regards you as odd, remember that Jesus was odd too, as a single man in his thirties in the Middle East, so you are in good company. If you have to be married to be a good leader, does that mean Jesus was a bad leader?

Some mission workers have found it helpful to explain their status by saying "I'm like a nun/monk/religiosa" or "I'm like Mother Teresa." If the listener respects nuns, this can enhance your status.

As a group, we can challenge assumptions such as "You must be gay if you're not married." We can point out that such assumptions cause damage, and can lead people to question their sexuality. It is perfectly acceptable to be single, without having to explain why.

Challenge 3: Childlessness
Not having children can lead to a sense of grief, especially for someone who has always expected that they would have a child. Some single women find it hard to be around pregnant women, and try to stay away from them. It can cause a sense of desolation. 'Barrenness' is a hard word to bear, and some cultures equate it to lacking value, as worth is thought to come through bearing children. In some cultures people are known by the name of their child (e.g. 'Mama David', David's mother). Childless people do not seem to fit in. People may assume that you have children (and, if you are older, grandchildren).

Response:
There are no easy answers for coping with childlessness. It can be very painful. Single woman and men have to face the fact that there is no one for them to pass the family line on to – not just genes, but family history, and on-going legacy.

Some people need to allow themselves to grieve for the children they will never bear. Crying, and even a ritual such as throwing petals in a river, helps some people say goodbye to their dreams of having their own child. The grief may return at various times, especially when women reach menopause and the chance of ever becoming pregnant fades.

As well as grieving the loss, people find it helpful to take positive action. Why should I only love a child I have created? We can love children even if they are not biologically our own. This may include working with children (in a school, orphanage, church group or children's club). Or it may involve acting like an auntie or godparent for children, and having fun with them. Many parents will be thrilled if you offer to play with their child or take them out. You can share the joys of helping to raise children without the huge costs parents pay (and the cost to the environment of bringing another child into the world). Some people sponsor a child (or a community), paying for food, education and other basic needs. Another option is to focus on 'spiritual children' – people you can mentor or disciple. They are your inheritance.

You might want to consider fostering or adopting children; single people as well as couples can do this (see chapter 15). This should be considered with advice and careful planning, considering the implications if you are doing this cross-culturally with children who don't share the same passport country as you. It should not be taken lightly, but it can work out very well. There are many children in the world who need a caring parent, and would love to become your family.

Don't assume that marriage would guarantee you happiness as a parent. About one in seven couples experience infertility.[138] Twenty percent of pregnancies end in miscarriage. Many children have disabilities or serious illnesses, and many children rebel against their parents, and God. In several research studies, parents have been found to have less life satisfaction, happiness and mental well-being than non-parents.[139] There can be sorrow through having children as well as sorrow from being childless.

We don't have a 'right' to have children. Jesus was childless. Whatever message a culture gives you, having no children does not mean that you are of less value. Our primary identity and value does not come from our family (or lack thereof) but from Christ.

Jesus promises, "Anyone who sacrifices home, family, fields – whatever – because of me will get it all back a hundred times over, not to mention the considerable bonus of eternal life" (Matthew 19:29, MSG).

Challenge 4: Having too much to do
Single mission workers are sometimes expected to work long hours because they have no family responsibilities. They are also required to raise support, produce prayer letters and reports and do household tasks on their own, with no-one to share the burden. Often there is no boundary between home and work, so they may continue to work in the evening as they have no family calling them. They may be expected to baby-sit other people's children, and to be more available than couples for responsibilities at evenings and weekends. Mission leaders often expect more of single people as they don't have children to care for. Single parents can find that people treat them as 'single' rather than as 'parent', forgetting that they need time for their children and that there is not another parent to share the load. It is easy to become over-busy, exhausted and drained. This can lead to neglecting your own spiritual growth, especially if there are few resources to spiritually sustain you, and no-one to pray with or talk to about your spiritual journey.

Response:
Continually seek God, and ask for his guidance. What does he want you to say "Yes" to, and what should you say "No" to? Even Jesus sometimes said "No" and didn't meet every need or request. Taking time out to enjoy God's presence can help us avoid burn-out or becoming over-busy.[140] Intimacy with God provides ultimate satisfaction, as we continue on our exciting journey of spiritual growth. Talk to anyone who puts you under pressure to work too much. Explain that single people need social time and relaxation too. Don't allow people to abuse the freedom and flexibility which your singleness provides. Set boundaries and safeguard your time and energy appropriately.

In chapter 2, Tim explains that he used to leave work around 7pm to have 'family time' with his plants. Could you do something similar?

If you are a single parent in mission, explain your limits to people, and ensure that you have enough family time.

1 Corinthians 7:9 states "It is better to marry than to burn with passion". The risk might be less 'burning with passion' than just 'burning out'! I suggest that 'it is better to tarry (or rest) than to burn out'!

Challenge 5: Sexual desire
Sexual feelings don't first appear when you walk down the aisle. Single people have sexual feelings too, and can long for sexual fulfilment. Cross-cultural mission can be a time of sexual temptation, for a number of reasons (see chapter 21).

Response:
It is normal to have sexual feelings and physiological arousal. This is such an important issue that we have spent a whole chapter on this issue, so see chapter 22 for suggested responses.

Challenge 6: Vacations
Holidays alone can seem a lonely or boring prospect, and can also be expensive (because single rooms often cost more per person). You might not want to go on holiday with spinsters and widows, or bachelors and widowers. You might be too far away to visit your family or friends from home.

Response:
Holidays are important so try not to miss them. Families often find aspects of holidays difficult too, so don't imagine that everyone else is having a better time. Make the most of your own situation. Try different ideas to find out what works for you. Are you able to plan a holiday with a friend or with family members – your own extended family, or perhaps joining a family you enjoy being with if? Is a package holiday your thing, perhaps with other single people? Some Christian organisations offer holidays with single people in mind.[141] Or would you like to try a retreat in a lovely location?[142] Do you prefer travelling by yourself? Think about

where in the world you would really like to go, or what you really want to do – you only have yourself to consider, so you can tailor-make a holiday to suit you. You could take your annual leave in parts (a few days at a time) if the thought of two weeks alone is off-putting. Psychological research suggests that holidays of 2-6 days can be the best, and the important thing is to plan in at least one really good experience (like one special trip or fun activity).[143] Have fun!

Challenge 7: Touch, and being harassed
Touch can be challenging in two ways. First, there might be a lack of appropriate touch (e.g. hugs). Appropriate touch can be very healing. A hug from someone you trust can reduce blood pressure, stress and anxiety.[144] Some people find it very difficult if they receive no touch for weeks on end. People from tactile cultures (such as South America) can really miss touch if they move to an arms length culture. Secondly, there may be inappropriate touch, such as groping by strangers. Unwanted touch can increase stress levels and raise blood pressure. There may also be other forms of harassment, such as strangers staring or making lewd comments. Sadly in some cultures this is extremely common.

Response:
Jesus touched lepers, the sick and children. He invited Thomas to touch him, and he welcomed loving touch when a woman poured perfume on him. Perhaps Jesus is calling you to bring healing through touching and praying for the sick or children, or others in need.

If you long for touch, are there any babies around whom it is appropriate for you to hold or cuddle? We need to take care that this is appropriate and ask the parent first. It is good to be part of a community which spans several generations. An older person might also crave touch, and appreciate an arm to hold while they walk.

Would you find it helpful to get a pet? Or to receive a back massage or makeover or hair-do? Or ask a friend for a hug?

Some suggestions about dealing with inappropriate touch (and comments and stares) are given in chapter 31. Being careful and travelling with others may reduce the risk of harassment, as might dressing modestly like local people and avoiding eye-contact. Even if you do all that, you might be harassed, and it is not your fault. Whether the harassment comes in the form of staring or someone masturbating against you in a bus, any time you feel violated it is important that you don't allow feelings of shame or embarrassment to stop you talking to someone about it or seeking help if you need to.[145]

If the unwanted touch comes from someone you know, tell them you do not want to be touched, as they may not realise that. If you are touched inappropriately by a doctor or someone else in authority, consider reporting them.

If unwanted touch occurs in a public place, shouting out or otherwise bringing attention to it can shame the offender and put a stop to it. Perhaps ask a local or expatriate friend how you could deal with this problem. Some people choose to ignore it, or to pray. Some respond with humour. Others put headphones on and play music so they don't hear comments. Choose a solution which works for you.

Challenge 8: Living arrangements
Living alone can feel unsafe or unsatisfactory, but options for sharing accommodation might not seem ideal either. Often families with children are given priority when housing is allocated, and single people are expected to put up with whatever is available, perhaps with frequent changes of house or housemates. Such changes are stressful. Sometimes single people in short-term mission teams are expected to share not only a room, but also a bed, with another single person of the same gender. Long-term mission workers may live with a local family which can provide a wonderful opportunity for learning the language and culture and building relationships, but may also be emotionally uncomfortable if they are expected to share a bed.

Response:
Review your living arrangements and the options available. Refuse to share a bed if you feel uncomfortable with that – perhaps offer to sleep

on the floor instead. Married couples are not asked to share a bed with other people so why should you be?

Sharing housing with a married couple can work in some situations but be unwise in others, particularly where polygamy is common and a single woman in the home might be perceived as a second wife.

Don't feel that you have to do what is expected (e.g. if single people are expected to share a house, but you would prefer to live alone, or if your organisation has provided somewhere for you to live alone but you would prefer to share). Pray, seek advice, try to understand what is acceptable in the local culture, explain your preferences, and make changes if necessary. If you will use your home for ministry (for example holding Bible studies, language lessons or inviting guests round), ensure that you will have enough room, privacy and quiet for this.

Ask for practical help in the house if you need it. Speak out. If you share a house, realise that some conflict is natural. Try to avoid getting too upset about it. Talk it through and work out a solution.

If you choose to live alone, ensure that your budget takes account of this, as this tends to be more expensive than sharing.

Some ideas about living arrangements are provided on the website www.missionarycare.com/singles/housing.htm. Further information and checklists for choosing a housemate are provided and in the book *Lord, send me: a handbook for single missionaries*.[146]

Challenge 9: Care for the elderly
You may be expected to care for elderly parents (because it is assumed that a single person is free to do this, having no children of your own). You may worry about who will care for you when you are older, and fear becoming old or sick alone.

Response:
Whether you are single or married, at home or away from home, there are likely to be questions about the care of ageing parents. These need to be considered prayerfully, seeking to know what God wants you to do. You may decide to leave the mission field for a time to care for family, and

God will honour that (see chapter 17). Or you may decide to stay, and God can honour that too.

Think ahead to your own later years. Perhaps your mission agency or supporters can help contribute towards a pension for you. Single people sometimes feel less lonely in later years than when they were younger, as many of their peers become widowed so singleness becomes the norm again. Some enjoy living in sheltered or residential accommodation, with people nearby for company. See chapter 1 for reassurance that single people can remain content, fulfilled and involved with meaningful relationships even in later life.

Challenge 10: Lack of affirmation
A husband and wife can affirm and encourage each other, but there may be no-one who affirms or thanks the single mission worker. Perhaps no-one seems to care about (or even to know about) most of what you do.

Response:
Intimacy with God can help us cope with *all* the challenges. When you know that God is pleased with you, affirmation from other people is less important. Try not to become bitter.

Dr Gary Chapman suggests that there are five 'love languages' or ways that we express and receive love: words of affirmation, quality time, gifts, acts of service and physical touch.[147] People have different primary 'love languages'. Perhaps the way you feel loved is through words of affirmation. If you don't receive affirmation, you may feel unloved, and empty. The great news is that God speaks all five love languages! Turn to the Bible, and receive words of affirmation from God. Listen to songs which speak of God's love for you.

If you speak one of the other 'love languages', God can speak to you this way too. If you need quality time, spend time with God, your beloved. If you yearn for gifts, as well as celebrating your birthday, make time to reflect on all the gifts God has given you, starting with the gift of his Son. If you feel loved when you receive acts of practical help, think of ways Jehovah Jireh (God our provider) has provided for you – perhaps in the area of strength, finance, health, or sending someone to assist you. If your love language is touch, as well as considering responses to the seventh challenge above, consider ways Jesus has touched your life, perhaps through others.

Be a grateful person, even if no-one seems grateful for what you do. Find small things to be grateful for, regularly. This has been found to lead to many benefits, including greater happiness.[148] If you model gratitude, other people might start to be grateful to you as well. If no-one else affirms you, affirm yourself and give yourself treats. Be a friend to yourself. Keep the perspective of eternity.

We live in a culture of entitlement. People feel it is their right to be happy and affirmed and to have a nice house and to marry and have children. In reality, these can be blessings but they are not rights. We came into this world with nothing, and every good gift is a blessing from God. I try not to focus too much on what I don't have. Nearly everyone has tough things to deal with in life, some people more than others. Our attitude is key to our experience of life. We can focus on what we lack, complain about what we don't have, and feel unhappy. Or we can accept that we feel sad about something, grieve what is lacking, but choose to focus on what is good in our life, and make the best we can out of a sad and difficult situation. We can learn to want what we have.

A story is told of an African man who kept asking for a pair of shoes, until one day he saw a man with no legs. Then he stopped asking for shoes, and started being grateful for his legs.

The people who have the least are often the most grateful people, while those who are comparatively rich tend to complain the most. Simon Guillebaud wrote,

> In the West we have a clear blue sky with a small cloud in the distance and we complain about the cloud, whilst out here [in Burundi] our African brothers have a cloudy sky with a small patch of blue, and they are grateful for that tiny break in the clouds. [149]

Being grateful does not mean that we should deny our problems, or that it is wrong to ask for help. Part of having a healthy attitude can be to seek help to cope with the grief, loss, disappointment and loneliness which can come with being single. It is a sign of strength, not weakness, to accept support such as debriefing, mentoring, spiritual direction, retreats, pastoral care and counselling if required. While we should not become overly dependent on an individual person to support us, support networks are very helpful. Formal support can be especially useful if we lack other relationships where we can express ourselves honestly and receive adequate time, interest and understanding. See Appendix 2 for suggestions about where to find such support.

In response to our question about what to say in this book, one single mission worker wrote, "Find out what God wants you to do and do it...single or married! If we are in God's will he will take care of everything."

Mission worker Jeannie Lockerbie wrote something similar:

> When I think back to the times when I asked, or even demanded of the Lord that he gave me this person or that thing the way I wanted, I shudder. The only way I have found to have joy and fulfilment is to concentrate on doing what the Lord wants me to do now, at this moment in the circumstances in which he has put me. Leave the future entirely in his hands. Don't ask me how it works. I just know that when you stop plotting and designing, God takes over. He then gives peace and contentment.[150]

Or as Jesus said (according to the paraphrase in *The Message*),

> Steep your life in God-reality, God-initiative, God-provisions. Don't worry about missing out. You'll find all your everyday human concerns will be met. Give your entire attention to what God is doing right now, and

don't get worked up about what may or may not happen tomorrow. God will help you deal with whatever hard things come up when the time comes (Matthew 6: 33-34, MSG).

Even if you do not receive much affirmation from others, you can still be content. Happiness is associated with many of the factors which have already been discussed in this book, including:

- Connecting with God
- Building close relationships (with friends and family)
- Helping others
- Having a sense of meaning
- Expressing gratitude
- Exercising, and other healthy behaviours.

When we do these things, we tend to be happier.[151]

Benefits of being a single person in ministry

Involvement with mission has the potential to provide a fulfilling lifestyle, and great joy. Being single in ministry can be better than being single 'back home' (see chapter 18). There can be great joy in doing meaningful activity and living in a different culture, hopefully with caring, like-minded people around. A sense of call can help sustain us during the hard times. Henri Nouwen wrote:

> Knowing that the place where you live and the work you do is not simply your own choice but part of a mission makes all the difference. When difficulties arise, the knowledge of being sent will give me the strength not to run away but to be faithful. When the work proves tiring, the facilities poor, and the relationships frustrating, I can say, 'These hardships are not a reason to leave, but an occasion to purify my heart.' [152]

The important things in life are loving God, having a sense of purpose, and good relationships. Being involved in ministry encourages these, as the ministry has meaning, we need to trust God, and deep relationships are built with both expatriates and local people.

What are some of the advantages of being a *single* mission worker, rather than a married one? As the chapters of this book illustrate, many people enjoy the single lifestyle. The research discussed in chapter 37 found that on the whole, single mission workers agreed with the statement "I am content in being single." [153] The same research found that a major advantage of singleness was the freedom to make decisions for yourself and do what you want, without needing to consider a partner or children. [154]

The celibate life can be a life of fulfilment and depth. Celibacy can be a spiritual discipline of abstinence, like fasting, drawing us closer to God (see chapter 12). Celibates can be single-hearted in their devotion to Christ. They are free to devote more time to God and ministry, without being distracted by the concerns of marriage and family (1 Corinthians 7:32-34). They are often more productive. They turn to God rather than to a spouse at times of need. They can be generous in their relationships to many people, because they have not promised to put a spouse (and children) above everyone else. Single people are generally more able than married people to respond spontaneously to a needy person and take a diversion in order to help (like the Good Samaritan). It can be harder to put an injured man on a donkey, or in a car, when it is already full of children.

Before his disastrous marriage, John Wesley wrote a pamphlet entitled *Thoughts on the single life*, which celebrates the benefits of singleness. Elsewhere, Wesley encouraged people to,

> Do all the good you can. By all the means you can. In all the ways you can. In all the places you can. At all the times you can. To all the people you can. As long as ever you can. [155]

Single and married people both do what they can, but single people often have the availability and flexibility to do more. A lot of time and energy can be required to maintain a healthy marriage and cope with the challenges of parenthood (including sleep deprivation, sibling rivalry, tantrums, childhood illnesses, and getting children to eat the right food and do their homework). The single person can devote this time and energy to other matters.

Single people may enter more deeply into a new culture, and have rich relationships. They might learn a language more easily, as they are not tempted to talk to their partner and children in their own language, and they have more time for study. Families often leave the mission field because of their children's educational needs or because one partner is not satisfied with their ministry; [156] single people don't need to give up for the sake of their children or spouse.

Some ministry settings are not suitable for families. Many Christian NGOs which send people to work in war-zones and other dangerous locations only send unaccompanied staff, not families, for reasons of safety. In case of evacuation, they want to move as few people as possible. A team house may be provided, with no accommodation for couples. Frequent travel may be more suitable for a single person than a couple, as it leaves little quality time for a marriage. It is cheaper and less complicated to travel and make changes (such as moving to a new location) as a single person than as a family. Some settings are regarded as unsuitable by families because of a lack of schooling options.

Single mission personnel connect easily with single people in the new culture. Young people often choose to build a friendship with single people rather than married ones, because they feel they have more in common. Single people may be asked questions like "Are you lonely?" or "Why don't you have a baby even if you aren't married?" Such questions provide an opportunity to witness, explaining that God is always with us and our priority is to obey him, not to get married or have children.

Henri Nouwen wrote:

> Celibacy is a lifestyle in which we try to witness to the priority of God in all relationships. This involves every part of our life… It is an openness to being loved first by God. The celibate life is bound to touch those we encounter because it is an ongoing street theatre

constantly raising questions in people's minds about the deeper meaning of their own existence. [157]

You may not wish to be an "ongoing street theatre"! But as mission workers that probably describes all of us, whether married or single. People watch to see how married people behave in their marriage and family, and how single people live out a celibate lifestyle. If we are going to be like clowns anyway, watched by all, then we might as well see this as an opportunity to show the love of God. Single people have unique opportunities to answer questions about how they cope with being alone, and why they don't seek sex as their goal.

Not having everything we desire in life helps us to identify with other people who lack. Some people lack adequate food, housing or friends. Many lack the peace, forgiveness and sense of meaning which come through having a relationship with God. If we know what it is like to lack something (such as a marriage partner and children), we gain credibility in the eyes of people who are poor in some way. They don't want someone who seems to have everything. If we don't have all that the world offers, and yet we continue to trust God and are fulfilled in him, we have something to share. Jesus became poor to identify with people (Philippians 2: 5-8). We too, in our areas of poverty, allow room for God to work.

Single people avoid the stress, disagreements and disappointments which are often part of marriage. People who have never married don't need to face the challenge of trying to spend time with two families (including returning 'home' for significant events for both families, and caring for elderly or ill relatives on both sides). Sadly the stress of mission life often increases marital discord, and sometimes the couple have to decide whether to keep the marriage but give up ministry, or to break up the marriage. It takes a lot of time and energy to maintain a good marriage, and this can mean less time for other matters, including personal walk with God, ministry, friends, and personal leisure time. In twenty years of counselling mission workers, I have met some single people who have struggled with being single, but many more married people who have struggled with their marriage. Single people are just as likely as married people to live happily ever after. Asking married friends to talk honestly about the difficult aspects can help create a realistic view of marriage and childrearing.[158]

The testimonies in this book say much about benefits of being a single person in ministry. It can be a fruitful, exciting, meaningful, satisfying life, with the joy of knowing you are walking with God and doing his will. You can make wonderful friends along the way, and experience interesting cultures.

One single mission worker wrote:

> What if we could show the world the benefits of being single, so that others could see for real that it's a truly blessed lifestyle? Then people might see that singleness can be more than just a time of waiting for the right [partner]; that it can mean a life of fulfilled contentment. The single people who are younger than us might learn not to fear singleness in the way that we did when we were younger. Wouldn't that be awesome?
>
> …Let's live life to the full, making the most of every opportunity to develop our gifts and form deep relationships. This life is all about relationships, but not just of the romantic, life-long partnership kind. Invest in the friendships you have. Seek out new friends. Make time to really get to know other people; develop bonds of shared experiences and emotions. Be generous with your love… Most importantly, invest time and energy in your relationship with God. He is there, waiting for us to turn to him, longing for us to know him as he knows us. He wants all of us, not just half an hour in the morning, but all day, every day. He loves us with a passion no human could ever match. Why settle for anything less than a fully intimate relationship with our Lord? [159]

There are joys and challenges in both singleness and marriage. Wherever we find ourselves, we can ask God to help us be content in him, and keep our focus on him, as he goes through the hard times with us. Jesus was a single man, in ministry, crossing cultures. He understands, and he does not leave us alone. One day, you will be rewarded for your faithfulness.

"God is not unjust; he will not forget your work and the love you have shown him as you have helped his people and continue to help them" (Hebrews 6:10).

"Marriage is a major preoccupation here, but not [after death]… All ecstasies and intimacies then will be with God" (Luke 20: 34, 36, MSG).

Appendices

Appendix 1 - Topics to discuss if you are considering a cross-cultural marriage

*This appendix is by **Janet Fraser-Smith** (see chapter 30).*

Marriage brings two people with their two distinct identities together in a legal contract and they make a vow for their relationship to be life-long. In a cross-cultural marriage, culture plays an important role in the adventures and opportunities, challenges and losses. The purpose of this appendix is to encourage couples to consider some of the implications and enter marriage wisely and with a good foundation.

To use the analogy of an iceberg, dating takes place in open waters, but in marriage you discover a lot more below the surface. If you are reading this you have probably lived away from 'home' for a sufficient length of time to have learned how to adjust to new surroundings, but you may not realise how much of your initial formation remains part of who you are. In a marriage, the tendency to react spontaneously in ways that feel normal must be tempered until a new shared way is discovered.

The key to understanding cultural clashes is in knowing not just what we do, but why we do it. A couple may agree on an action but disagree, for example, on the criteria for respect, on the need for connections and accomplishments, on immediacy and planning, on the use of control, or on the right to choose. What happens if we are not willing to give up control? Why is being given our own space unthinkable? How vulnerable are we prepared to be? Do we prefer to do lots of things at once or not? How forceful and insistent should we be on our own ways? Do we place a high value on care for others? Marriage depends on the balance of power/leadership, submission/cooperation, gentleness/firmness, care/encouragement, honour/respect, and on our understanding and handling of good/evil and forgiveness/obedience. As Christians we may have to challenge what our cultural background has taught us to consider okay.

Discovering *why* we do things a certain way comes as we reflect on *what* we do automatically, our own action clashing with the expression of a different value. The cross-cultural couple must not fear discussion.

There are four key areas which influence a cross-cultural marriage: personality; extended family; community of origin (both local and national); and the legal dimensions of citizenship. It is in the context of these that a clash of values can occur. Below are some questions to explore. As you reflect on your own answers and those of your partner, note the areas that would be hard for you to change.

Personal identity factors (personality)
Our identity as individuals is composed of our genetic makeup and our attitudes, our ability to communicate and respond to crises, our faith and our friends, our gender and our roles, and the effect our choices have had on us, among other factors. The development of our gifts, skills, education and past experiences reflect cultural background. What do you value about yourself, and about each other? What interests do you both have, and how do you like to spend free time? What do you like to eat and how and who with? Do your musical tastes overlap?

Our character may also have cultural overtones. Friendliness, or a buoyant spirit, may be as much national characteristics as are seriousness or high levels of confidence. It will help if you have a good understanding of how you recognize and deal with conflict. Do either of you get angry easily? Do you shout or sulk? What experience do you have of intercultural conflict already? Were you satisfied with the resolution? How well do you communicate? How do you make decisions?

Finances are a well known source of stress. How will you manage financially? Is one of you better at managing money? What are the priorities when spending money? What are your views on giving, including when someone asks for money? How would you like to furnish and decorate your home? What could you live without?

Sharing time and possessions keeps couples in touch with others. Do you welcome visitors at all times and enjoy being surrounded by people, or do you like space, privacy and time alone? When would you be happy to let people outside your family use your belongings?

Personal faith is integral to our identity as Christians. How has your Christian faith developed and how do you express it? Is your style of worship reserved or expressive, liturgical or exuberant? What church will you attend together? How do you plan to share your daily walk with God with each other, or is this a private affair? What has been your experience of suffering and grief?

Being accepted as we are is one key to the long-term blessing of marriage. Acceptance is easy enough while the joys of initial love are supporting the relationship. What will help you to enjoy being together in the future? How will you nurture your partner?

Extended family
Identity within the context of family is in part related to whether you are a son or a daughter, and what your sibling position is both in age and assumed responsibility.

The western view sees the family unit primarily as a safe place for the couple and secondarily as a place for launching children into adulthood as independent decision makers in their own right (although nowadays many young people in their twenties still live with their parents). To a greater or lesser extent, collective family structures see both parents and children as integral, responsive members of the whole community wherever they live. Obligations vary, but may include a willingness to support a family network. Will the extended family always be welcome at your door? How would you describe your family of origin, and your social class?

It is within the family that the child observes gender relations and roles and responsibilities. What are your views on maleness and femaleness? What makes a good husband or wife? What makes a good son-in-law, daughter–in-law or parent-in-law? What is the relationship between mother and son, or eldest siblings to younger ones? Where is the power base? Who takes the final decision and why? How does one challenge such a decision?

How do men and women view their responsibilities in the home and in general? One couple resolved a possible tension as follows. When inside the home the husband acted as men should in the wife's culture (as an equal, helping with the housework). When outside the home, the wife acted as wives should in her husband's culture where they were living (giving him the respect that a husband is due). Note that it is on the whole hard for a Western woman with her need for independence to adjust readily to a man from a collective culture.

Has anyone in your family had learning difficulties, major health problems or psychological difficulties? Might any of these have a genetic component?

If possible develop positive relationships with your own family and in-laws.

Community of origin: Places and cultures where each partner grew up
Subjects such as history, traditions, languages, geography, music, food, landmarks, schooling, healthcare, transport, commercial sector and form of government all reflect values that underlie our expectations and

attitudes. It is good to discuss these areas. Is the beginning of life more important than its end?   What foods are grown locally?   Who goes hungry, and why?   Is it good to leave food on your plate, or is that wasteful? What are your political views? Do you think democracy is more effective than dictatorship, and why?

Language is big part of a society's identity. How many languages are spoken in your culture? How many do you speak? What language will you speak between you and with your children?

How would you be treated as an intercultural couple in the country where you now live, and in your partner's country? How are immigrants and foreigners regarded? What might be called racism in some countries is accepted as normal elsewhere. What is it like to be part of a minority?

In most cases, at least one partner will have little knowledge of the other's community, not having lived in the country where the other has grown up. It helps if cross-cultural couples gain as much understanding as they can of their own and each other's countries, ideally spending at least six months together in each other's countries, especially if one partner has never lived in a different culture. This might allow you to get to know each other's extended family, church and significant friends.

Citizenship and its legal obligations and responsibilities
For couples who do not share a common citizenship or passport, the legal area can have practical and financial implications. You may need to move between countries at different times, depending on factors such as job availability, visa renewal, evacuation, education options for children and the health of your parents. It is understandable to feel that when it happens, "We will cope." But some personalities are better at coping than others. It is wise to find out in advance what some of the challenges might be.

Consider the ramifications of the immigration process. What are the visa requirements for spouses in both countries – could you live in either country if necessary? Is a marriage conducted in one country recognised in the other?   Do foreign nationals have the right to work or own property?   What are the procedures for getting work permits?   Will retraining be necessary?   Is it possible to obtain citizenship without relinquishing your own? What are the advantages and disadvantages of having different citizenships? Can the forms be understood, or is there a language barrier? Will you need a translator? Being required to pass a driving test in another country having driven for years in your own or being required to retrain in order to validate your professional qualifications can be humbling (and frustrating).

The inter-relation of these four areas in the daily dynamics of marriage
The interplay between these four topics is illustrated in the following diagram.

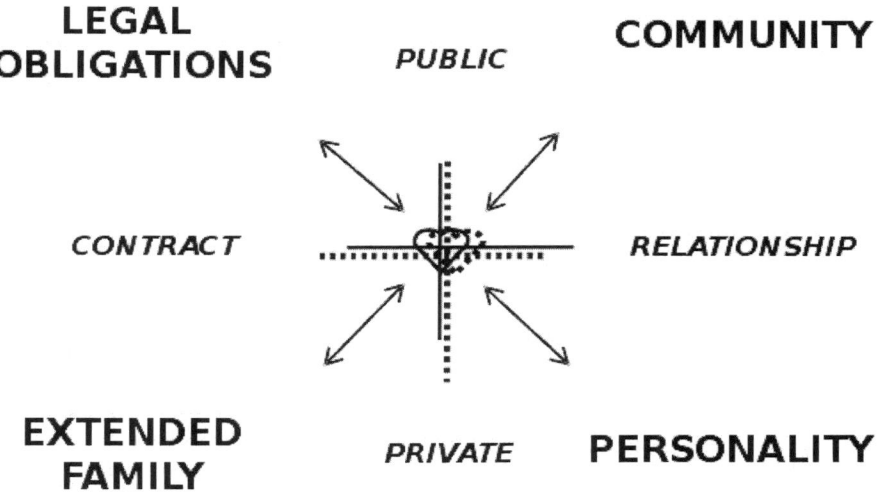

Figure 1 - Dynamics of an Intercultural Marriage

In the centre are two separate hearts representing the spouses. Each spouse is distinct from the other, bringing to the marriage their own experiences as a gendered person, their personality and family backgrounds. To some extent these aspects are private. Each partner also brings their experiences of life in their community, with its laws. These are publicly experienced.

The horizontal axis illustrates the balance between the poles of marriage as a contract ("we stay together because we are married") or a relationship ("we stay together because we want to"). The marriage contract may bring certain rights and opportunities, and status as a husband or wife. It may lead to citizenship in the partner's country.

Marrying into a culture that seems to offer safety and a future may seem to be a way out of difficulties. A greater focus on the friendship underlines the shared interests and the desire to spend time together for sheer enjoyment and compatibility. If friendship is the most important for one partner and the contract for the other, there may be tensions. For most couples the balance will vary from time to time.

The overlapping of the two hearts in the centre of the diagram represents the marital unit where intimacy takes place. It is the place where the couple work out the creative expression of their cultures so they can both feel at home and have a stable base. It is also the place where the pressures that come in from the outside are absorbed, discussed and worked through such as how much to let the family 'interfere', and issues related to children.

According to your culture, what makes a good marriage? Western people may have ideas related to romance, deep friendship, partnership, sharing labour, and spending time alone as a couple. People from other cultures may concentrate more on the husband providing income and the wife raising children, and all being part of the extended family and community, frequently joining in with family events.

How much will the extended family want to influence you as a couple? How are the names of children chosen? Do they need to be named after members of the family? How close will you live to your own family of origin and your in-laws, and how much time will you spend with them? How often will you visit family? What will happen if your parents need more care? Do you plan to support them financially or to live with them? How much time will you spend on the internet or phone, keeping in touch with family members? Do you have a shared language with your in-laws? Will translation be needed for the wedding service and family visits? Where will the wedding be held and who will be invited?

How many children do you want? How soon do the grandparents want grand-children? What are your views on contraception? Who will be the main carer for your children? How will you discipline children? What do you think of smacking? What opinions do your in-laws and extended family have on child-rearing, how much influence will they want to have, and how will you resolve any discrepancies? Where will children go to school? Which languages will you speak in your home? How will each of you retain some of your own cultural traditions?

The vertical axis focuses on the people who have input in the lives of the couple. This includes people known privately, such as the extended family and friends as well as people known in a more professional or public manner, such as lawyers, medical professionals, teachers or neighbours. Do the partners agree about how much time they want to spend with people privately and in public? Do they agree about which aspects of their marriage are private, and which are public? These groups of people may have expectations that are felt unequally by the couple.

The arrows between the couple and the topics represent the reciprocal interplay between the couple and the factors influencing them. In a marriage, the tendency is to react spontaneously in ways that feel 'normal' until a new shared third way is discovered.

A final point: where you live matters
The dynamic of your relationship will alter to some degree whenever you move. Some people recommend that the intercultural couple should live in a third culture, and not in the culture that either of them comes from. This avoids the situation of one feeling at home while the other feels like a foreigner (who might grow resentful for having to give up their culture and family while their spouse seems to win everything). Keep in mind the question of citizenship and retirement.

For other couples the best solution is to live in the culture from which one of them comes. Friends and family members are nearby to provide support and be an extended family for any children, and it might be easier to get work. Do you have a preference for rural or urban life? Are you willing to live in your partner's country? How often will you be able to visit other family members? There is no right or wrong solution here, but it is important for each couple to consider carefully what is best for them, and what the role expectations are for couples within that culture.

One of the challenges for the Christian couple is weighing up whether the call to marriage has a higher priority than the original call to mission. Marriage may well lead you away from the culture and people to whom you felt called. Do you have a shared sense of call, and if so, what is that calling? If you leave the mission in the future, what sort of work might you be able to find in another context? In which countries would you be happy to live, and why? What is it like to live there and how expensive is it?

If you both wish to stay in your ministry at least for a while, there are other questions to ask. If you are with a mission organisation, will your spouse also join the organisation? Some organisations insist that you resign when you get married, and then reapply as a couple. Some might not accept your spouse as a member if he or she will be unable to raise support. Deputation in each other's countries might involve a change of role and language.

Conclusion
Sometimes couples fear that their relationship is falling apart and that they no longer love each other because they experience many arguments. It can be a relief to discover that the root problem of the arguments may be due to intercultural differences, and not personality or a loss of love. Such difficulties can be overcome and a healthy marriage can blossom.

Help yourselves by researching the specific cultural values of your respective cultures. If you have very different views, it is good to be aware of these, and to work out ways to cope or accept the need to live with the dissonance.

Once you have expressed your observations and feelings about your personal experiences, your family background, the influence of your background community and cultural experiences and the cultural values that underpin them, you will be more certain about whether you want to commit yourself to a life with someone from another culture. If you choose not to marry, then you can be grateful for having had the opportunity to get to know someone from another culture and yourself well enough to be sure you made the right decision. If you choose to marry, along with the cultural challenges there will be many experiences and enrichments that you will enjoy and that you can offer to your children and to others. Above all, feed the love for God which draws you together.

For further information, see:

Books
- Fraser-Smith, J. (1997). *Love across latitudes: A workbook on cross-cultural marriage.* Loughborough: Arab World Ministries
- Shelling, G. & Fraser-Smith, J. (2008). *In love but worlds apart: Insights, questions, and tips for the intercultural couple.* Self-published: AuthorHouse

- Apupoaicei, M. (2009). *Your intercultural marriage: A guide to a healthy, happy relationship.* Chicago: Moody
- Dugan, R. (2008). *Intercultural marriage: Promises and pitfalls.* Yarmouth, ME: Intercultural Press Inc
- Gilbert, R. & Gilbert, R. (2011). *Marriage Masala: 52 spices for a healthy marriage.* Wytheville, VA: Elemental Publishing LLC

Website
www.crossculturalworkers.com (select the resources on marriage)

Appendix 2 - Useful resources

There are too many helpful books and websites to list here, so we have just selected a few. Others are mentioned in relevant chapters of this book, and in the footnotes.

Adoption
- Small World Adoption: www.swa.net (A Christian charity which assists with international adoptions in certain countries)

Bereavement
- www.cruse.org.uk (Information about grief, and support by email)

Celibacy
- Clark, K. (1986). *Being sexual ... and celibate*. Quezon City, Philippines: Claretian Publications

Counselling
Counselling services for mission personnel worldwide are listed at:
- www.globalmembercare.org (click on "Global map")
- www.oscar.org.uk/service/pastoral
- www.linkcare.org/resources

Debriefing, support and information for mission personnel
- www.resilientexpat.co.uk (Debbie & David Hawker's website)
- www.syzygy.org.uk (Tim Herbert's website)
- www.globalmembercare.org (Global Member Care Network – lists other resources)

Depression
The following websites provide free cognitive behavioural therapy (CBT) self-help programmes for people suffering from depression:
- http://moodgym.anu.edu.au
- http://bluepages.anu.edu.au

Emotional health
- www.membercareradio.com (Download free member care radio programmes on many topics related to emotional health, including friendships)

Loneliness
- Page, J. (2012). *Freedom from Loneliness: 52 ways to stop feeling lonely*. Self-published: CreateSpace Independent Publishing Platform

Rest
- Horsfall, T. (2010). *Working from a place of rest*. Abingdon: BRF

Retreats and spiritual direction
- www.singlevisioninternational.com (retreats for single mission workers)
- www.elimretreats.org (low-cost retreats in the USA for mission personnel)
- www.penhurst.org.uk (retreat centre in the UK specialising in mission workers)

Same-sex attraction
- www.truefreedomtrust.co.uk (Support for people with unwanted same-sex attraction, but does not aim to 'cure' homosexuality)

Sexual wholeness
- www.membercareradio.com (select "emotional health" then "addictions and dependencies" to download programmes)
- Cusuck, M. J. (2012). *Surfing for God*. Nashville: Thomas Nelson
- Duin, J. (1988). *Sex and the Single Christian*. London: Marshall Pickering
- Ethridge, S. (2009). *Every Woman's Battle*. Colorado Springs: WaterBrook Press
- Smith, A. (2013). *Celibate Sex: Musings on being loved, single, twisted and holy*. Colorado Springs: NavPress
- Stoeker, F. & Arterburn, S. (2009) *Every Single Man's Battle*. Colorado Springs: WaterBrook Press.

Singleness
- Danylak, B. (2009). *Redeeming singleness: How the storytelling of Scripture affirms the single life*. Wheaton, IL: Crossway
- Hsu, A. (1997). *The single issue*. Leicester: IVP
- Payne, R.A. (1994). *Embracing the single life*. Melbourne: Acorn Press
- Towns, J. (2012). *Validating Singles: Strategies for living single*. Bloomington, IN: WestBowPress
- www.thesinglesnetwork.org (includes an extensive list of other books on topics related to singleness)
- http://storage.cloversites.com/mmctmobilemembercareteam/documents/MMCT%20Communique,%20August%202010%20-%20Singleness.pdf (list of other resources on singleness)
- www.singleness.org (support for single Christians who desire to live purposeful lives)
- www.oscar.org.uk ("Oscar active" includes a singles group, where people interested in mission can discuss issues related to singleness)
- www.crossculturalworkers.com (Includes a free e-book on singleness for cross-cultural workers)

Single parents
- Farmer, A. (1998). Single parents and the church. Appendix A in *The rich single life: Abundance, opportunity and purpose in God*. Free at http://www.sovereigngracestore.com/Product/B3155-00-11/The_Rich_Single_Life_Abundance,_Opportunity_Purpose_in_God.aspx

Stress and trauma in cross-cultural work
- www.headington-institute.org (free online training on stress, trauma and resilience)

Appendix 3 - 40 ideas for coping with loneliness and sad times

1. Find someone to visit, phone or contact by internet. Perhaps a friend, family member, or someone who is elderly, unwell or in difficult circumstances and might appreciate being contacted.
2. Go out for a walk or to a shop or café, and start a conversation.
3. Visit a beautiful place, or look at pictures of one (a mountain or water, or somewhere with grass, trees, flowers, or animals, or a sunrise, sunset or the clouds or stars).
4. Go somewhere you enjoy e.g. a café, a swimming pool, an art gallery, museum or concert, a church, a shop.
5. Listen to music you like (worship music or other).
6. Plan something to look forward to – a holiday, special outing, treat, or a party.
7. Invite people to join you for a meal – whether in your home, or eating out. Order a takeaway if you don't want to cook.
8. Focus on things you are thankful for. Perhaps write your own poem, prayer, psalm or song.
9. Go for a walk, run, swim, cycle or to the gym. Exercise is a natural anti-depressant and releases tension.
10. Dance on your own.
11. Impersonate a chicken.
12. Watch or play a sport. Tennis is good for singles, as there are lots of singles matches. It's not a romantic game, because love means nothing in tennis!
13. Be creative – paint, write, plant something, make a model, knit, cross-stitch, or take photos.
14. Take a bath or shower (warm or cool).
15. Have a spiritual retreat, either led or on your own.
16. List all your friends and family members and decide which you want to invest more in (which might include forming new friends). Work out the first step to take, and do it.
17. Ask people to pray for you.
18. Light a candle, and spend time in silent prayer and reflection.
19. Read a good book or magazine.
20. Watch a film, alone or with others.
21. Think about things you have enjoyed in the past, and plan some again.

22. Talk to a counsellor about your feelings.
23. Think about your long-term goals, and what you need to do to bring them about.
24. Write a letter.
25. If you like order, try to tidy, clean or iron something.
26. If you like to make a mess, do it (trying not to irritate others).
27. If you like children, spend time with some.
28. Forgive someone.
29. Help someone.
30. Spend time being aware that God is with you.
31. Eat something nice.
32. Whistle, sing or read aloud.
33. Pretend you're happy. Smile – it improves your mood.[160]
34. Look at your photos and remember happy times.
35. Play a game (on the computer if necessary).
36. Create a competition.
37. Have a massage, or a haircut.
38. Be very aware of the present moment – everything you can hear and see.
39. Thank someone for something.
40. Come up with a better list than this, and try out your own ideas.

> Be creative! One mission worker who missed being able to go to a beach found that sitting with her eyes closed and her feet in a big bowl of warm water helped her relax, and she was able to imagine that she was at the seaside. Another stressed mission partner felt much better after going clothes shopping with her twin sister – even though they were in different continents. They 'met up' to shop online together!

Appendix 4 - Abuse

Women who have been physically or sexually abused are less likely to be married or to be in stable, long-term cohabiting relationships than other women.[161] A history of abuse can lead to avoiding intimate relationships. Therefore, although some married mission workers may have a history of abuse, this may be more common among single workers, both men and women.

A history of abuse does not mean that we should automatically reject an application to serve in mission. It is important to consider how the person has been affected by the abuse, and how they have coped with life since it happened. Some people who have been abused become very effective mission partners. It can be helpful to consider carefully the best location and role for them. For example, although they might be drawn by compassion to work with trafficked women and abused children, this is not always the best place for them if it provokes too many reminders of their own painful past. Likewise, working in a location where prostitutes (including children) are very visible can cause a lot of pain and anger to someone who has been abused. It is worth choosing the placement carefully, and offering counselling if needed.

While serving in mission, single people (especially women) may be more at risk of being sexually harassed or even raped than married people, as they lack protection. Good security training and providing personal alarms may help reduce this risk.

For guidelines on action to take after rape or assault, see http://globaled.us/peacecorps/rape-response-handbook.asp.

Footnotes

[1] In Hoke, S. & Taylor, B. (2009) *Global Mission Handbook*. Downers Grove, IL: IVP, p.174.

[2] The Bible teaches against 'fornication' or 'sexual immorality' (Greek word *porneia*) – e.g. Galatians 5:19. Most evangelical Christians assume that this refers to all sex except that between a husband and wife.

[3] See chapter 37. See also Danielson, E.E., Cummings, B. & Fry, M. (1991) *Lord, send me: a handbook for single missionaries*. El Cajon, CA: E.D. Publishing. Marti Smith puts the figure at six women to each man in her chapter 'Choosing how to live in a Muslim context: case studies from missionary women' in Eitel, K. E. (2008) *Missions in Contexts of Violence*. Pasadena, CA: William Carey Library.

[4] Foyle, M. (2001) *Honourably Wounded: Stress among Christian workers*. Second Edition, London: Monarch.

[5] "Member care is the preparation, equipping and empowering of missionaries for effective and sustainable life and ministry." (www.globalmembercare.com).

[6] In a personal communication, Dr Ritchey (see chapter 36) stated that she also noticed this desire for protection when she interviewed Latino single women in mission.

[7] See chapter 35 for a discussion of such statements.

[8] Rupp, J. (1988) *Praying our goodbyes*. Notre Dame, IN: Ave Maria Press.

[9] Moon, S. (2013) *The Korean Missionary Movement: Dynamics and Trends (1988-2013)*. Unpublished paper.

[10] Center for the Study of Global Christianity (2013) *Christianity in its Global Context, 1970 – 2020: Society, Religion and Mission*. Gordon-Conwell Theological Seminary (http://wwwgordonconwell.com/netcommunity/CSGCResources/ChristianityinitsGlobalContext.pdf)

[11] Philippines Mission Mobilization Movement is a global movement of Filipino Church and partners committed to glorify God by mobilizing, equipping and deploying a million tentmakers and career missionaries to disciple unevangelized peoples by 2020. See Taniajura, R. *The Philippines Mission Movement: An Update* (available at http://philippinemissionsassociation.com/pdf/Philmissionsmovement2010.pdf)

[12] A condo (condominium) is a freehold apartment.

[13] Georgia Department of Corrections. *Offenders in Georgia: Child sex offenders* (available at www.dcor.state.ga.us/Research/Standing/Sex_offenses_against_children.pdf)

[14] In some Asian countries, the locals consider some foods as 'heaty' and some as 'cooling'. Heaty foods are those that make a person's body feel hot, such as hot peppers, spices, and fried foods. Cooling foods help to cool down the body, such as cucumber, yoghurt, and watermelon. In Asian cuisine, one is supposed to eat a balanced diet of such foods in each meal in order to stay healthy.

[15] http://www.servantsasia.org

[16] Clark, K. (1986) *Being Sexual... and Celibate.* Quezon City, Philippines: Claretian.

[17] Abu-Lughod, L (2006).The Muslim woman *Eurozine*, 09-01. (available at www.eurozine.com/articles/2006-09-01-abulughod-en.html)

[18] *New Revised Standard Version Bible* (1989) Division of Christian Education of the National Council of the Churches of Christ in the United States of America.

[19] Dave Pollock was co-director of these early conferences.

[20] *The Holy Bible King James Version (1611; revised in 2004)*. Peabody, MA: Hendrickson.

[21] 'Home' is in inverted commas because it often doesn't feel like home after returning

[22] Calhoun, A. A. (2005). *The Spiritual Disciplines Handbook.* Downers Grove, IL: IVP.

[23] See Knell, M. (2007). *Burn up or splash down: surviving the culture shock of re-entry.* Waynesboro GA: Authentic books.

[24] Both quotations are from Hawker, D. (2013) *Debriefing aid workers and missionaries: A comprehensive manual.* London: People In Aid. Available at www.peopleinaid.org

[25] Storti, C. (1991) *The art of coming home.* Yarmouth, ME: Intercultural Press.

[26] Swindoll, L. (1982) *Wide my world, Narrow my bed: Living and Loving the Single Life.* Portland: Multnomah Press

[27] You can read about Simon's work in Burundi at http://www.greatlakesoutreach.org

[28] This comes directly from Simon Guillebaud's diary, printed with his permission. An adapted account of this experience is also published in his book Guillebaud, S. (2011) *Dangerously Alive: African adventures of faith under fire.* Oxford: Monarch Books

[29] www.love146.org

[30] Ainsworth, M., Miles, G. & Taylor, K. (2013). *Sexual Integrity of Expat Christian Men in Cambodia - Removing Planks*. Presentation to Heads of Foreign Agencies, January 2013. Email glenn@love146.org for information.

[31] For example, support www.daughtersofcambodia.org, www.love146.org or www.chabdai.org. Or be a volunteer with www.mstproject.com which challenges expatriates who are looking for sexual encounters.

[32] Retreats are held annually in Asia and Europe - see www.SingleVisionInternational.com.

[33] Roni is from the USA. Currently she serves as the Missionary Care Provider for World Mission Ministries. She helps coordinate the Mental Health & Missions Conference and serves on the board of the Global Member Care Network. She is working on her second Ph.D (in Intercultural Studies).

[34] O'Donnell, K. & O'Donnell, M.L. (1992) Understanding and managing stress. In K. O'Donnell (Ed.). *Missionary Care*. Pasedena, CA: William Carey Library, p.110-122.

[35] Cain, K., Postlewait, H. & Thomson, A. (2005). *Emergency Sex (and other desperate measures)*. London: Ebury Press.

[36] See chapter 21

[37] Smith, A. (2013). *Celibate Sex: Musings on being loved, single, twisted and holy*. Colorado Springs: NavPress, p. 136.

[38] Lewis, C.S. (1960; revised 1991). *The Four Loves*. Fort Worth: Harcourt Brace, p. 91, 94.

[39] Bonhoeffer, D. cited in Cusuck, M. J. (2012). *Surfing for God*. Nashville: Thomas Nelson, page x.

[40] Clark, K. (1986). *Being sexual... and celibate*. Quezon City, Philippines: Claretian Publications, p. 176.

[41] Traditional Christian teaching refers to sex outside marriage as 'sexual immorality' or 'fornication', classed in the Bible as a sin. Dwelling on lustful thoughts is also classified as sinful (Matthew 5: 28).

[42] Introduction to Song of Songs in Peterson, E.G. (2004). *The Message*. Colorado: NavPress.

[43] Smith, A. (2013). *Celibate Sex: Musings on being loved, single, twisted and holy*. Colorado Springs: NavPress, p. 101-102.

[44] Lewis, C.S. (1996). In W. Hooper (Ed.) *The weight of glory, and other addresses.* New York, Simon and Schuster, p. 25-26.

[45] Reported in Daniel, K. T. (2012) Like sex or chocolate. *Psychology Today*, 21 February. (http://www.psychologytoday.com/blog/naughty-nutrition/201202/sex-or-chocolate)

[46] Patton, M. S. (1985). Masturbation from Judaism to Victorianism. *Journal of Religion and Health*, 24 (2), 133–146.

[47] Many studies indicate this. For a simple summary see http://en.wikipedia.org/wiki/Masturbation

[48] National Survey of Sexual Health and Behavior (2010); Kinsey, A. C., Pomeroy, W. B., Martin, C. E. (1948). *Sexual Behavior in the Human Male*. Philadelphia: W. B. Saunders; Kinsey, A. C. et al. (1953). *Sexual Behavior in the Human Female*. Philadelphia: W.B. Saunders.

[49] Gerressu M, Mercer C.H, Graham C.A, Wellings K., & Johnson A.M. (2008). Prevalence of masturbation and associated factors in a British national probability survey. *Archives of Sexual Behavior*, 37, (2), 266–278.

[50] Huggett, J. (1985) *Dating, sex and friendship.* Downers Grove, Illinois: IVP.

[51] Quoted in Smith, A. (2013) *Celibate Sex: Musings on being loved, single, twisted and holy.* Colorado Springs: NavPress, p. 135.

[52] Dennerstein, L. et al. (1994) The relationship between the menstrual cycle and female sexual interest in women with PMS complaints and volunteers. *Psychoneuroendocrinology,* 19,(3), 293-304.

[53] Smith, A. (2013) *Celibate Sex: Musings on being loved, single, twisted and holy.* Colorado Springs: NavPress, p. 134.

[54] White, J. (1977) *Eros Defiled.* Leicester: IVP.

[55] Dobson, J. (2002) *Breakaway Magazine,* Focus on the family, July 2002.

[56] Cited in Huggett, J. (1985) *Dating, sex and friendship.* Downers Grove, Illinois: IVP, p. 165.

[57] Cusuck, M. J. (2012) *Surfing for God.* Nashville: Thomas Nelson, p.15.

[58] Dr Roni Pruitt (see chapter 21), personal communication, 6th June 2013.

[59] www.interhealth.org.uk

[60] http://johnsteley.co.uk

[61] Oxford University Press (2013) *Oxford dictionaries* (at http://oxforddictionaries.com/definition/english/pornography)

[62] http://en.wikipedia.org/wiki/Pornography

[63] Name and identifying details have been changed

[64] Other options are listed at http://www.truefreedomtrust.co.uk/book/export/html/1199, or see http://en.wikipedia.org/wiki/Accountability_software. Alternatively, type 'accountability software' into your search engine and see what is available.

[65] Ward, K. *Gay people as missionaries: an interrogation of the silences*, available at http://www.anglicancommunion.org/listening/book_resources/docs/kevin%20ward.pdf

[66] Goddard, A. & Harrison, G. (2011) *Unwanted same-sex attraction: issues of pastoral and counselling support*. London: Christian Medical Fellowship; Diamond, L. (2008) *Sexual fluidity: Understanding women's love and desire*. Harvard: Harvard University.

[67] Diamond, L. M. (2003) What does sexual orientation orient? A biobehavioral model distinguishing romantic love and sexual desire. *Psychological Review*, 110, 173-192.

[68] Dr Roni Pruitt (see chapter 21), personal communication, 6th June 2013.

[69] De Pomerai, D. (2008) Biological mechanisms in homosexuality: A critical review. In P. Groves (Ed.) *The Anglican Communion and Homosexuality: A resource to enable listening and dialogue*. London: SPCK, p.268-292.

[70] Chalke, S. (2013) The bible and homosexuality – part 1. *Christianity*, January 22 2013. http://www.christianitymagazine.co.uk/sexuality/stevechalkeextended.aspx

[71] Goddard, A. & Harrison, G. (2011) *Unwanted same-sex attraction: issues of pastoral and counselling support*. London: Christian Medical Fellowship.

[72] Evangelical Alliance (2012) At http://www.eauk.org/church/resources/theological-articles/resources-for-church-leaders-biblical-and-pastoral-responses-to-homosexuality.cfm

[73] Ward, K. *Gay people as missionaries: an interrogation of the silences* At http://www.anglicancommunion.org/listening/book_resources/docs/kevin%20ward.pdf

[74] www.truefreedomtrust.co.uk is an organization which supports gay Christians who want to be celibate.

[75] www.bsfinternational.org

[76] Ward, K. *Gay people as missionaries: an interrogation of the silences*, available at http://www.anglicancommunion.org/listening/book_resources/docs/kevin%20ward.pdf

[77] Intersex refers to people who are born with a variation in sex characteristics including chromosomes, gonads (ovaries or testicles) and/or genitals which mean that they cannot be distinctly identified as either male or female. There is no need to exclude such people from mission work. They should be subject to the same application procedure as other candidates.

[78] See chapter 21 for information about Dr Pruitt.

[79] Friesen, L. J. (1989) *Sexuality: a biblical model in historical perspective*. Unpublished dissertation, Fuller Theological Seminary.

[80] Ryken, L., Wilhoit., J.C, Tremper, L. (Eds). (1998) *Dictionary of biblical imagery*. Downers Grove, ILL.: InterVarsity Press.

[81] Trible, Phyllis. (1978) *God and the Rhetoric of Sexuality*. Philadelphia: Fortress, p.99.

[82] We are grateful to Dr Jessie Ritchey (see chapter 36) for ideas in this paragraph.

[83] For example Apostoli, A. (1995). *When God asks for an undivided heart: Choosing celibacy in love and freedom*. Slough: Pauline Books and Media; and Clark, K. (1982) *An experience of celibacy*. Notre Dame, IN: Ave Maria Press.

[84] See www.oscar.org.uk/oscaractive/articles/cooper.htm

[85] Goldsmith, E. (1996) *God Can be Trusted*. Milton Keynes: Authentic Media, p.57.

[86] Interview with John Stott, in Hsu, A. (1997) *The single issue*. Leicester: IVP, p. 85-86.

[87] Ritchey, J. (2013) *Should we even bother sending single women cross-cultural workers to serve in an Islamic context?* Unpublished paper.

[88] Some of the ideas in this chapter were first printed in Swinney, J. (2012) *Love on-line* Liberti, Jan-March 2012. Jo has also written a book called *Cheerful Madness: How eleven couples made it to marriage* (2008, London: Monarch Books), which is an interesting read for anyone wondering how couples get to the point of marriage. See www.joswinney.com.

[89] McKay, L. (2012) *Love at the speed of email*. Washington DC: Karinya Publishing

[90] www.yoursiteontop.co.uk/only-dating-in-the-usa/

[91] www.christianconnection.co.uk

[92] McKay, L. (2012) *Love at the speed of email*. Washington DC: Karinya Publishing, p. 224

[93] www.christianconnection.co.uk/safety. For more information about scammers, see www.RomanceScams.org

[94] Rivers, F. (2001). *Redeeming Love* Sisters, Orgeon: Multnomah Press

[95] See chapter 21 for information about Dr Pruitt

[96] Janet Fraser-Smith and her husband have an intercultural marriage. Since 1976 they have served in the Middle East, France, and latterly in the UK. Janet is author of the book *Love across latitudes*, and co-author of *In love but worlds apart*. She has led seminars in several countries on cross-cultural marriage.

[97] A TCK is a person who grows up in a different culture to that of their parents, due to their parents' work – e.g. the child of mission or development workers.

[98] Personal conversation with Anne Yeardley

[99] Thomas, G. (2000) *Sacred Marriage*. Grand Rapids, Michigab: Zondervan Publishing House

[100] Heartstream exists to care for mission workers and other cross-cultural workers worldwide. It offers Intensive Care Programs for crisis care and recovery, Member Care Training Courses, retreats, counselling and a variety of other programs. Resources are also available, including the three volume series 'Global servants: cross-cultural humanitarian heroes'. See www.heartstreamresources.org.

[101] UK results taken from *Singularly Significant* survey, reported in Wraight, H. (1995) *Single: The Jesus model.* Leicester: Crossway Books, p. 100. Australian results taken from the 2001 National Church Life Survey, retrieved from www.ncls.org.au/default.aspx?sitemapid=23 on 30/5/13.

[102] There are also other differences between these studies, especially the dates of the research. The mission worker study took place more than 10 years after the other 2 studies, and as the divorce rate has risen during this time, it is even more surprising that the proportion of divorced mission workers was much lower. There was also a higher proportion of widowed people in sending churches (24% of the singles in church vs 2% of single mission workers). This is likely to be due to the fact that a large proportion of church attenders are elderly. The proportion of widowed people is smaller on the mission field, as people retire from mission as they grow older, so most of the widowed people are former mission workers rather than currently serving. Of widowed mission

workers, many lost their spouse at a young age 'in service' as a mission worker (e.g. death in a traffic accident, violent attack, or through tropical illness), rather than through a natural death later in life.

[103] Southey, R. (1820) *The Life of John Wesley*. London: Hutchinson; Faire, J. (1998) *Seven silver rings*. Northampton, UK: Multiply Publications, p.71. See also http://lexloiz.wordpress.com/2010/03/19/john-wesley-and-his-wife-part-2/

[104] There are different views on whether remarriage is acceptable after divorce. See www.reclaimingthemind.org/blog/2010/07/can-a-divorced-christian-be-remarried

[105] Song by J. F. Coots and H. Gillespie, 1934.

[106] There is a poem by Wendy Cope called 'Bl***y men are like bl***y buses' which suggests that after waiting a very long time, multiple offers might appear at once. For some of us, this never happens!

[107] Pinto, C. (2005) *Ministrando a Solteros En América Latina: Individuos Escondidos En Una Sociedad Orientada Hacia La Familia*. Unpublished paper.

[108] Kraft, M. and Crossman, M. (2013) Women in Missions. Available at www.thetravelingteam.org/articles/women-missions

[109] COMIBAM. (2007). COMOBAM III research project – phase 1. In *Connections*, 6,1, 20-24. Available at www.worldea.org/images/wimg/files/Comibam%20III.pdf.

[110] Cunningham, L., Hamilton, D.J. & Rogers, J. (2000) *Why Not Women? : A Fresh Look at Scripture on Women in Missions, Ministry and Leadership*. Seattle, WA: YWAM.

[111] Created by Headington Institute, and available at http://headington-institute.org/Portals/32/Resources/Test_Self_care_inventory.pdf.

[112] For methodological details, email Karen Carr at carrmmct@gmail.com. See also Carr, K.F. (November, 2011) *Resilient cross cultural living: Unique perspectives from single missionaries*. Unpublished paper presented at The Mental Health and Missions Conference, Angola, IN. Retrieved from http://storage.cloversites.com/mmctmobilemembercareteam/documents/Paper%20-%20Resilience%20%20Singles%20Plenary%20-%20Mental%20Health%20%20Missions%2011.pdf [7/6/13]. Also Crawford, N.A. & Carr, K.F. (2013). *The relationship between marital status and missionary resilience*. Unpublished manuscript. Rosemead School of Psychology, La Mirada, CA.

[113] Danielson, E.E., Cummings, B. & Fry, M. (1991) *Lord, send me: a handbook for single missionaries*. El Cajon, CA: E.D. Publishing.

[114] This difference was statistically significant.

[115] Crawford, N.A. (1999). *Perceived ministry roles and measures of well-being among missionary women*. Dissertation: Wheaton College, Wheaton, IL.

[116] Help mate or helper – see Genesis 2: 18

[117] Edwards, K.J., Crawford, N.A., & Cerny, L.J. (2013). *Life stages and measures of cross-cultural stress among married and single workers*. Unpublished manuscript. Rosemead School of Psychology, La Mirada, CA.

[118] See www.cernysmith.com

[119] Bell, R. (2007). *Sex God: Exploring the endless connections between sexuality and spirituality*. Grand Rapids, MI: Zondervan.

[120] This point is made in Farmer, A. (1998). *The rich single life: Abundance, opportunity and purpose in God*. Louisville, KY: Sovereign Grace Ministries.

[121] Foster, R. (2005). *Freedom of simplicity*. New York: HarperOne, p. 172, 76.

[122] Danylak, B. (2009). *Redeeming singleness: How the storytelling of Scripture affirms the single life*. Wheaton, IL: Crossway.

[123] Hsu, A. (1997). *The single issue*. Leicester: IVP, p.37.

[124] Smith, H.I. (1990). *A Singular Devotion: 366 Portraits of Singles Who Have Changed the World*. Old Tappan, New Jersey: Fleming H Revell Co.

[125] Pope John Paul II (1981) *Apostolic Exhortation of His Holiness: The role of the Christian family in the modern world*. St Paul Editions, p.29-30.

[126] Chapter 6 lists resources related to security. For general preparation guidelines you can freely download, go to www.syzygy.org.uk/guides/going. For an online preparation course, see www.allnations.ac.uk. For a good book, see B, S. (2010). *Cross cultural Christian*. Nottingham: St John's. For a toolkit, see the *'Do it well' mission toolkit*, available from www.pcimissionoverseas.org.

[127] For example, *Servants to Asia's Urban Poor* is good at modelling community, as this is one of the key values of the organisation (www.servantsasia.org). See chapter 9.

[128] Williams, K. *Spiritual warfare for sexuality on the mission field*. Cited in Tissingh, A. *Tran-cultural stress and human sexuality*. Unpublished paper.

[129] See the next chapter, and Appendix 2

[130] Married couples are encouraged to consider how satisfied they are with their marriage, and to take steps to enrich it; singles can also try to enhance their satisfaction.

[131] Mintel study, 2005, available at http://news.bbc.co.uk/1/hi/uk/4262739.stm.

[132] Baumeister, R.F., & Leary, M.R. (1995) The need to belong: Desire for interpersonal attachments as a fundamental human motivation. *Psychological Bulletin,* 117, 497-529.

[133] Carr, K. (2012). Personal resilience. In Schaefer, F.C. and Schaefer, C.A. (eds.) *Trauma and Resilience: Effectively Supporting Those Who Serve God.* Fresno, CA: Condeo Press.

[134] Graybill, R. A. The emotional needs of women in the mission field. Available at www.mrnet.org.

[135] Clark, K. (1986). *Being sexual... and celibate.* Quezon City, Philippines: Claretian Publications, p. 49.

[136] Page, J. (2012). *Freedom from Loneliness: 52 Ways To Stop Feeling Lonely.* CreateSpace Independent Publishing Platform.

[137] Clark, K. (1986). *Being sexual... and celibate.* Quezon City, Philippines: Claretian Publications, p. 177.

[138] Morgan, R. (2013). *Living with infertility – a Christian perspective.* Abingdon, England: BRF.

[139] See Powdthavee, N. (2009, April) Think having children will make you happy? *The Psychologist,* 22, (4), 208-211.

[140] See Horsfall, T. (2010). *Working from a place of rest.* Abingdon: BRF.

[141] E.g. www.richmond-holidays.com and www.oakhall.co.uk

[142] See Appendix 2 for some retreat options.

[143] See Jarrett, C. (2011). *Wish you were here?* The Psychologist, 24, (8), 574-579. Available at www.thepsychologist.org.uk/archive.

[144] Light, K.C., Grewen, K.M. & Amico, J.A. (2005). More frequent partner hugs and higher oxytocin levels are linked to lower blood pressure and heart rate in premenopausal women. *Biological Psychology,* 69 (1), 5-21.

[145] See Van Dalen, E. (2001). Raising resilient daughters in dark places. In J. R. Blomberg & D. F. Brooks (Eds) *Fitted Pieces.* St. Clair Shores, MI: SHARE Education Services

[146] Danielson, E.E., Cummings, B. & Fry, M. (1991). *Lord, send me: a handbook for single missionaries*. El Cajon, CA: E.D. Publishing.

[147] Chapman, G. (2010). *The 5 Love Languages*. Chicago: Moody Publishers.

[148] Emmons, R. A. (2008). *Thanks! How practicing gratitude can make you happier*. Boston: Houghton Mifflin Company.

[149] Guillebaud, S. (2011). *Dangerously alive*. Oxford: Monarch Books, p. 47.

[150] Lockerbie, J. 1983). *By ones and by twos*. Pasadena, CA: William Carey Library, p.38.

[151] There is a lot of research about each of these factors. For a simple summary, see Davis-Laack, P. (2013) 10 things happy people do differently. *The Huffington Post,* 25/1/2013. Available at www.huffingtonpost.com/paula-davislaack/happiness-tips_b_2325700.html?view=print&comm_ref=false

[152] Nouwen, H. (1990). *The Road to Daybreak.* New York: Doubleday

[153] Single respondents rated this statement on average 3.67, on a scale from 1 (strongly disagree) to 5 (strongly agree).

[154] Single workers reported that they see their freedom as a benefit. However, in chapter 35 Alison warns that singles might not appreciate married people who say "I wish I had your freedom." Such a comment minimises the cost that can come with the freedom.

[155] Attributed to John Wesley, but not found in his published writings.

[156] Deane, H. (2008). *Good and faithful: New Zealand missionaries and their experience of attrition.* Mairangi Bay: Daystar.

[157] Nouwen, H.J.M. (1979). *Clowning in Rome: Reflections on solitude, celibacy, prayer and contemplation.* New York: Image Books, p. 50.

[158] Married people should avoid giving the impression that marriage is harder than singleness, as if in a competition for pity (see chapter 35). The point is that each lifestyle has its challenges and its joys.

[159] http://fionalouisecooper.blogspot.co.uk/2008/11/joy-of-singleness.html

[160] E.g. Neuhoff, C.C. & Schaefer, C. (2002). Effects of laughing, smiling and howling on mood. *Psychological Reports,* 91, 1079-1080.

[161] Cherlin, A.J., Burton, L.M., Hurt, T.R. & Purvin, D.M. (2004). The influence of physical and sexual abuse on marriage and cohabitation. *American Sociological Review* December, 69 (6), 768-789